THE CIVIL WAR IN MISSOURI

Shades of Blue and Gray Series
Louis S. Gerteis, Series Editor

The Shades of Blue and Gray Series offers Civil War studies for the modern reader—Civil War buff and scholar alike. Military history today addresses the relationship between society and warfare. Thus biographies and thematic studies that deal with civilians, soldiers, and political leaders are increasingly important to a larger public. This series includes books that will appeal to Civil War Roundtable groups, individuals, libraries, and academics with a special interest in this era of American history.

THE CIVIL WAR IN MISSOURI

A Military History

LOUIS S. GERTEIS

UNIVERSITY OF MISSOURI PRESS
COLUMBIA

University of Missouri Press, Columbia, Missouri 65211
Printed and bound in the United States of America

First paperback printing, 2015

Cataloging-in-Publication data available from the Library of Congress.
ISBN 978-0-8262-2078-3

∞™ This paper meets the requirements of the
American National Standard for Permanence of Paper
for Printed Library Materials, Z39.48, 1984.

Design and composition: Jennifer Cropp
Typefaces: Inscription, Minion, Engravers, and Trajan

In Memory of

James Neal Primm

Mentor and Friend

Contents

Preface

In the history of the United States nothing rankles more than the tensions and enmities of the Civil War. In this military history of the war in Missouri, I have tried to offer a balanced account of the conflict's triumphs and defeats. At the same time I recognize that all histories are shaped by the perspectives and experiences of the historians who write them. Perhaps some observations about my own background will help to locate this work in a usable context.

I have dedicated this book to my late colleague James Neal Primm, an economic historian with a particular interest in banking policy. His knowledge of Missouri history was deep and wide, and in the arena of Civil War disputes and historiography, he was as surefooted as anyone I have known. Primm was from a Unionist family in Edina, in northeast Missouri, a region where proslavery and pro-southern sentiments clashed harshly with the free labor and northern-oriented interests of the region's commercial farmers and merchants. In the Unionist view, Missouri was not a southern state but an essential national corridor linking East and West. After World War II, Primm entered graduate school at the University of Missouri and studied history at a time when Revisionist historiography dominated interpretations of the Civil War Era. Among the most influential of the Revisionists was Avery O. Craven of the University of Chicago. Craven and the Revisionists generally downplayed the importance of slavery as a cause of the Civil War. More important were the irresponsible zealots on both sides of the sectional divide and the pandering politicians who empowered them. It was an interpretation of the Civil War that Primm understood but never accepted: he always knew that slavery was the cause of the war because his father told him that it was.

So it is with me. My interest in history and my understanding of the past are shaped by family memories. I was born in Kansas City, Missouri. Neither of my parents had immediate family ties to the Civil War, but the war was never very distant from our lives. My father's German ancestors immigrated to the United States immediately after the Civil War and eventually settled in eastern Kansas. My mother's family moved into southwestern Missouri after the Civil War and settled in Neosho. My parents met and married in Kansas City where, I suspect, they believed they had left behind the parochial concerns of a distant sectional conflict. With the outbreak of World War II, my family moved to Arlington, Virginia, and my father began working for the federal government. In Arlington, the Civil War emerged from the landscape, and sectional identities informed social relationships. In the woods surrounding our apartment complex overgrown earthworks revealed the remains of the Civil War defenses of Washington, DC. Arlington House, Robert E. Lee's mansion overlooking the Potomac, was close at hand, and the sites of the battles of Ball's Bluff and Bull Run revealed the magnificent Potomac River valley and the rolling hills of the Virginia Piedmont rising to the distant Blue Ridge Mountains. My schoolmates who were native Virginians offered me a degree of acceptance because I came from a "slave state." They were southern in sentiment and pointed out with pride that Baileys Crossroads (still a crossroads at the time) was the location of a skirmish during a daring raid by the Confederate partisan John Singleton Mosby.

During summers, my family frequently made automobile trips back to Missouri and Kansas. During one trip we visited friends of my mother in Neosho (at some point I learned that the town had been the Confederate capital of Missouri) before driving into eastern Kansas to visit an elderly aunt of my father. My great-aunt had been a longtime member of the Unitarian Church in Lawrence, Kansas, and remembered the congregation's somber annual observance of William Quantrill's murderous raid of August 1863. From her youthful memory my great-aunt retold terrifying stories shared with her by survivors. Before we left, I think it was at my mother's suggestion, my sisters and I sang to her what we knew of the Battle Hymn of the Republic.

My formal study of history began at Antioch College in 1960 and continued at the University of Wisconsin to 1969. For me the study of history coincided with the centennial of the Civil War and with the civil rights movement. I studied with historians who actively rejected Revisionist historiography and worked to recover a long-suppressed abolitionist narrative of the Civil War Era. It was in this intellectual climate that I had the opportunity to hear a lecture delivered by Avery O. Craven, retired from the University of Chicago at this point. At Wisconsin he offered a series of undergraduate lectures as a visiting professor. The topic of his lecture was the sectional bifurcation of the Democratic Party at its nominating convention in Charleston, South Carolina, in late April and early May of 1860. It was a critical moment in history, Craven said: if the Democratic Party could have maintained its institutional unity, in all likelihood Stephen A. Douglas would have been elected president and the Union would have been preserved. Tragically it was not to be. Craven constructed vivid descriptions of the passions of the moment as moderate men of sound principle were undone by zealots. Douglas failed to secure the requisite two-thirds majority of delegates after dozens of ballots. In frustration and anger, the party's northern and southern delegates dispersed. Craven lectured brilliantly but, for me, unconvincingly. For

Craven the Civil War was an unmitigated tragedy that should have been avoided. In my experience the war was a catharsis: a bloody, brutal, epic, heroic struggle that changed the character of the nation. Writing about the war in Missouri has given me a fresh appreciation of the reasons the Civil War continues to rankle, and to fascinate.

Louis S. Gerteis
St. Louis, Missouri
January 6, 2012

Erratum: On the map of "Missouri in 1861" following the front matter and on the maps appearing on pages 127 and 184, the town of Franklin on the Meramec River is indicated as the point at which the Northern Pacific R.R. headed west to Jefferson City and Sedalia. The town of Franklin is also mentioned in the text on page 184. While the town of Franklin was originally platted in 1852, it was renamed Pacific when incorporated in 1859. See Bill Earngey, *Missouri Roadsides: The Traveler's Companion* (Columbia: University of Missouri Press, 1995), 85. The author extends his thanks to Edward A. Ruesing II of St. Louis for this correction.

ACKNOWLEDGMENTS

This work began after a conversation some years ago with Clair Willcox, editor-in-chief of the University of Missouri Press. Willcox had long wanted to publish a one-volume military history of the Civil War in Missouri. The approaching sesquicentennial of the war seemed to offer a propitious occasion for such a project, and he asked me if I would be interested in undertaking it. I agreed, and as the project progressed I have benefited from the involvement of a number of individuals.

I have been repeatedly encouraged (and urged forward) by Clair Willcox, who would have preferred to see this work published a year earlier, at the beginning of the sesquicentennial commemoration. Jon Wakelyn, one of the editors of the Shades of Blue and Gray Series, offered his strong support. The two anonymous readers of the manuscript for the University of Missouri Press provided insightful criticisms and useful suggestions. One reader, noting that I have relied almost entirely on published primary sources, correctly observed that this work will not be the final word on the subject. A second reader encouraged me to think of Missouri as part of a larger Confederate effort (largely unsuccessful) to establish a secure northern border in the trans-Appalachian West.

At the Press, Assistant Managing Editor Sara Davis strengthened and improved the manuscript in a number of ways. I benefited greatly from the close scrutiny and fine attention to detail provided by my copyeditor, Pippa Letsky. I am fortunate as well to have been able to enlist the services of the cartographer Erin Greb. I also benefited from a timely grant from the University of Missouri Research Board, which made it possible for me to devote an entire semester and a summer to research and writing and substantially hastened the completion of the project.

In the past it was common for historians to thank individual librarians and archivists who assisted them in their research. It is still appropriate to do so, although in the new age of digitized resources acquired from the Internet, it is necessary to do so anonymously. Nevertheless, the willingness of librarians and archivists across the country to make their collections available for online research has revolutionized the historian's task.

Finally, as is always the case, all errors and omissions in the manuscript are the sole responsibility of the author.

THE CIVIL WAR IN MISSOURI

Missouri in 1861

Introduction

This is a work of traditional military history: it focuses on strategy, tactics, and terrain; on the organization, movement, and deployment of troops; and on the victories and defeats experienced by armies in the field. It requires some familiarity with the historiography of the Civil War in Missouri and with the lingering ideology of the Lost Cause to appreciate why, in the second decade of the twenty-first century, such a traditional military history is needed.

The historiography of the Civil War in Missouri is nicely summarized in the recent edition of the nation's leading textbook on the Civil War and Reconstruction. In a map of the principal campaigns of the war appearing in the front of *Ordeal by Fire* (2009), James M. McPherson and James K. Hogue depict Missouri as a blank slate. The authors discuss the Battle of Wilson's Creek (August 1861), they mention the Battle of Lexington (September 1861), and they briefly comment on the defeat of Confederate General Sterling Price at the Battle of Westport (October 1864). Overall, however, the authors concluded that conventional warfare in Missouri was "peripheral to the principal military campaigns of the war." While organized Union and Confederate armies clashed elsewhere, Missouri experienced a continuation and expansion of the vicious antebellum Border War between proslavery Missourians and Free State settlers in Kansas. McPherson and Hogue concluded that irregular warfare overwhelmed the state: Missouri suffered "more than any other state from raids, skirmishes, and guerrilla actions." Missouri sank into an abyss of undifferentiated guerrilla attacks and Federal retaliations. The state was brutalized but marginalized in relation to the mainstream of Civil War military history.[1]

There is no reason to dispute the significance of guerrilla warfare in Missouri. But, the impact and significance of conventional warfare in the state requires reconsideration. McPherson's and Hogue's characterization of the Civil War in Missouri arises from a scholarly and popular historiography that has overemphasized the role of guerrillas. This was not always the case. The first military histories focused on conventional warfare and were written by participants who chronicled the battles and campaigns they experienced in the Union and Confederate armies.[2] John N. Edwards, who served as Confederate General Jo Shelby's adjutant during the war, led the way. His *Shelby and His Men* (1867) contributed to the early military history of the war. But the fiery and partisan tone of his work suggested that Edwards was motivated by purposes that diverged from the pride and nostalgia of a veteran soldier. A journalist by trade, Edwards became a leading figure in the construction of the ideology of the Lost Cause. His singular contribution was the creation of the mythic Jesse James, whose resistance to the tyranny of invaders during the war gave rise to social banditry in the postwar years. Edwards found a highly receptive popular audience for his celebration of a defiant and indomitable southern spirit and by the early twentieth century Jesse James and other guerrilla warriors-turned-bandits became legendary figures.[3]

The ascendance of Jesse James in popular memory invested guerrilla warfare with greater valor than conventional warfare. Academic historians resisted the tendency to romanticize the guerrillas, but they too made guerrilla warfare central to the war in the West. Richard S. Brownlee led the way with *Gray Ghosts of the Confederacy* (1958), a sometimes chilling account of guerrilla warfare. Michael Fellman's *Inside War* (1989) made guerrilla warfare the central wartime experience in Missouri. Fellman brought the horrors of guerrilla warfare to the forefront as never before, but he did so without distinctions of chronology, region, or social identity. In Fellman's portrayal, guerrilla warfare engulfed the state. Fellman's portrait of Missouri guerrillas sought to reverse the mythology of the Lost Cause. The guerrillas were driven, he argued, by a deep ideological hatred of the forces that eroded slavery and the way of life it sustained in Missouri. T. J. Stiles, a recent biographer of Jesse James, emphasized this ideological divide as he debunked Edwards's Jesse James mythology. More recently, the historian Mark W. Geiger linked Missouri guerrillas to wider kinship networks and to specific financial interests that gave them good reason to resist Federal authority and attack their enemies close to home.

Nevertheless, the tendency to give greater emphasis to guerrilla actions than to conventional warfare persisted. In this historiographical environment Edwards's popular mythology of guerilla valor lived on. As audiences learned from John Wayne's (1969) and Jeff Bridge's (2010) depictions of the fictional character Reuben J. "Rooster" Cogburn in the film "True Grit," it was a point of pride for Cogburn that he rode during the war with the guerrilla leader William Quantrill and not with Confederate General E. Kirby Smith. Cogburn named his cat Sterling Price, offering a nod of recognition to the Confederate general who commissioned Quantrill a colonel. But that nod of recognition underscored the larger point that Gogburn operated with guerrillas outside of the mainstream of conventional Civil War military operations. In this regard, the resilience and fortitude of Rooster Cogburn, Edwards's eulogies of Jesse James, Fellman's exploration of social anarchy, and Stiles's portrait of unrelenting hatred formed an unintended historiographical junction: as McPherson and Hogue summarized the literature, the chaotic violence in Missouri was peripheral to the military history of the Civil War.[4]

This characterization of the war in Missouri is badly overdrawn and it tends to overlook a body of work by historians who have examined the state's many battles, its shifting command structure, and its leading military figures. In the mid-twentieth century William E. Parrish published the first scholarly account of the administrative, political, and military history of Civil War Missouri. Two excellent biographies of Sterling Price appeared in the next decade and offered descriptions and evaluations of his major military campaigns. William Piston and Richard Hatcher's study of the Battle of Wilson's Creek, published in 2000, added substantially to this historiography by offering the first detailed scholarly examination of a conventional military campaign in Missouri. Piston and Hatcher located the Battle of Wilson's Creek in its national context, as the second battle of the Civil War, and in its regional significance as a pivotal part of a military campaign that also involved clashes at Boonville, Carthage, and Lexington. McPherson and Hogue drew on this work when they included the Battle of Wilson's Creek in their textbook. But Wilson's Creek—and the military campaign of which it was a part—was not an isolated phenomenon. Conventional military forces clashed continually in Missouri from the spring of 1861 into the fall of 1864. Guerrillas roamed the countryside, to be sure, but organized military forces also maneuvered and fought for strategic advantage.[5]

Conventional warfare took on added significance in Missouri because of the intensity of guerrilla activity. Although all armies produced stragglers, lawless deserters, and acts of wanton destruction, they are not organized to do so and they self-consciously police themselves to minimize such tendencies. As the historian Daniel Sutherland has recently pointed out, it was the instability produced by guerrilla activities that ultimately harmed the Confederate cause. Legitimate governments, sustained by an organized military, provide stability and security. Guerrillas wreaked havoc on occupying military forces but they did so at the expense of stability and security. Conversely, as Mark Neely has shown in his study of limited warfare during the Civil War, the presence of regular Confederate forces in Missouri, particularly during Price's 1864 Expedition, brought with it a degree of order. Discipline was lax in Price's command and it declined rapidly as the Confederate army moved across the state. But Price and his commanders recognized what their generation understood to be the laws of civilized warfare and, overall, they adhered to them.[6]

Conventional warfare focused an army's capacity for violence and destruction on enemy combatants, not on civilians. The ability of conventional military forces to maintain stability and security always stood in sharp contrast to the ruthlessness of guerrilla actions. But the relationship between the two has yet to be explored. Eventually guerrilla warfare in Missouri will be best understood in terms of its conflicts and interactions with conventional military forces. If a traditional military history of the Civil War in Missouri can clarify the scope, scale, and chronology of conventional warfare, it should become possible to introduce a new level of sophistication to the study of the Civil War in the Border States and its impact on civil society.

This work offers a comprehensive narrative of conventional warfare in Missouri. It contends that Union and Confederate authorities saw the strategic importance of Missouri and fought for military advantage in that state throughout the war. At the beginning of the war, it was the nascent Border State policy of neutrality that offered the greatest advantage to the Confederacy and posed the greatest threat to Federal interests. For two months after the fall of Fort Sumter, Missouri and Kentucky embraced a policy of armed neutrality and effectively offered the Confederacy a northern border in the West stretching for six hundred miles from the Appalachian Mountains in eastern Kentucky to the Ozark Mountains and the Indian Territory in western Missouri.

Missouri's newly elected governor, Claiborne Jackson, hoped eventually to maneuver Missouri into the Confederacy, but he realized that Conditional Unionists were dominant in the state. While most Missourians opposed immediate secession they supported a policy of neutrality. When former Missouri governor Sterling Price took command of the newly formed Missouri State Guard, he negotiated an agreement with General William Harney, the Federal commander in Missouri. To avoid war, Harney agreed to keep Federal forces out of the interior of the state. Harney never fully supported the "armed" part of Governor Jackson's policy of neutrality but he and his powerful ally in Washington—Lincoln's new attorney general, the St. Louis attorney Edward Bates—hoped to maintain peace in Missouri through the Price-Harney agreement. Lincoln's decision to allow the St. Louis Republican leader Frank Blair to remove Harney from command sealed the doom of the Price-Harney agreement and with it any Federal accommodation of the policy of armed neutrality. By the time Lincoln openly rejected armed neutrality in his July 4, 1861, address to the special session of Congress, Harney's replacement, General Nathaniel Lyon, had moved into central Missouri to break up the Missouri State Guard.

Early in September the policy of armed neutrality collapsed in Kentucky as well. There Confederate general Leonidas Polk fortified Columbus, Kentucky, and Belmont, Missouri, on the Mississippi River. General Ulysses Grant—commanding Federal forces at Cairo, Illinois—countered Polk's move by occupying Paducah, Kentucky, near the mouth of the Tennessee and Cumberland Rivers. In Missouri, as in Kentucky and Virginia, rival armies maneuvered and fought, intent upon establishing the authority of the governments they represented. Guerrillas operated in the context of this conventional warfare.

Lincoln proclaimed in his July 4 address to Congress that to recognize the status of neutrality "would be disunion completed." Neutrality "would tie the hands of the Union men, and freely pass supplies from among them, to the insurrectionists." Neutrality, concluded Lincoln, "recognizes no fidelity to the Constitution, no obligation to maintain the Union; and while very many who have favored it are, doubtless, loyal citizens, it is, nevertheless, treason in effect."[7]

Lincoln could have added that, in Missouri, any successful concentration of rebel troops in the center of the state raised other threats as well. The richest slaveholding counties and the largest concentration of potential rebel soldiers lay along the Missouri River valley. Rebel control of the river corridor across Missouri would threaten the fragile Free State settlements in eastern Kansas and, more broadly, US access to the Far West. Rebel forces in Missouri threatened the aspirations of the United States to control a continental empire stretching from sea to shining sea.

The political maneuvering that led to the removal of General Harney from command in Missouri offered early indications (in April and May of 1861) that Lincoln had no intention of allowing a policy of armed neutrality to take hold in Missouri. Nevertheless, a mentality of armed neutrality persisted in Missouri for some time. Fighting between Federal forces and the Missouri State Guard quickly brought Confederate troops into Missouri but the Missouri Guardsmen did not hasten to become Confederate soldiers. For more than three months following the collapse of the Price-Harney agreement the integrity of the Missouri State Guard as a state military force remained intact. For the first six months of the war (and arguably for its duration) Missouri rebels identified first and foremost with their state.

Lincoln's decision to reject neutrality assured that war would come to Missouri. Soon the war in Missouri focused on two strategic goals central to the larger struggle over nation and empire: control of the lower Mississippi valley and control of the Missouri River corridor to the West. The battles and campaigns examined in this work determined the outcome of this aspect of the national struggle and they were distinct from the irregular skirmishes, raids, and acts of banditry that plagued the state. This distinction between significant battles and irregular armed conflict draws on the work of the Federal Civil War Sites Advisory Commission, created by Congress in November 1990. Congress charged the commission with the task of identifying all of the militarily significant battlefields of the Civil War. The creation of the commission had been prompted by a proposed new shopping mall in northern Virginia the construction of which would alter the landscape around Manassas, the site of the First and Second Battles of Bull Run. Eventually the Federal government bought enough land to protect the battlefield landscape. But, with the goal of averting future threats of the sort, Congress created the commission and directed it to "examine comprehensively the state of battlefield preservation" everywhere in the country. The commission distinguished "principal" battles from the thousands of armed conflicts that took place during the Civil War. Leading the research was ex-officio commissioner and former chief historian of the National Park Service, Edwin C. Bearss. The commission defined four categories of principal battles. At the most significant level a battle had "a decisive influence on a campaign and a direct impact on the course of the war." At the second level of significance, a battle had "a direct and decisive influence" on a campaign. At the third level of significance, a battle had an "observable influence on the outcome of a campaign." At the lowest level of significance a principal battle had "limited influence" on the outcome of a campaign, but it achieved "important local objectives." Within these categories of analysis, the commission identified 384 principal battles in the American Civil War.

This inventory of Civil War battles provides a valuable starting point for a military history of the Civil War in Missouri. It underscores the point that Missouri played a significant role in the larger military history of the war. The principal battles identified by the commission occurred in twenty-six states with Missouri ranking third (with 29 battles) behind Virginia (with 123) and Tennessee (with 38). Moreover, the commission ranked only forty-five battles at the highest level of significance. Three of these battles took place in Missouri. At the second level of significance, another three battles took place in Missouri (all associated with Sterling Price's Missouri Expedition of 1864). The remainder of Missouri's twenty-three principal battles (about 80 percent of the total in the state) fell into the third and fourth levels of significance, as did more than 60 percent of the principal battles fought elsewhere in the nation.[8]

The three battles in Missouri with the highest level of significance clearly link the state with the wider Civil War at critical points in time. They offer a preview of how the war in Missouri should be integrated into the wider military history of the Civil War. The victory of the Missouri State Guard and its Confederate allies at the Battle of Wilson's Creek in August 1861 occurred shortly after the Confederate victory at the First Battle of Bull Run near Washington, DC. These early rebel victories created jubilation in the South and foreboding in the North. The Federal victory at New Madrid Bend and Island Number Ten in the late winter and early spring of 1862 (a battle that ended just a day after the Federal victory at Shiloh) opened the lower Mississippi valley to Federal advances that culminated in the capture of Vicksburg. Finally, the Federal victory at Westport in October 1864 marked the bitter end of Price's ill-fated assault on the Missouri River corridor at a time when Grant laid siege to Petersburg, Virginia, and Sherman prepared to launch his march across Georgia. Federal victories on all three fronts—the defeat of the Confederate threat to the Missouri corridor, the Federal invasion of the Confederate heartland, and the Federal penetration of the defenses of Richmond—brought the Civil War to an end.

Although the military history presented in this work emphasizes the significance of the Civil War in Missouri, it must be acknowledged at the outset that a vast disparity of scale distinguished the fighting in Missouri from the military campaigns in the East. At the Battle of the Wilderness in Virginia (May 1864) and the Battle of Westport in Missouri (October 1864), Confederate generals Robert E. Lee and Sterling Price each lost about 17 percent of their troops. Both battles had major consequences in their respective theaters. In Virginia, Grant moved his Federal army south of the Confederate defenses on the Rappahannock River. In Missouri, Price retreated from Westport having lost the offensive capacity of his army. But Lee commanded sixty-five thousand men compared to the eighty-five hundred troops under Price's command. The smaller scale of warfare in Missouri helps to explain why historians have devoted far more attention to fighting in the East, but it does not justify marginalizing or ignoring the military history of the Civil War in Missouri. If this work is successful, it will help to locate Missouri in the national Civil War and provide a conventional military context for future examinations of the impact of the war on civil society.

Chapter One

"Your First Allegiance"

Small-scale slavery flourished in Missouri in 1860. In the state's largest slaveholding counties, small slaveholders defined and defended a distinctive southern culture in close proximity to Free State communities in Illinois and Kansas—and in St. Louis, a booming city at the confluence of the Missouri and Mississippi Rivers that identified itself economically and politically with the Northeast. With the exception of Cape Girardeau and New Madrid Counties in the Boot Heel and Greene County in southwest Missouri, slaves and slaveholders in Missouri clustered in the Mississippi River counties bordering Illinois from Lewis County south to St. Charles County and then along the Missouri River westward from Warren County to Buchanan, Platte, and Jackson Counties on the border with Kansas.[1]

In the presidential election of 1860, Missouri's small slaveholders showed little sympathy for the Southern Rights candidate John C. Breckenridge. None of Missouri's largest slaveholding counties supported Breckenridge. Several supported the Unionist Democrat Stephen A. Douglas, including Chariton, Howard, and Cooper Counties in central Missouri and Franklin, Lincoln, St. Charles, and Jefferson Counties near St. Louis. All the rest of Missouri's largest slaveholding counties supported the Constitutional Unionist candidate, John Bell. Abraham Lincoln carried two counties in Missouri (St. Louis and Gasconade, both with large German populations) but Lincoln carried only 10 percent of the vote across the state and posted the smallest tally of the four presidential candidates.[2]

Outside of St. Louis, small-scale slaveholders commanded Missouri's agricultural economy and its politics. These Missourians viewed themselves as southerners, and during the 1850s they had become increasingly radical in their defense of slavery. In the secession crisis they sympathized with the southern cause. But Missouri's small slaveholders were not eager for the civil war that soon engulfed them. Their support for Douglas and Bell reflected their desire to avoid a sectional conflict. This pairing of proslavery radicalism and conservative Unionism produced a distinctive demeanor, at once wary of secession and hostile toward the intrusion of outside influences. As the secession leader Basil Duke noted, Missourians were "ardent" in their sympathy for the southern cause but they were not "open and active" in expressing it. Impatient for action, Duke soon left Missouri to fight with his father-in-law, John Hunt Morgan.[3] Throughout the war Confederates similarly found Missourians friendly but cautious. Missourians often lent their aid and support to those who took up arms against the Federal government but they never fully embraced the Confederacy. Missouri's Confederate leaders never enjoyed the outpouring of popular support that they exhorted and seemed to expect. Federal forces found the populace sullen: undemonstrative but hostile and subversive in the face of a Federal military presence. For North and South in the Civil War, Missouri remained an unpredictable, unstable, and contested border.

Claiborne Fox Jackson, the man Missourians elected governor in 1860, understood the temper of his state. In his political campaign, Jackson declared his support for Douglas. But those who knew Jackson well recognized him as a strong supporter of Southern Rights. He was, in his heart, a Breckenridge man. In the state senate in 1849, it was Claiborne Jackson who lent his name to the "Jackson Resolutions" that attacked Senator Thomas Hart Benton for his opposition to the expansion of slavery. In the words of Thomas Snead, who worked with Jackson to lead Missouri into the Confederacy, the Jackson Resolutions had taken "high Southern ground" to support extending slavery into the West. Jackson, wrote Snead, "was ever after recognized as one of the ablest leaders of the . . . Southern Rights' Democrats."[4]

In his inaugural address, Jackson unequivocally broke with Stephen Douglas. As Douglas lent his support to the new Lincoln administration, Jackson declared that Missouri would "stand by her sister slave-holding States." Missouri, said Jackson, would remain "devoted to the union . . . so long as there is any hope that it will maintain the spirit and guarantees of the Constitution." But, if the "Northern States" were determined that no new slave states should be admitted or if they otherwise intended to interfere with slavery in existing states, it was they who had "abandoned the Union" and Missouri would not submit to a government "on terms of inequality and subordination."[5]

The governor did not yet openly embrace secession, but he left no doubt that he wanted to mobilize the resources of his state to support the Confederacy. A resource of enormous importance was the Federal arsenal in St. Louis, the largest cache of military supplies west of the Mississippi River. To gain control of the Arsenal became Governor Jackson's compelling interest. Politically, St. Louis was in the control of the Republican Party. But only a small detachment of Federal troops controlled access to the Arsenal. Under the right circumstances, Jackson believed that the resources of the Arsenal could be appropriated by the state.

Jackson knew that he had important allies in St. Louis. Throughout the 1850s, the St. Louis business elite had aligned the city's economic interests with the Northeast, but southern ties and sympathies remained strong in the city. Moreover, the presence in the city of a large Irish and German immigrant population assured a volatile urban setting that could prove favorable to Jackson's goals. Jackson worked closely with the Minute Men, a pro-secessionist militia formed in St. Louis early in January 1861. The Minute Men challenged the Republican "Wide Awakes," a largely German paramilitary force that guarded Republican rallies and marches. A wealthy St. Louis businessman, Charles McLaren, founded and funded the Minute Men. But bolder, younger men—notably Basil Duke, Colton Greene, and J. R. "Rock" Champion—emerged as the leaders of the secessionist militia.[6]

Although an avowed secessionist, McLaren displayed the cautiousness of an established businessman. He undoubtedly hoped that Missouri would join the Confederacy and he lent Governor Jackson his assistance to advance that goal, but McLaren probably considered himself too old for military service, and in any case, he was not willing to abandon his St. Louis business interests. Missouri's Union Provost Marshal Papers indicate that McLaren took the loyalty oath. As St. Louis historian Walter B. Stevens noted, "When the Civil War was in progress St. Louis brain and St. Louis capital were developing the mineral wealth in Montana." McLaren was among the St. Louis businessmen engaged in this enterprise.[7]

Duke, Greene, and Champion were younger than McLaren and they were relatively new arrivals to St. Louis. They were anxious to fight for the cause of southern nationhood wherever they could. All three were impetuous, but the Irish-born Rock Champion stunned contemporaries with his boldness. Listed in the 1857 and 1858 St. Louis city directories as a "steamboat mate," Champion undoubtedly knew his way around the waterfront districts of St. Louis and other river towns. When he died near Corinth, Mississippi, in September 1862, his commander noted the fallen captain's "reckless daring and intrepid boldness."[8]

Duke and Greene also distinguished themselves in battle, but they displayed a more disciplined courage that led to their rise to the rank of brigadier general in the Confederate army. A native of the bluegrass region of Kentucky, Duke studied law at Transylvania University before moving to St. Louis in 1858. Duke was in his early twenties in 1861. Also in his twenties was Colton Greene who moved to St. Louis from South Carolina in the mid-1850s. Greene had begun to establish himself as a retail grocer in St. Louis when his home state seceded and he prepared to go to war.[9]

Duke, Greene, and Champion believed that southern men should act swiftly to seize the advantage in Missouri. They hoped that the Minute Men militia would give them an opportunity to do so. Indeed, the men who joined the Minute Men were ardent and bold secessionists. An older and somewhat improbable companion in this endeavor was twenty-nine-year-old Pittsburgh native James R. Shaler, an agent of the Pennsylvania Railroad in St. Louis. Shaler's economic interests were oriented to the North but he cast his lot wholeheartedly with the Confederacy. Duke described Shaler as "the bravest and most efficient colonel whom Missouri gave to the South."[10]

Two other Minute Men veterans, Samuel Farrington and Overton W. Barrett, soon joined Confederate artillery units. Farrington later died, as Duke put it, "under the Southern flag." Irish-born Arthur McCoy became, perhaps, the most notorious veteran of the Minute Men militia. McCoy had joined the California gold rush before settling in St. Louis in the mid-1850s. In his mid-twenties when the war began, McCoy fought with Jo Shelby during the war. After the war, he joined the James-Younger gang.[11]

The Minute Men eagerly took up arms and they hoped to precipitate a fight in St. Louis while Union forces remained relatively unorganized and vulnerable. Duke in particular hoped that by flying a home-made rebel flag from their Minute Men headquarters in the Berthold Mansion at Fifth and Pine they could goad the Germans into attacking them. If this happened, Duke believed that the state militia brigade (recently returned from the Border War with Kansas) and many of the city's Irish would come to their aid. Amid the turmoil, Duke believed that a determined band of Minute Men could take control of the Arsenal and deliver its munitions to Governor Jackson. As it happened, the Germans did not attack the Minute Men, but at a more fundamental level Duke's plan failed because older men acted with caution—far too much caution in Duke's opinion.

Undoubtedly, Daniel Frost was the most important of the cautious older men who frustrated the zeal of the Minute Men. Frost commanded the brigade of Missouri militia. These men—numbering about five hundred men and eighty officers—had recently fought in western Missouri against Kansas Jay Hawkers. The Minute Men leaders hoped that these experienced troops would be their allies. But Frost would not act rashly. A native of Schenectady County, New York, Frost graduated near the top of his class at West Point in 1844 and served with distinction under Winfield Scott in the Mexican War. Stationed at Jefferson Barracks in the early 1850s, he married into a St. Louis family. After suffering a severe wound in a skirmish with Indians in Texas in 1853, Frost resigned his army commission and devoted himself to his business interests in St. Louis. In 1858, he accepted an appointment as brigadier general in the Missouri militia.[12]

Despite Frost's northern birth, Governor Jackson knew him to be reliable on the issue of Southern Rights. Shortly after Jackson took office in January 1861, Frost reported to the governor that he had met with the commander of the St. Louis Arsenal, Major William H. Bell, a North Carolina native. "He is with us," reported Frost. "The Arsenal," he continued, "if properly looked after, will be everything to our state, and I intend to look after it; very quietly, however." It was Frost's quiet approach that frustrated the hopes of the Minute Men. By mid-February, the five companies of the Minute Men mustered into the state militia under Frost's command.[13]

Jackson and Frost mistakenly believed that the state constitutional convention —authorized by the state legislature on January 18, 1861, and scheduled to meet on February 28—would take Missouri out of the Union. When this happened, the governor and the St. Louis militia commander expected Bell to transfer the Arsenal to the state. While Jackson and Frost awaited the deliberations of the convention, however, word of Bell's meeting with Frost reached General of the Army Winfield Scott who promptly replaced Bell with Brevet Major Peter V. Hagner. A forty-five-year-old West Point graduate and Mexican War veteran, Hagner was a native of Maryland, but he shared the conservative Unionist views of the Federal commander of the Department of the West, Tennessee-born General William S. Harney. Harney and Hagner hoped to avoid armed conflict over the Arsenal, but neither man would do the bidding of Governor Jackson or militia commander Frost.[14]

Well aware of Governor Jackson's collaborations with the Minute Men and Daniel Frost, Union men in St. Louis also acted with determination to take matters in hand. Early in January, leading Republicans in St. Louis organized the Committee of Safety to arm a Unionist militia and coordinate with Federal military forces to protect the Arsenal and other Federal property in the city. It was not until the end of April that the committee received official recognition in an order from Secretary of War Simon Cameron (endorsed by President Lincoln) to General Harney directing him to collaborate with the committee. At that time, Cameron formally identified the members of the committee as Oliver D. Filley, John How, James Broadhead, Samuel T. Glover, J. J. Witzig, and Francis P. Blair, Jr. In fact, however, these men had been brought together by Blair who knew them to be both influential in the St. Louis community and politically reliable. Kentucky-born Francis P. Blair, Jr. (known as Frank), played a leading role among Unconditional Unionists in Missouri. He was the proprietor of the *St. Louis Missouri Democrat*, an antislavery paper founded in 1851 that became the voice of the Republican Party in the state. He also had powerful family ties to the Lincoln administration. His father, Francis P. Blair, Sr., led antislavery Democrats into the Republican Party and presided over that party's first presidential nominating convention. The elder Blair became a close advisor to Lincoln, and the new president chose Frank Blair's older brother, Montgomery, for the powerful patronage office of postmaster general.[15]

The men Blair gathered around him as the Committee of Safety were all Unconditional Unionists, but they also represented the key elements of Unionist support in Missouri. Most of that support was centered in St. Louis, but there were similar pockets of Unionist support across the state. Across Missouri, Unionists drew support from businessmen who had personal and financial ties to the Northeast, from slaveholders who looked to the Federal government for protection, and from German immigrants. Blair took care to have each of these groups represented in the Committee of Safety. Oliver Filley and John How were wealthy businessmen and prominent Republicans. Filley was a native of Connecticut who in his late twenties had moved to St. Louis in 1833 and soon had been joined by his brother Giles. The Filleys built a highly successful stove manufacturing company, and both of the Filley brothers served as wartime Republican mayors of St. Louis. Born in Philadelphia in 1813, How had become wealthy as a merchant in St. Louis and had twice been elected mayor of the city—in 1853 as a Democrat and in 1856 as a Republican. He ran for mayor again in 1861 but lost to a candidate who ran as a "Union Anti-Black Republican."[16]

How's defeat at the polls in 1861 underscored the fact that many Unionists in St. Louis did not embrace abolitionism. As in the rest of Missouri, they favored slavery, or like Frank Blair, they linked emancipation with racial separation and colonization. The fact that How had been attacked and defeated as a Black Republican suggests he was viewed as a friend of emancipation. If Unionists could be identified simply with emancipation, they would find little support anywhere in the state. Blair had always made racial separation the centerpiece of his antislavery appeal. And in John Broadhead and Joshua Glover, Blair identified two prominent St. Louis attorneys who shared his support for the Union and his hostility to what he described as the abolitionist wing of the Republican Party. Like Blair, Broadhead and Glover were men of southern origins. Broadhead moved from Virginia to St. Charles County in 1837. He later served as provost marshal for Missouri from May 1863 to January 1864. Glover was a native of Kentucky. He had practiced law in Hannibal before moving to St. Louis. A Republican and a colonizationist, he declared in a public address that "The separation of the white and colored races is demanded by the best interests of both."[17]

John J. Witzig filled out the committee and provided Blair with a vital tie to the German community. Born in Mulhouse, Germany, in 1821, Witzig was a railroad engineer who had worked in France and Italy before moving to St. Louis in 1851. By 1859 he was superintendent of the Iron Mountain Railroad, a post he held until 1865.[18]

It was the goal of the Committee of Safety to secure Unionist control of Federal resources in St. Louis, the most important being the Arsenal. In the months preceding Lincoln's inauguration in mid-March, this was not a simple or straightforward task. The administration of President James Buchanan supported the accommodationist course adopted by General Harney. This policy left Governor Jackson free to collaborate with the Confederacy. As long as Federal forces in St. Louis were few in number and uncertain in loyalty, Harney's accommodation of Jackson probably made sense. When Hagner took command of the Arsenal in January, the forty men available for its defense could easily have been swept aside by Frost's brigade. By the time of Lincoln's inauguration in mid-March, however, Federal forces in St. Louis were steadily gaining cohesion and strength. The Federal buildup began in late January and early February. Among the new troops were a number of future military leaders whom Blair found useful in his effort to stiffen Federal resistance to pro-Confederate elements. A striking figure in this new alignment of Federal forces was Captain Thomas Sweeny, a native Irishman who had immigrated fifteen years earlier to New York City, at a time when the country prepared for war with Mexico. Sweeny soon joined a volunteer regiment. Although a severe wound had required the amputation of his right arm, military life suited him well and he accepted a commission as a second lieutenant in the regular army in 1848. After the Mexican War, Sweeny served in the West, rose to the rank of captain, and in January 1861 received orders to move to St. Louis with two companies of regular troops in order to reinforce the Arsenal.[19]

Also redeployed to St. Louis was Captain James Totten. Born in Pittsburgh, Pennsylvania, Totten graduated from West Point in 1841. He served in Kansas in 1857 and 1858 during the harshest period of the Border War. In November 1860 he became commander of the Federal arsenal at Little Rock, Arkansas. Although Arkansas did not formally secede from the Union until May 1861, thousands of pro-Confederate volunteers flocked to the state capital and threatened his command. At the behest of the state's governor, he withdrew his forces to St. Louis early in February 1861. He served as an artillery commander and remained in Missouri under John C. Fremont and Henry Halleck.[20]

The most important new arrival proved to be Captain Nathaniel Lyon who came to the Arsenal from Fort Riley, Kansas, on February 6. Lyon quickly forged a powerful partnership with Frank Blair and took the lead in placing Federal forces in St. Louis on a strong military footing. Born in eastern Connecticut in 1818, Lyon attended West Point and won commendation for his "gallant and meritorious conduct" during the Mexican War. The army stationed Lyon briefly at Jefferson Barracks before sending him to California for several years. Lyon went to Kansas in the spring of 1858 and remained there until ordered to St. Louis. In Kansas, Lyon maintained an official demeanor of neutrality but acted to aid the Free State forces wherever he could. While in Kansas, Lyon also demonstrated his willingness to confront senior officers when their actions seemed to him to be irresponsible or misguided. As Blair quickly learned, Lyon was not a man who would accommodate enemies of the Federal government.[21]

Predictably, Lyon's strong Unionist views and his aggressive demeanor soon brought him into conflict with Hagner and Harney. Both men wanted Federal forces in St. Louis to maintain a low profile to avoid armed conflict. By contrast, Lyon feared for the security of his troops and wanted to act quickly to strengthen the Federal presence. Lyon was also eager to assert military control and suppress displays of defiance by Minute Men and other southern sympathizers. Signs of disloyalty were everywhere to be seen. On February 16, when the War Department ordered two companies of troops to move to the Arsenal from Jefferson Barracks, the soldiers expected to face resistance. Captain Albert Tracy recorded in his journal the prevailing sense of danger. A New Yorker and a veteran of both the Mexican War and the Federal Utah Expedition, Tracy noted that the troops began the march to St. Louis "with ten rounds of ball-cartridge." They expected that their movement would attract opposition. They "went up with as little noise as practicable," Tracy reported. As they approached the Arsenal the soldiers prepared for a "scrimmage." As it happened, no enemy appeared and they reported to Major Hagner without incident. Lyon continued to fear an attack and continued to press for a stronger military presence at the Arsenal. Soon the Federal forces defending the Arsenal numbered nearly five hundred men.[22]

To Governor Jackson's great disappointment, Unionists prevailed at the state convention, which adjourned on March 21, 1861. But Jackson continued to believe that he could position his forces to seize the Arsenal. He took what he hoped would be a significant step in that direction on March 23 when the state legislature passed a bill giving the governor of Missouri and not the mayor of St. Louis control of the city's police force. Under the new legislation (modeled after legislation passed in New York state to reform the police force in New York City), control of the St. Louis police rested with a police board. The mayor sat on the board ex officio but the governor appointed all of the voting members. Jackson placed secessionists on the board, including Basil Duke and Charles McLaren, and hoped that the police force could help Frost's brigade gain control of the Arsenal.

Harney continued to accommodate Jackson in ways that raised the suspicions of Blair and Lyon regarding the commander's loyalty. Harney's motivation continued to be his desire to avoid armed conflict, but when he tried to promote friendly relations between Federal forces and the state militia, he raised the hackles of the Unconditional Unionists. Early in April, amid the growing crisis at Fort Sumter in Charleston harbor, General Harney held a dinner party at his home in St. Louis. Harney's battles with Lyon concerning the fortification of the Arsenal had intensified since Lincoln's inauguration, and the commanding general probably hoped to find new allies among his guests. Captain Albert Tracy recorded in his journal that the guests included himself, Captain Rufus Saxton, and Colonel Benjamin L. E. Bonneville. The French-born, West Point–educated Bonneville commanded an infantry regiment stationed at Benton Barracks, north of St. Louis. Bonneville had served in the Mexican War, but he was best-known as an army explorer in the Southwest. He impressed Tracy with his gracious manners. Saxton was an abolitionist from Massachusetts who graduated from West Point shortly after the Mexican War. He commanded an artillery battery at the Arsenal. Another guest was Samuel Bullitt Churchill, publisher of the *St. Louis Bulletin* and a colonel in General Frost's brigade. Tracy thought that Harney intended to promote camaraderie among the Federal and state military men. The effort failed, Tracy concluded. Certainly Harney was not aware of Saxton's views. The commander had misjudged Tracy as well. Tracy described Churchill as "a sallow, black-haired Secessionist, who if he were not employed to ascertain our temper about [secession], certainly succeeded in developing it."[23]

On April 12, 1861, as Confederate General P. G. T. Beauregard ordered Confederate forces to open fire on the Federal garrison at Fort Sumter, the defenders of the St. Louis Arsenal received reports that they, too, were about to be attacked.

Albert Tracy noted that Lyon "exhibits restlessness and even anxiety." At 11:00 p.m. that night, Lyon held a meeting with his trusted officers. Four officers were excluded from the meeting: two because Lyon did not fully trust them and two because they were openly disloyal. Of the latter two, Moses Wright of Tennessee resigned in May to join the Confederacy. Also openly disloyal was Richard Bland Lee of Virginia who had been placed under arrest, as Tracy noted, "as a secessionist, giving entrance to spies." Lyon now openly took charge of the defenses of the Arsenal. Captain Sweeny commanded riflemen behind sandbags on the north wall. Sweeny took command of a howitzer aimed at the gate on that side of the Arsenal. Captain Saxton commanded the defenses of the west wall, including the main gate to the street. Tracy commanded troops located in several brick buildings commanding the southern approach to the Arsenal. Tracy also commanded a howitzer positioned to fire on the west wall if attackers gained entrance on that side. Lyon expected the enemy to attack with artillery from the high ground to the west of the Arsenal. If the enemy tried to do so, it was agreed that Tracy would storm the battery before the rebel gunners could begin firing. "Gentlemen," declared Lyon as the meeting closed, "if that man Hagner, interferes with you in any way, put him in irons, and in the guardhouse." "And if he interferes with *me*," Lyon concluded, "I'll shoot him in his tracks." The expected attack never came, but Tracy, who was subsequently transferred to protect the powder magazine at Jefferson Barracks, watched nervously for several days as groups of armed men gathered on the west bank of the Mississippi River. They seemed to be examining the magazine and its defenders.[24]

The surrender of Fort Sumter on April 14 and Lincoln's subsequent call for troops placed greater pressure on Governor Jackson to determine the military course he intended to follow. The same events brought John M. Schofield back into the US army and into a position of leadership in Missouri. A native of New York, Schofield grew up in Freeport, Illinois, and graduated from West Point in 1853 near the top of his class. He taught for a time at West Point, but in the summer of 1860, seeing no opportunity for promotion from lieutenant to captain, he secured a year's leave of absence and accepted a professorship in physics at Washington University in St. Louis. After Lincoln's election, Schofield (now thirty years old) realized that "military force would be required by the government to maintain its authority in the Southern States." Accordingly, he informed the War Department that he was prepared at any time to resume active duty. When Lincoln called for troops, Schofield received orders to muster in the troops required from Missouri. On April 16, Governor Jackson received from Secretary of War Simon Cameron a call for four thousand Missouri troops to be made available for service under the authority of the United States. Schofield's orders directed him to present himself to the governor and receive the four fully organized regiments demanded by the president. "I called upon Governor Jackson for his regiments," Schofield recalled, "but received no reply."[25]

On April 17, Jackson made his position clear: he would not authorize Missouri troops to participate in Federal military operations against the seceded southern states. "Your dispatch of the 13th instant . . . has been received," wrote the governor. Expressing his view that states had the right to secede from the Union he continued, "Your requisition . . . is illegal, unconstitutional, and revolutionary in its objects, inhuman and diabolical, and cannot be complied with." On the same day, Jackson traveled to St. Louis to confer with secessionist leaders Basil Duke and Colton Greene. He directed them to travel to Montgomery, Alabama (then the capital of the Confederacy), and secure arms from President Jefferson Davis. In an attempt to gauge the strength of his military support in St. Louis, Jackson also met with General Frost and with the president of the new police board. Jackson did not yet know (though he would learn it shortly) that Missouri's leading Unconditional Unionist, Frank Blair, had returned to St. Louis from Washington, DC, with authorization from the War Department to draw five thousand muskets from the Arsenal to arm a home guard and muster them into the Federal service as United States Volunteers.[26]

The Federal troops that were quickly mustered in were largely German immigrants, and this fact worried Harney. Less than a decade earlier, St. Louis had twice witnessed deadly anti-German riots and Harney feared renewed civil disorder. Harney protested the War Department directive to his friend and supporter Attorney General Edward Bates who had been a leading member of the nativist Know Nothing Party in St. Louis in the 1850s. Harney clearly hoped that with the attorney general's support the Germans could be kept quiet. But the order to arm the Home Guard withstood Harney's protest, and by the evening of April 21 the commanding general had capitulated. In the next few days, Lyon and Blair worked with Schofield to muster in four regiments of volunteers. The First Regiment, commanded by Colonel Frank Blair, was composed for the most part of native-born Americans. The rest of the regiments—commanded by colonels Henry Boernstein, Franz Sigel, and Nicholas Schuettner—were German. A fifth regiment of German troops was also mustered in and commanded by Colonel Charles E. Solomon. This recruitment activity more than filled the original Federal quota.[27]

The day after Blair and Lyon began arming the German regiments in St. Louis, Governor Jackson (on April 22) invoked the state Militia Act of 1859 and called for a statewide militia muster. As commander of the St. Louis Military District, General Frost hoped to locate the militia camp near the Arsenal to facilitate its capture. Lyon's defensive actions thwarted this plan, however, and Frost located his camp at Lindell Grove on the western edge of the city.

On one level, the German troops represented the salvation of the Union cause in St. Louis, but they also posed problems for Blair and Lyon. Blair had an important political link to the German community in John J. Witzig of the Committee of Safety, but Witzig's influence waned as military mobilization advanced. New

German leaders quickly emerged. The fact that most of the new troops spoke little English became the object of humor on the minstrel stage as "delineators" performed the popular song "I'm going to fight mit Sigel." The song presented the German soldiers as resolute and patriotic but the use of dialect evoked laughter. Each verse ended with a chorus: "Yaw! Daus is drue, I shpeake mit you, I'm going to fight mit Sigel." The song also attested to the importance that Franz Sigel had assumed not simply among Germans in St. Louis but across the North.[28]

Of all the German commanders in Missouri, Sigel had the most extensive military training and experience. For reasons that became clearer in coming months, Blair and particularly Lyon deferred to Sigel. Although Sigel towered over the other German regimental commanders in military reputation, his fellow officers played essential roles in the organization and direction of the German troops. An intellectual, Boernstein was in his mid-fifties when the war began. Born in Hamburg in 1805, he had served five years in the Austrian army before settling in Vienna where he became a journalist and playwright. With the failure of the liberal revolutions of 1848, Boernstein joined the German emigration to the United States, and in 1850 he became the editor of the St. Louis German language daily, the *Anzeiger des Westens*. Boernstein also owned a hotel and a brewery and operated the city's largest theater as an opera house. A leading figure in the St. Louis German community, Boernstein understood that his contributions would be cultural and political, not military. Although he organized and deployed his troops effectively, Boernstein left the army when his initial period of enlistment ended. Shortly thereafter, Lincoln appointed him US consul to Bremen.[29]

Nicholas Schuettner won election as colonel of the Fourth Regiment because of his reputation for bravado in defending the German community and the Union cause. Born in Germany, he was about forty when the Civil War began. A carpenter with little formal education, he led the Schwarze Jaeger, a German hunting club that took to the streets of St. Louis to counter the influence of the pro-Confederate Minute Men. When Anthony Niederwieser (proprietor of the Tivoli restaurant) planted an American flag opposite the Minute Men headquarters (flying its improvised secessionist flag), forty members of the Schwarze Jaegers stood guard. Members of the Schwarze Jaeger made up the core of the Fourth Regiment. Schuettner's regiment took part in the capture of Camp Jackson and was then deployed in Cairo, Illinois, and at Bird's Point, Missouri (just south of Cairo). Toward the end of July 1861 they patrolled in Callaway County with two companies detached to protect the Pacific Railroad. The regiment was mustered out on July 30, 1861, although many members joined different units.[30]

Charles E. Solomon, commanding the Fifth Regiment of Volunteers, had been born in Germany in 1822. Trained as a surveyor, he became active in railroad construction. He fled to the United States in 1849 and settled in St. Louis the next year. In 1860 he won election as county engineer, defeating fellow candidate Ulysses S. Grant, who described the position as "an office of respectability and emolument," which he badly needed at that time. Admitting to having been a member of the Know Nothings, Grant complained that his "opponent had the advantage of birth over me (he was a citizen by adoption) and carried the prize." Grant soon left St. Louis to work as a clerk in his father's store in Galena, Illinois. When the Fifth Missouri Volunteers mustered out, Solomon found that family ties enabled him to take command of a Wisconsin regiment. During the war he rose to the rank of brevet brigadier general.[31]

As the German troops organized, General Frost presided over a militia muster of fewer than seven hundred men at Lindell Grove, soon known as Camp Jackson in honor of the governor. At the same time, Duke and Greene carried out their mission to the Confederacy promptly and successfully. In a meeting with President Davis in Montgomery, they received authorization to draw the artillery and muskets they requested from the former Federal arsenal at Baton Rouge, Louisiana. The commander of the Baton Rouge arsenal provided the Missourians with two twelve-pound howitzers, two thirty-two-pound siege guns, about five hundred muskets, and a corresponding quantity of ammunition. Duke and Greene then traveled south to New Orleans, chartered the riverboat, the *Swan*, and made their way back to Baton Rouge. After loading and concealing their military cargo, Duke traveled north by train to New Madrid, Missouri, where he waited to meet Greene and the *Swan* before proceeding to St. Louis. While Duke and Greene made their way north with weapons from the Confederacy, state militia forces seized the small Federal arsenal at Liberty, Missouri.

As Duke and Greene traveled north from New Madrid, the clandestine military cargo on the *Swan* faced detection at Cairo, Illinois, where Federal military authorities required riverboats to stop and submit to inspection. Duke had watched the inspectors carefully on his way down river and found them to be careless. He found them to be equally ineffective on his return trip. The *Swan* arrived in St. Louis on May 9, and Duke and Greene delivered their weapons to General Frost at Camp Jackson that night. Duke was eager to put the weapons to use in an assault on the Arsenal. But when he visited with Frost on the evening of May 9 and again at seven in the morning on May 10, he found the commander reluctant to take action. Indeed, Frost took care to keep the militia muster at Camp Jackson from becoming an act of overt hostility against the United States. As Frost later pointed out, he had required "every officer and soldier in my command" to raise their hand and swear that they would "faithfully serve the State of Missouri" and "sustain the Constitution and laws of the United States." One could argue, as Blair and Lyon did, that it had become impossible to serve Claiborne Jackson's Missouri faithfully and sustain the Constitution of the United States. But Frost clearly took care not to commit treason against the United States.[32]

Disappointed, Duke and Greene left St. Louis for Jefferson City early in the morning of May 10 to report to Governor Jackson. They found about a thousand men gathered at the capital's fairgrounds. Fellow Minute Men Rock Champion and Samuel Farrington were among the new recruits rallying to support Governor Jackson. Captain Joseph Kelly brought his company of Irishmen to Jefferson City rather than to Camp Jackson. Kelly took command in Jefferson City and began training the recruits. Duke found Governor Jackson in Jefferson City to be as caution as General Frost in St. Louis. Duke feared that "active hostilities in Missouri would be indefinitely postponed." Eager for action, he took a leave of absence from the Missouri militia and went to Kentucky. There, in June, he married his fiancée, the daughter of John Hunt Morgan. Although Duke returned to southeast Missouri in late August 1861, he soon returned to Kentucky and was in the field with Morgan's cavalry throughout the war. "It was my fate," Duke later recalled, "to be separated from the noble band of Missouri troops." Nevertheless, he took pride in the "noble behavior of our Missouri boys" who supported Governor Jackson.[33]

The caution displayed by General Frost and Governor Jackson seemed to reassure Harney who continued to battle with Lyon over Federal policy toward state troops. Harney believed that the interests of the Union were best served by avoiding any confrontations between Federal and state troops. Although Jackson had refused to comply with Lincoln's call for troops, Harney let the matter pass and viewed the militia muster at Camp Jackson (beginning on May 6) as a constitutional exercise of state law. Harney did what he could to thwart Lyon. Nevertheless, on April 30, a few days before Camp Jackson opened, Lyon responded to the coming muster by deploying Totten's battery on the high ground west of the Arsenal. Also on April 30, Lyon received orders specifically authorizing him to do what he had been doing since he first arrived in St. Louis early in February: work in collaboration with the St. Louis Committee of Safety to secure St. Louis for the Union.

After ordering the militia muster, Jackson directed Lieutenant Colonel John S. Bowen to disband those elements of the Southwest Battalion still deployed along the Kansas border to deter Jay Hawker raids. Bowen left a company of mounted riflemen and a light battery in the field and brought all the men and officers belonging to the St. Louis Militia District to Frost's encampment. A native of Georgia, Bowen had graduated from West Point in 1853. Stationed for a time at Jefferson Barracks, he met and married his wife in St. Louis. Like Frost, Bowen left the army, but during the Border War with Kansas, he accepted a commission in the Missouri state militia. At Camp Jackson, Bowen commanded the Second Regiment of Missouri Volunteers. After the capture of Camp Jackson, Bowen accepted a parole from Lyon and early in June traveled to Richmond where he accepted a commission as colonel in the Confederate army. In May 1863, he rose to the rank of major general.[34]

Less dedicated to the Confederate cause was Lieutenant Colonel John Knapp who commanded the First Regiment at Camp Jackson. Born in New York City in 1816, Knapp moved to St. Louis with his parents in 1820. He joined a regiment of

Missouri Volunteers and fought in the Mexican War. Knapp was a wholesale grocer and, with his brother, proprietor and publisher of the conservative *St. Louis Republican*. After Lyon forced Claiborne Jackson out of Jefferson City, however, Knapp supported provisional governor Hamilton Gamble and proposed and helped to lead the Enrolled Missouri Militia.[35]

At Blair's suggestion, a number of Union men quickly left Frost's militia muster. Thomas Snead identified "Colonel Pritchard" as one who led a number of Union men out of Camp Jackson. This may have been Levi Pritchard, a thirty-year-old Ohio native who in 1856 had settled in DeKalb County in northwest Missouri. Pritchard probably served in the Southwest Battalion. The owner of a general store and DeKalb County's postmaster before the war, Pritchard served as a Federal inspecting officer in the Central District of Missouri. While in Jefferson City, he possessed sufficient wealth and self-esteem to commission a full-length oil portrait of himself. The portrait, attributed to George Caleb Bingham, showed Pritchard (probably in 1862) as a captain in the Fourth Regiment of Missouri State Militia Cavalry. In March 1864, Pritchard joined the newly formed Twelfth Regiment Missouri Cavalry which, in June, was assigned to Tennessee.[36]

Also departing from Camp Jackson was the German native Major Frederick Schaeffer. Before the war, Schaeffer directed a military academy for children in St. Louis and organized two militia companies. He resigned as a major in the Missouri militia and joined Boernstein's three-month Second Missouri Infantry as a lieutenant colonel. When the regiment mustered out late in August 1861, Schaeffer became a colonel in the three-year Second Missouri Infantry.[37]

Frost's adjutant, John S. Cavender, also resigned. Like Schaeffer, Cavender joined Blair's newly formed First Regiment of Missouri Volunteers, enlisting as captain of Company G. Born in New Hampshire in 1824, he had moved to St. Louis with his family in 1836. His father, also John Cavender, became a prominent member of William Greenleaf Eliot's Unitarian Church. (The elder Cavender was also a founding member of the Mercantile Library and the first treasurer of Washington University.)[38]

Answering the call to muster at Camp Jackson were portions of the Minute Men and several pro-southern private militia companies, including the St. Louis Grays, the Laclede Guards, the Washington Blues, and Basil Duke's Missouri Videttes. Frost detached Captain Kelly's company to carry arms and gunpowder acquired in St. Louis to the governor in Jefferson City. This left Frost with about 630 men at Camp Jackson, a relatively small force compared with the growing Federal army under Harney and Lyon.[39]

On April 30, with the five regiments of Missouri Volunteers mustered in and armed, Lyon received authorization to raise another five regiments. These troops would not be immediately mustered into the US army but would be organized as a US Reserve Corps commanded by Thomas Sweeny. General of the Army Winfield Scott acknowledged that to arm this body of men, without mustering them in as US soldiers, was an extraordinary measure, justified only by "revolutionary times."[40]

As was the case with the Volunteer Regiments, the Reserve Corps was composed predominately of Germans. In a tacit acknowledgment of Frank Blair's political influence, Sweeny appointed John McNeil colonel of the Third Reserve Regiment and B. Gratz Brown colonel of the Fourth Reserve Regiment. Both men were in their forties and neither had any military training or experience, but both men were close allies of Frank Blair and no one doubted their hostility to secessionists. A native of Nova Scotia, McNeil's fur-trading interests brought him to St. Louis in 1840. Noted for his unyielding hostility to southern sympathizers, McNeil fought guerillas in Missouri and would be remembered for his order to execute pro-Confederate prisoners at Palmyra, Missouri, in October 1862. B. Gratz Brown was a native of Kentucky and a graduate of Yale University who had moved to St. Louis in 1849. He soon won election to the state legislature as an antislavery Democrat and joined his cousin Frank Blair as editor of the pro-Republican *Missouri Democrat*.[41]

The remaining regimental commanders of the Reserve Corps were Germans. Henry Almstedt of the First Regiment was the oldest and had the most military experience. Born in Germany in 1817, he emigrated to St. Louis and served as a lieutenant in the Mexican War. Thereafter he was known in St. Louis as Captain Almstedt, commander of the light artillery in the Missouri Volunteer Militia. It was Captain Almstedt who "fired his national salute at sunrise" on the Fourth of July in 1851 at the ground-breaking festivities for the Pacific Railroad in St. Louis. With the formation of the Republican Party, Almstedt became an active member of the paramilitary Wide Awakes. After a parade of Wide Awakes in September 1860, the *Missouri Democrat* reported that "a few Douglas bullies" confronted Almstedt and other German Republicans outside a beer hall. In the altercation that followed, one of the Douglas men drew a pistol and fired a shot through the saloon window. No one was hit, but when another attacker cocked a pistol, "the weapon was instantly wrested from him by Captain Almstedt, whose utmost exertions were then needed to save the foolish fellow from merciless punishment."[42] Colonel Herman Kallmann of the Second Regiment Reserve Corps was the youngest of the Reserve Corps commanders. Born in Silesia (then a province of Prussia) in 1823, he participated in the failed revolution of 1848 and then escaped to the United States. An engineer by training, Kallmann settled in St. Louis and became active in railroad construction. Kallmann's regiment protected the Iron Mountain Railroad during its three months of service. Colonel Charles G. Stifel of the Fifth Regiment Reserve Corps was the prominent and wealthy owner of a brewery that bore his name. Born in the Kingdom of Worttenberg in 1819, he emigrated to New York in 1837 and moved to St. Louis in 1849.[43]

With approximately ten thousand men under arms, Lyon and Blair now had the resources they needed to close down Camp Jackson and secure St. Louis for the Union. Lyon confirmed on May 9 that Frost's men had in their possession cannon taken from the US Arsenal at Baton Rouge. Although the Committee of Safety did not agree that Frost's possession of US artillery justified a Federal attack, Blair strongly agreed with Lyon that the moment for action had arrived. General Harney continued to oppose the deployment of German troops and he had traveled to Washington, DC, to argue his case. Harney, if present, would certainly have opposed a confrontation at Camp Jackson. Lyon and Blair agreed to act before Harney returned.

On the morning of May 10 a heavy rain delayed the Federal movement. But Blair marched his regiment into the city from Jefferson Barracks. He was joined by Captain Sweeny's two companies of regular US troops. At about 1:00 p.m., Lyon began to deploy his forces. Lyon took command of Blair's regiment, Sweeny's two companies and Major Franz Backof's artillery battery and led the first column. Backof provided Lyon with an experienced artillery officer. Forty-eight when the Civil War began, Backof was born in Germany and trained in artillery in the German army. He had joined the Revolution of 1848 and briefly fought with Franz Sigel. Captured and jailed when the revolution failed, Backof emigrated to St. Louis when he was released in 1851. Back in the field with Sigel in 1861, Backof joined Lyon's column as it moved west on Laclede Avenue to the western end of Lindell Grove. Lyon then followed a lane north to Olive Street and then turned east on Olive to deploy on the northern edge of Camp Jackson.[44]

Boernstein's Second Regiment of US Volunteers left their barracks at the Marine Hospital south of the Arsenal and marched west on Pine Street to Lindell Grove. There they linked up with Lyon's column and deployed on the west side of Camp Jackson. Sigel's Third Regiment and Nicholas Schuettner's Fourth Regiment of US Volunteers moved out of the Arsenal and marched north on Broadway toward Olive. Sigel turned his regiment west onto Elm and then followed Tenth Street north. As the regiment passed Turner Hall at Tenth and Walnut Streets, Colonel McNeil's Third Reserves let out a rousing cheer. Sigel then moved west on Olive while Schuettner's regiment formed a parallel column and marched west on Market Street.[45]

In addition to the regular US troops and the US Volunteers, Lyon also deployed four regiments of the new US Reserve Corps. Almstedt's First Reserves followed Laclede Avenue to Lindell Grove and deployed south of Sigel's regiment on the east side of Camp Jackson. Kallmann's Second Reserves marched north to Olive from Soulard Market and then followed Olive to Lindell Grove. Kallmann positioned his regiment alongside Sigel's regiment at the northeastern corner of Camp Jackson. McNeil's Third Reserves probably followed Clark Street west from Turner Hall and deployed at the southeastern corner of Camp Jackson. Gratz Brown led the Fourth Reserves from the center of the city to the northeastern corner of the camp on Garrison Street.

Within two hours Lyon had deployed about eight thousand troops and surrounded the fewer than seven hundred men at Camp Jackson. At 3:15 p.m., Lyon demanded that Frost surrender his command:

HEADQUARTERS UNITED STATES TROOPS

St. Louis, MO., May 10, 1861

Sir: Your command is regarded as evidently hostile towards the Government of the United States. . . .

You are openly in communication with the so-called Southern Confederacy, which is now at war with the United States; and you are receiving at your camp, from the said Confederacy, and under its flag, large supplies of the material of war, most of which is known to be the property of the United States

These extraordinary preparations plainly indicate . . . hostilities to the General Government and co-operation with its enemies.

In view of these considerations . . . it is my duty to demand, and I do hereby demand, of you an immediate surrender of your command, with no other conditions than that all persons surrendering under this demand shall be humanely and kindly treated. Believing myself prepared to enforce this demand, one-half hour's time, before doing so, will be allowed for your compliance therewith.

Very respectfully, your obedient servant,
N. Lyon
Captain, Second Infantry, Comdg. Troops
General D.M. Frost, Commanding Camp Jackson

To this ultimatum Frost replied briefly and bitterly:

CAMP JACKSON, MO. May 10, 1861

Sir: I never for a moment having conceived the idea that so illegal and unconstitutional a demand as I have just received from you would be made by an officer of the United States Army. I am wholly unprepared to defend my command from this unwarranted attack, and shall therefore be forced to comply with your demand.

I am, sir, very respectfully, your obedient servant,
D.M. FROST
Brig. Gen., Comdg. Camp Jackson, M. V. M
Capt. N. LYON, Commanding U.S. Troops.[46]

The bitterness expressed by Frost as he surrendered to Lyon arose in part from the fact that Frost had worked hard to keep the Missouri militia muster within the letter of the law. His caution in this regard had been noted by Basil Duke. Frost's behavior after the surrender of Camp Jackson also suggests a degree of ambivalence on his part toward Claiborne Jackson's course of action and, more broadly, toward the Confederacy. Lyon paroled Frost after the capture of Camp Jackson, and unlike many of his men Frost initially respected the terms of the parole. Frost did not try to join Jackson and Price in central Missouri, nor did he immediately try to make his way into the Confederacy. Instead, he retired to his estate in Hazelwood, Missouri. It was not until March 1862 that Frost accepted an appointment as brigadier general in the Confederate army.[47]

Lyon's demand for the surrender of Camp Jackson outraged Frost, but it was the events that followed the camp's capitulation that outraged Conditional Unionists across the state and strengthened Claiborne Jackson's hand with the state legislature. As the Missouri militiamen surrendered, Lyon divided them into two groups and marched them onto the Olive Street plank road. Schuettner's and Sigel's regiments remained at the camp to secure weapons and equipment. At Lyon's direction, Boernstein moved his regiment east along the north side of the camp and formed a column behind Blair's regiment. Blair's troops enclosed one group of the prisoners; Boernstein's men enclosed the other. Lyon placed a band at the head of the procession, followed by himself and his staff. At about 6:00 p.m. the band played "The Star Spangled Banner" and the column began its march to the Arsenal.

Suddenly shots rang out and before officers restored order scores of civilian men, women, and children had been killed or wounded. Several soldiers had also been killed or wounded. Different observers reported different sequences of events, but all agreed on certain points. The inexperienced German Volunteers and Reserves had been the targets of angry taunts as they marched to Camp Jackson and particularly as they prepared to march their prisoners to the Arsenal. Angry civilians had also thrown rocks at the soldiers and some had probably fired pistols as well. The *Missouri Republican*, a Democratic paper that defended the legality of the militia muster and denounced the German troops for killing "unoffending spectators," noted that the unspecified "conduct of a few . . . desperadoes" preceded the shooting by the soldiers. In the confrontational climate that followed the surrender at Camp Jackson, the regular US troops held their fire. It was the Germans who first fired a warning volley over the heads of the crowd and then fired a deadly volley directly into the crowd. Lyon reported very little regarding the violence that followed the surrender: "During the surrender of Camp Jackson and their passage into our lines a mob attacked our force." He said he would forward a published account of the events, presumably from Blair's *Democrat*.

Harney returned to St. Louis on May 11 and resumed command of the Department of the West. Although he officially gave his "entire approval" to Lyon's actions at Camp Jackson, he promised to use only regular army troops—not the German volunteers or reserves—to maintain the peace in St. Louis. On May 14, the state legislature, incensed by Lyon's actions in St. Louis, passed "An Act to Provide for the Organization . . . of the Military Forces" in Missouri. The "military bill," as it came to be called, had been proposed by Governor Jackson. It prohibited all private militias, required that all commands be given in English, divided the state into nine military districts (corresponding to the state's Federal congressional districts), and authorized the governor to appoint a brigadier general for each district and a major general to assume overall command. It was the duty of the district commanders to raise and train a new militia, the Missouri State Guard. To fund this force, the legislature appropriated all of the revenue and credit available to the state. Clearly, if the State Guard engaged Federal forces in combat, a state of insurrection existed in Missouri. Harney hoped to avert such a crisis.

As Governor Jackson acted to enforce the military bill, Harney issued a relatively stern warning. Harney described the legislation as "an indirect secession ordinance" and declared it "a nullity" that "cannot and ought not to be upheld." At the same time, however, Harney continued to promote a conciliatory policy toward the governor. The general expressed his desire not to "interfere in any way with the prerogatives of the State of Missouri or with the functions of its executive or other authorities." But he promised "to suppress all unlawful combinations of men, whether formed under pretext of military organization or otherwise."[48]

On May 18, Jackson appointed Sterling Price major general, commanding the new Missouri State Guard. In the wake of the Camp Jackson affair, Price had largely abandoned his Conditional Unionist stance. With a new sense of purpose, Price accepted Jackson's appointment. Aware of Harney's desire to avoid further bloodshed, Price immediately sought a meeting with the Federal commander. On May 20, Harney agreed to meet with Price in St. Louis. The next day, the two commanders conferred and agreed to cooperate to maintain "peace and good order to the people of the state." The agreement stipulated that "General Price . . . undertakes, with the sanction of the governor of the state . . . to direct the whole power of the state officers to maintain order within the state among the people thereof." As for Federal authority in Missouri, the agreement declared that Harney "can have no occasion, as he has no wish, to make movements which might otherwise create excitement and jealousies which he most earnestly desires to avoid." In conclusion, the commanders expressed their hope that "the unquiet elements, which have threatened so seriously to disturb the public peace, may soon subside, and be remembered only to be deplored."[49]

Unbeknownst to Harney, Frank Blair had obtained orders from the War Department that removed Harney from command. The orders were dated May 16 and reached Blair on May 20. The orders were accompanied by a note from President Lincoln (dated May 18) asking Blair not to deliver the orders to Harney unless "in your judgment it is *indispensable*."[50]

As Harney and Price drafted their agreement, Governor Jackson moved forward to organize the State Guard. On May 21 the governor appointed the nine brigadier generals authorized by the military bill. Jackson acted deliberately but not as brashly as many ardent southern men desired. To command the First Military District in southeastern Missouri, Jackson initially appointed Nathaniel W. Watkins whom he had known as a state legislator. A native of Kentucky, Watkins settled in Cape Girardeau County in 1820 and practiced law there until his death in 1875. Watkins went into camp and began to organize his district but he was in his mid-sixties and soon decided to resign. By late July 1861 Meriwether Jeff Thompson took command. Lately the mayor of St. Joseph, at the opposite corner of the state, Thompson was seen by many to be an interloper, but he cut a dashing figure in his gray flannel shirt and broad red sash holding his saber, pistol, and Bowie knife. He was, as he recalled, "a rip-squealer and my name was Fight." He was the popular choice of the men in Watkins's camp.[51]

It was Thompson's eagerness to fight that brought him to southeastern Missouri. Born in Harpers Ferry, Virginia, in 1826, he moved to northwestern Missouri in 1848 and served as mayor of St. Joseph from 1858 to 1860 (he presided over the opening of the Pony Express there in April 1860). An ardent supporter of the Confederacy, Thompson initially looked with suspicion on Sterling Price's appointment as commander of the State Guard. Thompson viewed Price as a Union man and the Price-Harney agreement seemed to him to confirm that Price would not be the military leader that Missouri secessionists needed. Thompson went to Jefferson City and worked with Basil Duke and Colton Greene to urge Governor Jackson to take action. Thompson grew further disgusted with Jackson's "temporizing" when the governor appointed the moderate Alexander W. Doniphan brigadier general for Thompson's home district (the Fifth Military District). Thompson then made his way to southeast Missouri and joined the gathering Confederate forces in the Memphis (Tennessee), New Madrid (Missouri), and Pocahontas (Arkansas) region. As brigadier general of the Missouri State Guard in the First Military District, Thompson commanded an area that was lightly populated, rugged, and made difficult to traverse by swamps and numerous rivers. Thompson's ability to maneuver in this terrain gave rise to his nickname, the Swamp Fox of the Confederacy.[52]

The Second Military District encompassed the counties of northeastern Missouri but stretched southward to include the Missouri River counties of Callaway, Montgomery, Warren, and St. Charles. For a commander, Jackson ceremoniously turned to a prominent new resident of the district, Thomas Beverly Randolph, the son of Thomas Jefferson's cousin William Randolph. Born in Virginia in 1793, Randolph graduated from West Point in 1812 and served in the War of 1812. Late in life he moved to Missouri, and following the death of his wife in 1859, he lived with his son in northeast Missouri. In his late sixties when the Civil War began, Randolph predictably declined Jackson's appointment and the command of the district soon passed to thirty-five-year-old Thomas A. Harris, a native of Virginia, who settled in Hannibal and was serving as judge of the Lewis County Court when the war broke out. Harris successfully raised troops in his district, and in July 1861 the new Federal commander in the area, Colonel Ulysses S. Grant, moved against him. Grant believed that Harris was encamped near the town of Florida, in Monroe County. Grant later remarked about his mounting trepidation as he advanced toward Florida. Although a veteran of the Mexican War, this was Grant's first command. Grant recalled that he expected an engagement with Harris. As it happened, Harris had been warned of Grant's advance and had withdrawn. "It occurred to me at once," Grant recalled, "that Harris had been as much afraid of me as I had been of him." From that moment, Grant remembered, "I never experienced trepidation upon confronting an enemy, though I always felt more or less anxiety!" In late August, Harris received orders to move south of the Missouri River to join Price's army.[53]

John B. Clark, Sr., commanded the troops he raised in the Third Military District in central Missouri, extending south from the Iowa border to include the Missouri River counties of Chariton, Howard, and Boone. Born in Kentucky in 1802, Clark practiced law in Fayette, Missouri. He had fought in the Black Hawk War and represented Missouri in Congress from December 1857 until he was formally expelled in July 1861 for taking up arms against the United States. Clark engaged in the early fighting in Missouri and was wounded at Wilson's Creek. He recuperated at Memphis and soon thereafter served as a delegate from Missouri to the Provisional Confederate Congress. He later served as senator from Missouri in the first Confederate Congress and as a representative from Missouri in the second Confederate Congress.[54]

Located just west of Clark's district the Fourth Military District extended from the Iowa border south to the Missouri River counties of Ray and Carroll. Governor Jackson appointed William Y. Slack brigadier general of this district. Born in Kentucky in 1816, Slack moved with his parents to Boone County, Missouri. He studied law, was admitted to the bar in 1837, and moved northwest to Chillicothe. During the Mexican War he raised a company of volunteers and served as captain in the regiment commanded by Sterling Price. Slack served in the legislature where he expressed his proslavery and pro-southern views. With General Clark of the Second Missouri Division, Slack fought at the Battle of Wilson's Creek where he was badly wounded. Slack recovered and fought at Pea Ridge where he died on March 20, 1862, at the age of forty-six.[55]

The Fifth Military District included the counties of northwest Missouri, including the volatile Missouri River counties of Atchison, Holt, Buchanan, and Platte. Jackson's first choice for brigadier general of the fifth district was Alexander W. Doniphan, a prominent slaveholding Whig who practiced law at Lexington and, later, at Liberty, Missouri. Doniphan had served with distinction with Sterling Price in the Mexican War. Jackson knew that Doniphan had strongly supported the proslavery forces in Kansas. But, as Jeff Thompson noted, Doniphan never supported secession. Doniphan vowed instead not to take up arms against the southern states or the United States. Thompson was convinced that Jackson's overture to Doniphan weakened the southern cause in northwest Missouri. The governor made his offer early in May, and Doniphan took several weeks to respond. Finally, on May 23, Doniphan wrote to Jackson declining the offer. Believing that the Price-Harney agreement "adjusted" matters in the state "to promote entire peace in the future," Doniphan saw no need for a state guard. In 1863, however, he left his western Missouri home for the security of St. Louis where he continued to practice law.[56]

When Doniphan declined Jackson's offer to command the Fifth Division, the governor turned to Alexander Steen. Born in St. Louis in 1827, Steen was the son of an army officer. Although he never attended West Point he received an army commission and served in the Mexican War. At the end of the war he resigned from the army but resumed his military career in the 1850s. Steen resigned again after the capture of Camp Jackson. Although his father remained loyal to the Union, Steen accepted Jackson's commission as brigadier general of the Missouri State Guard on June 18, 1861. Unable to recruit a division in the district assigned to him, Steen joined Price in southwest Missouri without a command. Price made good use of Steen's regular army experience to train his raw recruits. Steen helped direct troop movements at the Battle of Wilson's Creek.[57]

For the central Sixth Military District located south of the Missouri River, Jackson appointed the native Virginian M. Mosby Parsons. Although Basil Duke left Missouri before fighting began, members of his Minute Men militia became the core of the First Rifle Regiment of Parson's division. Migrating to Missouri, Parsons settled in Jefferson City where he was admitted to the bar in 1846. He served as a volunteer in the Mexican War in Alexander Doniphan's regiment. Parsons was appointed US attorney for the western district of Missouri and later served in the state legislature.[58]

South of Parsons's district, the Seventh District reached southward through the Ozarks to the Arkansas border. Jackson appointed James H. McBride commander. A native of Kentucky who became a merchant and manufacturer in Paris, Monroe County, Missouri, before moving to Springfield where he practiced law, McBride served in the legislature and won election as circuit judge.[59]

Jackson appointed James S. Rains commander of the Eighth Military District, which included the southwestern counties of the state from Jackson County (and Kansas City) south to the Arkansas border. Born in Tennessee in 1817, Rains moved to Sarcoxie, Missouri, in 1840. He served as a judge in Newton County and as a member of the legislature.[60]

The Ninth Military District included the counties of east central Missouri, including St. Louis. Jackson appointed Meriwether Lewis Clark, Sr., commander. Clark was the son of William Clark of Lewis and Clark Expedition fame. Born in St. Louis, Clark graduated from West Point in 1830 and fought in the Black Hawk War before resigning his army commission in 1833 and returning to St. Louis. Clark served with Missouri Volunteers in the Mexican War. Fervently pro-secessionist and unable to organize Confederate troops in the Federally controlled district assigned to him, Clark soon left St. Louis to join the Confederate army. As Clark's replacement, Jackson turned to Camp Jackson's commander,

Daniel Frost. But Frost, too, felt compelled to leave St. Louis in order to serve the southern cause. He became a brigadier general in the Confederate Army in March 1862. The Missouri State Guard never formally organized in the Ninth Military District.[61]

In the summer and early fall of 1861, seven of the nine brigadier generals appointed by Governor Jackson took the field with Missouri State Guard troops under the direct command of Major General Sterling Price. (Federal military actions prevented Daniel Frost and M. Jeff Thompson from joining Price until later in the war.) Among Price's commanders, Alexander Steen had the greatest military experience. As veterans of the Mexican War, Mosby Parsons and William Slack brought some military experience to Price's army. John S. Marmaduke, who served as colonel in Parson's Sixth Division, could have brought a great deal of experience to the Missouri State Guard. Indeed, Marmaduke should have been a great asset for his uncle, Governor Claiborne Jackson. The son of a prominent Saline County family, Marmaduke attended Yale and Harvard before entering West Point. During the secession crisis, Marmaduke returned to Missouri and although his father was a Unionist, he supported Jackson and the secessionist cause. However, an early disagreement with Jackson at the battle of Boonville prompted Marmaduke to leave the State Guard and join the Confederate army.[62]

Many of Price's commanders had little or no military experience. John B. Clark, Sr., who turned sixty as the Civil War began, had not seen action since the Black Hawk War, and James McBride and James Rains had no formal military experience. Similarly, Thomas Harris and Martin Green, whose troops from the Second Military District joined Price's army late in the summer of 1861, came without significant military experience. Poorly armed and with few experienced commanders, the Missouri State Guard appeared, even to ardent secessionists like Thomas Snead, more a mob than an army. Still, thousands of men rallied to Claiborne Jackson's banner and the governor expected to gain the active support of the vast majority of Missourians.

The Price-Harney agreement served Jackson very nicely but it soon came to an end. Convinced that the agreement encouraged pro-secession elements in the state, Blair delivered his removal order to a startled General Harney on May 30, and on May 31, Lyon took command of the Department of the West as brigadier general. Lyon did not immediately revoke the Price-Harney agreement. Hopeful that it could be continued under Lyon's command, Jackson and Lyon met on June 11 at the Planters House Hotel in St. Louis. Lyon attended the meeting with his aide-de-camp Major Horace Conant and with Colonel Frank Blair. Price and Jackson were accompanied by Price's aide-de-camp Thomas Snead. After more than four hours of fruitless discussion, Snead recalled that it was Lyon who suddenly brought the meeting to a close. Lyon remained seated, but he spoke "deliberately, slowly, and with a peculiar emphasis." He emphasized the supremacy of Federal authority in the state. He then rose to his feet to deliver his philippic.

"Rather than concede to the State of Missouri for one single instant the right to dictate to my Government in any matter however unimportant"—as he spoke he pointed in turn to Price, Snead, Blair, and Conant—"I would see you, and you, and you, and you, and every man, woman, and child in the State, dead and buried." Turning to Governor Jackson, Lyon then added, "This means war." Within an hour Federal officers escorted Jackson, Price, and Snead out of St. Louis.[63]

As soon as Jackson returned to Jefferson City (June 12, 1861), he issued a proclamation to the people of Missouri. In it, the governor explained the issues that compelled him to take up arms against the military forces of the United States. Jackson began his proclamation by assuring Missourians that he had sought peace at his meeting with Lyon in St. Louis. He had offered Lyon concessions that would have been "humiliating" to the governor if he had not been motivated by "the most earnest desire to avert the horrors of civil war." Jackson said that he offered to disband the new State Guard and not exercise his authority to call out the militia if the Federal military would disband the Home Guards "and pledge itself not to occupy with its troops any localities in the state not occupied by them at this time." Lyon bluntly rejected Jackson's terms. Lyon insisted that Jackson disband and disarm the State Guard without conditions. Furthermore, Lyon demanded that the governor declare the newly passed military act null and void. Lyon declared that the officers of the US Army would station troops wherever they deemed necessary. Lyon, reported Jackson, regarded Missouri to be in the "exact condition of Maryland," which had been the scene of violent clashes between Federal troops and its citizens in April. "Fellow-citizens," implored Jackson, "all our efforts toward conciliation have failed." He went on, "Military despotism" had "usurped the powers of the Federal Government," and their "minions" had invaded Missouri. It was Jackson's obligation as governor to call for fifty thousand men to rally to the defense of the state. "Your first allegiance is due to your own State," Jackson declared: "You are under no obligation whatever to obey the unconstitutional edicts of the military despotism which has enthroned itself at Washington." "Rise, then," concluded Jackson, "and drive out ignominiously the invaders."[64]

As Jackson issued his proclamation, Price began to deploy his troops: he directed that the forces of Clark's Third District march to Boonville and make contact with Parsons's forces in the Sixth District as they advanced toward that location from Tipton.[65] The elements for civil war in Missouri were now in place. Five days later, as Lyon advanced against the State Guard at Boonville, war began.

Chapter Two

"Formidable Preparations . . . By the Enemy"

As Claiborne Jackson and Sterling Price left St. Louis to make their way back to Jefferson City, they must have recognized that their ability to control Missouri's great city had eluded them. St. Louis was now the hub of Federal authority in the Trans-Mississippi West and in the Mississippi valley. Crossing the Gasconade River, Jackson and Price returned to the rural central Missouri valley where they made their homes. The Kentucky-born governor owned a plantation near Fayette in Howard County. Price, a Virginia native, prospered as a tobacco planter in Keytesville, Chariton County. Both men were prosperous slaveholders and prominent leaders of the proslavery Democracy in Missouri. Price had won election as governor of the state in 1852, and Jackson had won election to that office in 1860. Their proslavery views were well-known, but as yet, neither man had openly avowed secession. Jackson ran for governor as a Unionist Democrat in 1860, and Price presided over the state convention in February and March 1861 and joined with delegates who called for compromises to maintain the Union and preserve the peace. But Jackson and Price both aggressively promoted military preparedness in the state, and this suggests that eventually they intended to harness the resources of Missouri to the Confederate cause. St. Louis, for the time being, was firmly under Federal control. But the rest of the state—particularly the central Missouri valley—had much to offer the South in manpower and materials.

Returning to Jefferson City, Jackson and Price knew that Lyon intended to attack the Missouri State Guard as quickly as he could. As they contemplated the harsh realities of war, Lyon was by no means their only concern. Free states bordered Missouri on the east and north and the soon-to-be free state of Kansas bordered Missouri on the west. Under the circumstances, it would be difficult to maintain a significant state military presence north of the Missouri River. But it would take time for Federal forces in Illinois, Iowa, and Kansas to exert any influence in Missouri. Jackson and Price understood that they needed to act quickly, but they also knew that the central Missouri counties with the largest concentrations of slaves and slaveholders would be their principal source of support. With the collapse of the Price-Harney agreement, Jackson and Price needed to gather what men and supplies they could from these rich slaveholding counties —Callaway, Boone, Howard and Chariton—and concentrate them south of the Missouri. In southwest Missouri, within a day's march of Confederate armies gathering in Arkansas, Jackson and Price had a chance to maintain a military and political presence in the state and eventually concentrate military forces in the central Missouri River valley.

In Arkansas, the well-known Texas Ranger Ben McCulloch took command of Confederate forces. A brigadier general in the Confederate army, McCulloch's initial instructions directed him to defend the Indian Territory from Federal attack (most likely from Kansas). McCulloch made Fort Smith, Arkansas, his headquarters and assembled an army (eventually numbering twenty-seven hundred men) that included the Third Louisiana Infantry under Colonel Louis Hebert, seven companies of Arkansas mounted riflemen (the First Arkansas) under Colonel Thomas Churchill, and the Second Arkansas Mounted Riflemen under James M. McIntosh. McCulloch would later be joined by ten companies raised in Dallas, Texas, by Colonel Elkanah Greer and by two hundred Arkansas Infantry led by Colonel Dandridge McRae. In addition, closer to the Missouri border, at Mayville, Arkansas, West Point graduate Brigadier General Nicholas B. Pearce raised several regiments of Arkansas militia, eventually numbering about two thousand men. Although Pearce's troops were not yet Confederate soldiers, he was instructed by state authorities to cooperate with McCulloch. In June, when McCulloch learned that Lyon had brought an end to the Price-Harney agreement, he began moving his troops north from Fort Smith to join Pearce's brigade at Mayville. Now McCulloch received new instructions, to move into either Kansas or Missouri as circumstances required. Lyon clearly understood the challenge he faced. He had successfully broken up the state militia muster in St. Louis. Now he needed to disrupt militia musters in central Missouri and prevent Jackson and Price from forming a junction with McCulloch and Pearce in Arkansas.[1]

Jackson and Price expected to recruit successfully in central Missouri, but they realized that in order to do so they needed to gather their forces at a safe distance from St. Louis. They immediately moved the men and supplies gathered at the capital further up the Missouri River to Boonville. Jackson then dispatched Colton Greene to Fort Smith to meet with McCulloch. Greene arrived at Fort Smith on June 13 and met with both McCulloch and McIntosh. Greene explained that Jackson and Price were gathering men and supplies to support the southern cause. These efforts were threatened by Lyon out of St. Louis. If McCulloch would enter Missouri to support Jackson and Price, the men and resources of Missouri could substantially aid the Confederacy. Greene found McCulloch and McIntosh willing to enter Missouri if it became necessary to do so to carry out their orders to defend the Indian Territory. This was less than the unqualified support Greene had sought, but it marked the beginning of a discussion that became more productive over time.

Also on June 13, Jackson took command of the State Guard at Boonville as Price, who had fallen ill, returned to his Keytesville plantation to recuperate. On the same day, Lyon led a Federal army out of St. Louis to take control of Jefferson City and confront Jackson and Price in the center of the state. Two days after the momentous meeting at the Planters House Hotel, Missouri was on the brink of civil war.[2]

At Boonville, Jackson presided over a largely unorganized, untrained, and poorly armed aggregation of volunteers. Only Captain Joseph Kelly's company of St. Louis militiamen, the Washington Blues, functioned as a cohesive unit. Kelly's company had brought weapons and gunpowder to Jefferson City to support the State Guard and Jackson continued to rely on these men to guard his supplies. With the rest of his troops, Jackson faced tremendous challenges. Beyond his adventures as an infantry captain during the Black Hawk War, the governor had little in the way of military experience to guide him. With Price temporarily unavailable, Jackson was fortunate to have at his side his nephew, twenty-eight-year-old John Sappington Marmaduke. A West Point graduate, Marmaduke resigned from the US army in April to accept an appointment as colonel in the newly formed Missouri State Guard. Marmaduke surveyed the situation at Boonville and concluded that the town could not successfully be defended. The Missouri River provided Federal forces in Kansas and St. Louis with an invasion route and a line of supply. Marmaduke recommended moving the State Guard farther south to take up defensive positions near the town of Warsaw, south of the Osage River. Here, Marmaduke argued, the Guardsmen could rendezvous in relative safety and have time to organize and train before they were called upon to defend themselves and Jackson's government. Jackson rejected the advice. He hoped to hold his ground at Boonville. Located on bluffs on the south bank of the Missouri River, Boonville commanded heights from which Jackson hoped to control passage on the river. If the State Guard could hold Boonville, Jackson could control central Missouri long enough to give Price the time and resources he needed to raise an army. As soon as Jackson learned that Lyon had occupied Jefferson City and had begun to advance into central Missouri, the governor directed General Mosby Parsons at Tipton (about twenty miles to the south) to reinforce him at Boonville.

Jackson expected Lyon to move against him at Boonville. What Jackson did not know was that Lyon had also dispatched Thomas Sweeny with the volunteer regiments commanded by Franz Sigel, Charles Solomon, and B. Gratz Brown to southwest Missouri. Sweeny's brigade, supported by two artillery batteries (eight guns in all) under Major Backof, moved quickly by rail to Rolla and then more slowly by road to camps in Springfield and further west at Sarcoxie and Neosho. Along this line, Lyon intended to detect and block any movement by Confederates from Arkansas into Missouri and any effort by Jackson and Price to join Confederates in Arkansas. The last of Sweeny's troops left St. Louis on June 15,

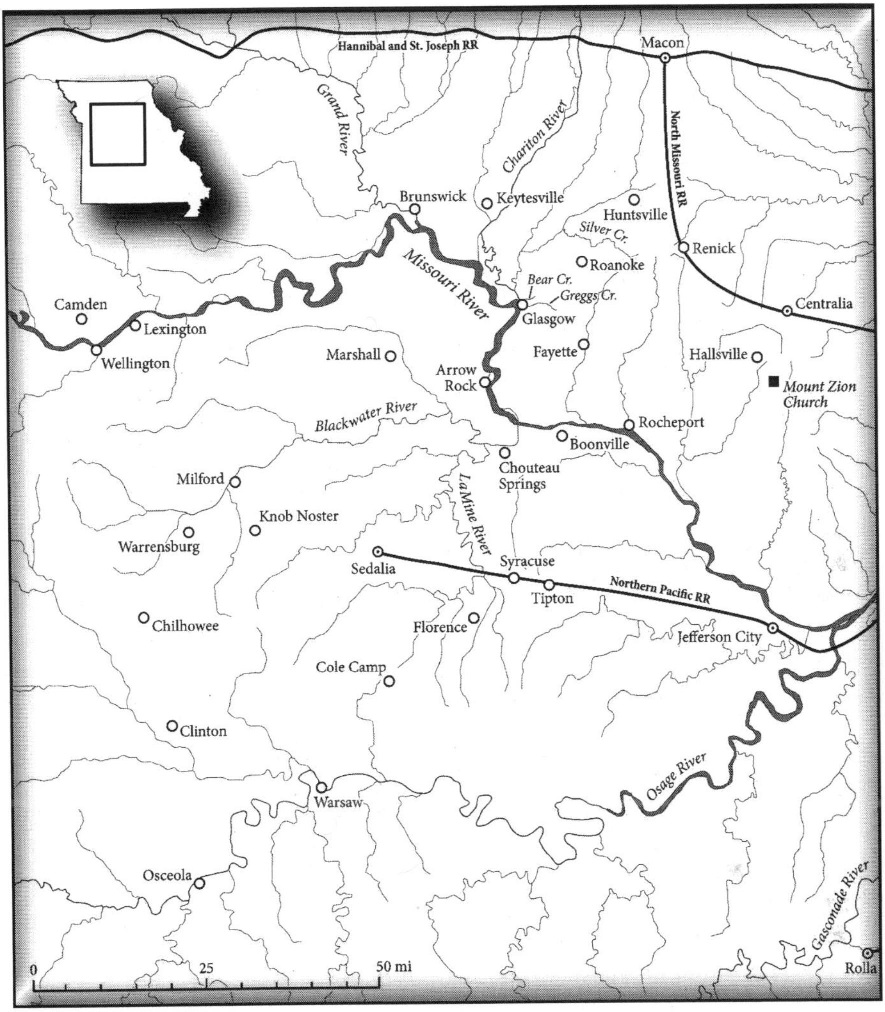

and Lyon urged his commander (George B. McClellan, whose Department of the Ohio briefly included Missouri) to send reinforcements into southwest Missouri. "I am fully persuaded," wrote Lyon, "that formidable preparations have been made by the enemy in that quarter."[3]

The force that Lyon led out of St. Louis for Jefferson City included James Totten's battery, Company F of the Second US Artillery, Company B of the Second US Infantry, two companies of regular army recruits, Frank Blair's First Regiment of Missouri Volunteers, and nine companies of Henry Boernstein's Second Regiment. With about two thousand men in all, Lyon moved up the Missouri River by riverboat to the state capital. He arrived at the capital about 2:00 p.m. on

June 15 and found that Jackson and Price had evacuated. The next morning Lyon detached Boernstein and three companies of his regiment to guard Jefferson City while Lyon continued west with the rest of his force (about seventeen hundred men) by three riverboats toward the reported State Guard camp at Boonville.[4]

Lyon moved as quickly as he could against the State Guard in central Missouri because he fully expected Ben McCulloch to lead Confederate forces into southwestern Missouri and he wanted to deny the Confederates access to the resources and recruits available to them in the central Missouri valley. Lyon must have known Ben McCulloch, at least by reputation. McCulloch had gained considerable renown in the West and across the nation as one of the original Texas Rangers. Fifty years old when the Civil War began, McCulloch had moved from his native Tennessee to Texas in 1835. There he fought with Sam Huston at the Battle of San Jacinto in 1836 and joined the Texas Rangers when they were first organized in 1840. During the Mexican War, McCulloch led a company of Texas Rangers as scouts. His bravery and bravado at the battles of Monterrey and Buena Vista brought him national recognition. After the Mexican War, McCulloch briefly joined the California gold rush but soon returned to Texas and made a quiet living as a cattle rancher. Restless in civilian life, he yearned for a military career. In 1855, when Congress authorized the formation of two new regiments of cavalry to patrol the southwestern frontier, McCulloch hoped to receive a commission as colonel. Perhaps because he had not attended West Point, the War Department offered him an appointment as major. McCulloch sullenly declined the commission. When Texas seceded, however, McCulloch quickly received the military command he had long sought. In March 1861, McCulloch became a brigadier general in the Confederate army.[5]

In their strategic thinking, Jackson and Price regarded McCulloch as a vital ally. A strong Confederate military presence in northern Arkansas would aid their efforts to bring Missouri (or a significant portion of it) into the Confederacy. For reasons that are not entirely clear, however, McCulloch seemed predisposed from the outset to regard with suspicion those Missourians who rallied to the southern cause. McCulloch's attitude was shaped in part by his disdain for Sterling Price. Like McCulloch, Price had not attended West Point, but this similarity in background did nothing to endear the Missourian to the Texan. Instead, McCulloch pointedly described Price as more politician than soldier. This perception may have been formed during the Mexican War when Price maneuvered openly and successfully for the political support that brought him promotion to brigadier general. But McCulloch also spoke disapprovingly of Price's recruits. Here there was more than personality involved. It was not the ragtag appearance of the Missourians that disturbed McCulloch. As a Texas Ranger, McCulloch was not one to follow formal military protocol. He wore a frock coat and hat into battle, not a general's uniform. But, McCulloch found the Missourians undisciplined in their bearing and untrustworthy in their behavior. Many of Price's men had participated in the Border War with Free State settlers in Kansas. While Mc-

Culloch was well versed in the tactics of irregular warfare that characterized the Border War, he nevertheless may have viewed the partisan warfare as a distraction from the larger goal of defending the new Confederate nation. The legacy of the Border War and the developing conflict between Federal and state forces in Missouri did not directly concern McCulloch. Indeed, while Jackson and Price argued with Lyon and Blair at the Planters House Hotel, McCulloch had traveled to the Indian Territory seeking strategic alliances with the Indian nations and recruits for his growing Confederate army of volunteers from Texas, Louisiana, and Arkansas. If Jackson and Price could provide a military buffer between Federal forces and his Confederate army, McCulloch had no reason to complain. But McCulloch saw northern Arkansas and the Indian Territory, not the Missouri valley, as the northern border of the Confederacy in the Trans-Mississippi West.

Lyon began his drive against Jackson and Price on June 16, a Sunday morning, when he left Jefferson City for Boonville. About fifteen miles below Boonville, Lyon tied up for the night and on the morning of the June 17 resumed his advance. After passing Rocheport on the north bank of the Missouri, Lyon's transports rounded a bend and approached Boonville. Lyon carefully examined both banks of the river with his field glasses and identified on the bluffs on the south bank about two miles east of Boonville two artillery pieces partially concealed by trees. Lyon concluded that the guns were positioned to offer some protection from an advance upriver against Boonville. This, Lyon concluded, was the site of Governor Jackson's camp. He did not challenge the rebel artillery. Instead he ordered his transports to land his men on the broad bottom lands on the south bank of the river about eight miles below Boonville and six miles from what he took to be the State Guard camp. To protect his three transports, Lyon detached a party of artillerymen with one eight-inch howitzer and a company of the First Missouri and instructed them to position themselves on the river within range of the rebel camp. Lyon's troops then advanced by land from the southeast along the river road known as the Rocheport Road. Lyon directed that the party guarding the transports open fire on the rebel camp from the river.[6]

Where Lyon landed, the Missouri bottoms extended about a mile south to a line of hills that stretched in a northwesterly direction to Boonville. As Lyon followed the Rocheport Road to the west, the bottoms narrowed and the line of hills drew closer to the river. Just east of Boonville, the bottoms disappeared and the Rocheport Road rose to higher ground. By 7:00 a.m. Lyon had completed his landing and he formed his men into a column. Ahead of the column Lyon deployed two companies of the Second Missouri as skirmishers. Lyon's company of regular US troops led the column followed by Totten's battery, the two companies of regular recruits, Blair's First Missouri, and the remaining four companies of the Second Missouri.[7]

As Lyon assembled his column along the Rocheport Road, Jackson prepared his defenses east of Boonville. Jackson decided to hold Kelly's company in the rear (presumably to continue to protect the weapons and gunpowder they had brought from St. Louis). Jackson directed Marmaduke to gather all of the rest of the troops he could find and confront Lyon. Jackson hoped that Marmaduke could delay Lyon long enough to permit Mosby Parsons to reinforce him from Tipton. Dutifully, but with little hope of success, Marmaduke gathered a band of about five hundred men to meet Lyon's advance.

As the Federal troops began to ascend to higher ground and follow the Rocheport Road to Boonville, their skirmishers drew fire from an advance party of Marmaduke's Guardsmen. The rebel fire was sufficiently brisk to cause Lyon to draw in his skirmishers (he gathered them into his right flank) and form a battle line. On the right side of the road, Lyon positioned Lieutenant Colonel Friedrich Schaeffer's Second Regiment of infantry. On the left side of the road was Lyon's company of regulars and Colonel Blair's First Regiment of infantry. Totten's battery remained in the rear. As the Federal line advanced, Marmaduke's men fell back about one mile to their main line of defense in and around the brick residence of William M. Adams, about three miles east of Boonville.[8]

As Marmaduke's pickets withdrew, the Federals advanced into what Lyon described as "high and open ground." Here, near the Adams house, the most serious fighting took place. Most of Marmaduke's men were in an open cornfield, although some found shelter behind fences, in a wooded thicket, and in the Adams house. Totten brought his guns to bear on the house and the woods. Two cannonballs demolished most of the eastern wall of the house, and the Guardsmen soon abandoned it. Artillery fire on the rebels in the woods scattered them as well. To Lyon's surprise Marmaduke did not answer the Federal guns with artillery fire of his own. Jackson had not deployed his two artillery pieces. They remained where Lyon had first seen them, on the high ground above the river about a mile away from the State Guard camp. They were not fired before Lyon captured them.

Marmaduke quickly realized that his men could not hold their ground. At the same time Jackson ordered Marmaduke to retreat in the direction of Parsons's force, thought to be approaching Boonville from the south. Unfortunately for Marmaduke, an orderly retreat under fire required a degree of training and discipline that his men did not yet posses. Soon, the retreat turned into a rout. Some of Guardsmen men ran off. Others cowered. When Marmaduke encountered one group of men huddled in a ravine seeking shelter from Totten's guns, he warned them that if they did not join him in retreat, the advancing Federals would kill half of them. Some of the fleeing Guardsmen returned to their camp, about a mile closer to town. But they soon scattered as the howitzer on the riverboat opened fire. A few of the routed Guardsmen took the opportunity to return home, but most straggled through town in the direction of Parson's presumed advance. It took them some time to find Parsons. As Parsons approached Boonville, he learned that the State Guard had been defeated and he withdrew to the southwest, to the vicinity of the towns of Syracuse and Florence. Eventually Jackson, with General John B. Clark and Colonel Marmaduke, caught up with Parsons and they completed an orderly retreat southwest to Warsaw. This was precisely the movement that Marmaduke had recommended to Jackson days earlier. The governor's refusal to recognize the superior military training of his nephew and Jackson's insistence that Marmaduke stand and fight at Boonville infuriated the younger man. Marmaduke resigned his commission in the State Guard, traveled as quickly as he could to Richmond, and joined the Confederate army.

The fighting at Boonville had been brief. Within twenty minutes, as one observer noted, the State Guard "melted steadily away." As Lyon's battle line advanced toward the hastily abandoned rebel camp and into the town beyond, the Union troops soon described Marmaduke's undisciplined retreat as the "Boonville races." It was the volunteers of Shaeffer's Second Regiment (on Lyon's right flank) who first entered the enemy's camp. It was clear that the Guardsmen had fled in haste. Jackson's men had been preparing breakfast when the Federal assault began and they left behind large amounts of food, arms, ammunition, and equipment. Lyon reported capturing Jackson's two artillery pieces and about five hundred guns of "all sorts." By 11:00 a.m. Lyon was in complete control of Boonville. Casualties on both sides had been light. Lyon reported four killed (two in battle and two from wounds), one missing, and seven wounded. Later accounts suggest that he suffered five dead and seven wounded. Marmaduke probably lost three dead and a half dozen wounded. Lyon also took about sixty prisoners whom he released "upon oath to obey the laws of the General Government."[9]

The military significance of the fighting at Boonville was slight; it had been little more than a skirmish. Jackson's retreat succeeded in part because of the onset of heavy rains and because of Lyon's need to assemble a supply train before he marched south away from the Missouri River. Lyon did not attempt an immediate pursuit. Indeed, fifteen days passed before Lyon moved south from Boonville. But the engagement at Boonville marked the first time that the State Guard and Federal troops had fired on one another. The Missouri Guardsmen were not yet Confederate soldiers (and they would not be for another six months). But at Boonville, Jackson cast off the veil of neutrality and Lyon engaged an enemy that he could unequivocally describe as being in open rebellion against the United States. Thomas W. Knox, a correspondent with the *New York Herald*, accompanied Lyon at Boonville and noted the nature of the loyalties of Jackson's men. "The rallying-cry at the time was in behalf of the State, and the people were told they must act for Missouri without regard to any thing else," Knox observed. But Knox's pro-Unionist eye found plenty of evidence in the flags captured at Boonville to indicate that for Jackson's men the interests of the state were rapidly blending with the interests of the Confederacy.

On the day after the skirmish at Boonville, Price, still weak from his illness, joined Rains and Slack in Lexington as they hastened to organize several thousand recruits in the area. Learning of Marmaduke's defeat at Booneville, Price placed Rains in command at Lexington and directed him to move as quickly as possible toward Lamar, beyond the Spring River in southwest Missouri. With a small escort, Price rode toward Arkansas to meet with McCulloch and urge the Confederate commander to enter Missouri to rescue Jackson and Rains. As Price made his way south, he steadily attracted more men. A mounted company, the Windsor Guards from Henry County, joined Price on the way to Arkansas. Also joining Price was Captain Leonidas St. Clair "Dick" Campbell who commanded a cavalry force of forty men recruited in Springfield and surrounding Greene County. Campbell's father-in-law, Daniel Dorsey Berry, was one of the earliest settlers in Greene County and by far the richest man in Springfield. Since Unionist sentiment ran strong in Springfield, Campbell quickly led his recruits to join Price at Cowskin Prairie near the Arkansas border. Others came in individually and in small groups. By the time Price reached Cowskin Prairie, his "escort" had swelled to a force of twelve hundred men. With weapons acquired from Pearce's Arkansas militia, Price began to arm and train his new recruits.[10]

While his men trained at Cowskin Prairie, Price traveled on to Maysville, Arkansas, to meet with McCulloch. Price quickly explained his situation to the Confederate commander. Just across the border, a body of well over a thousand men prepared to fight against Federal forces in Missouri. Thousands more men of southern sympathies were moving south from Lexington and Boonville. From Price's perspective, the situation was precarious because the Guardsmen at Cowskin Prairie and the Guardsmen moving south from the Missouri valley were separated by the Federal troops that he knew had taken control of Rolla, Springfield, Sarcoxie, and Neosho. McCulloch and Price fully recognized the vulnerabilities that Lyon and Sigel hoped to exploit. If the rebel forces in Missouri could not combine, they might be dispersed or destroyed separately. To avoid this calamity, McCulloch agreed to move swiftly into Missouri with the aim of defeating Sigel who could be trapped between McCulloch and Price to the south and Jackson's Guardsmen moving south from the Missouri valley. If Sigel could be defeated and the rebel forces combined, Lyon, pursuing Jackson from the rear, would be forced to withdraw or advance against an enemy of overwhelmingly superior strength.

Jackson met no significant opposition as he continued his retreat southward. As Marmaduke had predicted, the retreat to Warsaw provided Jackson with valuable time to organize, arm, and train his men. Jackson also benefited from the independent actions of State Guard units operating out of Warsaw. During his retreat, Jackson received word that a sizable body of German Home Guard stood in his path near the town of Cole Camp. As Jackson approached that location on June 18, he learned that a battalion of Guardsmen from Warsaw had badly beaten the Germans. The State Guard force had caught about 400 Home Guards asleep and killed or wounded about 100 of them and scattered the rest. The victorious Missouri Guardsmen (about 350 men with about a third of them mounted) had been composed of the Warsaw Grays, led by Lieutenant Colonel Walter S. O'Kane, and the Warsaw Blues, commanded by Major Thomas H. Murray. On the morning of June 19, as Jackson regrouped in Warsaw, O'Kane and Murray joined the State Guard and brought with them the weapons captured from the German Home Guards.

Also joining Jackson at Warsaw was Henry Guibor, recently paroled after his capture at Camp Jackson. Born in Alsace, France, in 1823, Guibor settled in St. Louis and served as a volunteer in the Mexican War. He also served as an artilleryman with John S. Bowen in the Southwest Expedition of 1860. Guibor now took charge of the four six-pounders taken from the Liberty, Missouri, Federal arsenal. John Q. Burbridge and a group of recruits from Pike County also made their way to Warsaw to join Jackson. They brought about 150 new muskets with them. Learning that Rains was moving to Lamar and that Price was in Arkansas, Jackson began moving his reorganized and strengthened force toward Lamar. By July 3, Jackson (with Parsons and Clark) had joined Rains and Slack at that location.[11]

The defeat at Boonville marked the end of orderly recruitment for the State Guard. But the fighting also heightened partisan sentiments in Missouri and thousands of new troops joined Jackson's army at Camp Lamar. The new recruits included Jo Shelby and a mounted force of veterans of the Border War now known as the Lafayette County Cavalry. At Lamar, Jackson attached Shelby and his men to Rains's Second Division. Shelby's decision to join the State Guard required an open break with an extended family that, for the most part, supported the Union cause. Shelby's cousins included Frank Blair and B. Gratz Brown, both of whom commanded Federal volunteer regiments.[12]

Born in Kentucky, Shelby had moved to Missouri in 1852 with another cousin, Howard Gratz, and settled near Waverly where they raised hemp and operated the Waverly Steam Rope Factory. In Waverly, Shelby married the daughter of his father's first cousin, also a wealthy planter. Over the next several years, Shelby and Gratz parted company, in large part because Shelby became increasingly active in the fight against Free State settlers in Kansas. Shelby also grew close to the Missouri guerilla leaders William Quantrill and Jesse and Frank James. During the Civil War, these fighters gained quasi-Confederate status by being attached to Shelby's cavalry division as what Shelby's biographer described as an "independent company of partisan rangers." Howard Gratz did not share Shelby's violent hostility to the Free State settlers. In the midst of the Border War, Gratz returned to his family's home in Lexington, Kentucky. Over time Shelby apparently bought out Gratz's interest in the rope factory. Although Shelby's proslavery and prosouthern views were well-known, Frank Blair continued to hope that his cousin would prove to be a Union man at heart. In May 1861, at Blair's request, Shelby visited St. Louis. There Shelby witnessed the capture of Camp Jackson and Blair, flush with victory, offered to seek a Federal military appointment for him.

Shelby declined the offer and returned to his Waverly estate. Following the birth of his second child in June, Shelby settled his family with relatives and joined Jackson at Lamar.[13]

At Camp Lamar, Claiborne Jackson surveyed his resources. Jackson commanded an army of nearly six thousand men under brigadier generals Rains, Parsons, Clark, and Slack. But about a third of the men were unarmed. Rains, for example, had recruited more than three thousand men from the Kansas City area to his Eighth Division, but about twelve hundred of them were unarmed. The best equipped and trained unit in Rains's division was a regiment of twelve hundred men commanded by Colonel Richard Hanson Weightman. A native of Washington, DC, Weightman, like Shelby, did not shrink from violence. He graduated from the University of Virginia in 1834 and attended West Point from 1835 to 1837. According to *Appleton's Cyclopedia of American Biography* published in the late 1880s, Weightman had been expelled from the academy "for cutting a comrade in the face in a personal encounter." After being admitted to the bar in the District of Columbia in 1841, the twenty-four-year-old Weightman moved to St. Louis and served as a captain of artillery during the Mexican War. After the Mexican War, he settled in the New Mexico Territory and, in 1851, won election to Congress as a territorial delegate. Weightman moved to Atchison, Kansas, in 1858 and to Independence, Missouri, in 1861. A veteran of the Border War, Weightman (now fifty-five) joined Rains's division.[14]

Rains's division also had about six hundred mounted troops commanded by Colonel James Cawthorn, who had moved to Missouri from Tennessee in the early 1840s. A slaveholder, he farmed land along the Sac River and won election as the first sheriff of Cedar County when it was created in 1845. The Eighth Division also had a three-gun artillery battery under Hiram M. Bledsoe, a Kentucky-born planter who had moved to Missouri in 1839. Bledsoe had seen action in the Mexican War with Doniphan, and he, like so many others in Jackson's army, had participated in the fight against Free State forces in Kansas.[15]

Parsons's Sixth Division had Henry Guibor's four-gun artillery battery and about six hundred armed men with Colonel Joseph M. Kelly commanding the infantry and Colonel William B. Brown commanding the mounted men. Kelly was an Irish immigrant and grocer in St. Louis who had served in the British army. He organized the Washington Blues in St. Louis in 1857. The Blues participated in the fight against Kansas Jayhawkers and later joined Daniel Frost's militia muster at Camp Jackson. They had left Camp Jackson shortly before its capture to guard a shipment of gunpowder and weapons acquired in St. Louis and transported to Governor Jackson in Jefferson City. They joined Jackson's army as it moved west to Boonville and then south to Warsaw and Lamar. Brown was a native of Kentucky who settled in Saline County and raised his mounted men there. He was said to rally his men in battle by blowing on an old hunting horn.[16]

At Lamar, Brigadier General Clark's Third Division began to take shape around a body of infantry consisting of about 350 armed men brought out of Louisiana in Pike County by John Q. Burbridge. Lyon's action at Boonville cut Clark off from his military district, which lay north of the Missouri River. As a result, Clark's command consisted of men, like those led by Burbridge, who made their way to the State Guard camps. As Burbridge marched through Lincoln, Montgomery, Callaway, Boone, and Howard Counties, he recruited about a thousand men, most of them unarmed. Burbridge and his men crossed the Missouri River at Glasgow and, by July 3, had joined Jackson's camp at Lamar. The men elected Burbridge colonel of the newly organized regiment.[17]

Colonel James P. Major, a native of Fayette, Missouri, commanded an aggregation of about three hundred mounted men who made up Clark's cavalry. Major had graduated from West Point in 1856 and served on the Texas frontier with the Second US Cavalry until he resigned in March 1861. Clark's entire division consisted of about six hundred men.[18]

Slack's Fourth Division consisted of about five hundred mounted troops under Colonel Benjamin Allen Rives (a physician in civilian life) and another seven hundred infantry under Sterling Price's cousin Colonel John T. Hughes. In his mid-fifties when the Civil War began, Hughes was a native of Kentucky who had moved to Missouri with his family as a young boy. After serving with Doniphan during the Mexican War, Hughes returned to Missouri and prospered as a slaveholding planter in Clinton County. Together, Parsons, Clark, and Slack had about eight hundred unarmed men.[19]

On July 4, while Jackson organized his troops at Lamar, McCulloch and Pearce joined Price in Missouri. On July 5, they learned that Lyon had been reinforced and was rapidly moving south to attack Jackson from the rear. The threat posed by Sigel—whose presence in southeast Missouri was still not known to Jackson—took on new urgency and McCulloch and Price pressed forward with their mounted men, leaving the infantry to follow.[20]

Lyon hoped to destroy Jackson. Reinforced by a regiment of Iowa volunteers shortly after the fighting at Boonville, Lyon also directed Federal forces at Fort Leavenworth, Kansas, to advance into Missouri and join him at Clinton, on the north bank of the South Grand River. Lyon knew that Governor Jackson and Generals Parson and Clark were retreating south from Boonville. He knew, too, that Generals Slack and Rains were heading in the same direction out of Lexington. Lyon hoped that the Federal cavalry from Kansas could cut off some of these men before they crossed the Osage. The commander of the Federal forces entering Missouri from Kansas was thirty-nine-year-old Pennsylvania-born Major Samuel D. Sturgis, an 1846 graduate of West Point and a veteran of the Mexican War. During the secession crisis, he had been stationed with the First US Cavalry at Fort Smith, Arkansas. Although many of his fellow officers joined the Confederacy, Sturgis led four companies of loyal troops (with all of the supplies they could carry) to Fort Leavenworth. Sturgis received the brevet rank of major in recognition of his initiative. The Federal force that he led out of Kansas City on June 24 consisted of two regiments of newly recruited, Kansas Infantry accompanied by a company of volunteer cavalry. In addition to these raw recruits, Sturgis brought a number of regular army units into the field. The regular troops included four companies of the First Cavalry and one company of the Second Dragoons, the latter armed with breach-loading Sharps and Maynard rifles. Sturgis organized a group of 255 new Federal recruits (recently arrived at Fort Leavenworth from Carlisle, Pennsylvania) into two infantry companies. Filling out the force of more than 2,000 men were three companies of the First Infantry, two companies of the Second Infantry, and a light battery of four guns.[21]

On July 2, Sturgis arrived in Austin, Missouri, and sent an advance force into Clinton to secure a crossing of the South Grand River. By July 4, Sturgis's entire force arrived in Clinton and awaited Lyon's arrival. The previous day (July 3, when Jackson moved into Camp Lamar), Lyon left Boonville with over two thousand troops. Four days later, in extreme heat, Sturgis welcomed Lyon's arrival in Clinton with an eleven-gun salute. In contrast to the rebel forces gathered at Lamar, Lyon's army at Clinton was well armed and equipped and led by officers described by Jackson's aide-de-camp as "educated soldiers." Nevertheless, Jackson had managed to put about a week's distance between his State Guard and Lyon's pursuing Federals.

What Jackson did not know was that Sweeny had arrived in Rolla on June 23 and dispatched Sigel and Solomon to Springfield and farther south and west to Sarcoxie and Neosho. Sigel knew that Price was to his south and that Jackson was at Lamar, about twenty miles north of Sarcoxie. As long as rebel forces in Missouri remained divided, Sigel hoped he could defeat Price and at least hold Jackson north of the Spring River while Lyon advanced from the north. Unfortunately for Sigel, as he prepared to lead his consolidated troops out of Sarcoxie on June 29, Price moved into camp at Cowskin Prairie, more than forty miles away. With Price out of reach for the time being, Sigel deemed it "my duty to give all my attention to the northern forces of the enemy." He turned north to attack Jackson.[22]

On the evening of July 4, Sigel left a company under Captain Joseph Conrad to guard Neosho and moved the rest of his command to the Spring River and camped just southeast of Carthage. The troops under Sigel's command included nine companies of the Third Missouri Volunteers (with an effective strength of 550), seven companies of the Fifth Missouri (about 400 men) and two artillery batteries with four guns each. As Sigel moved into camp near Carthage, a detachment of foragers from the State Guard camp at Lamar discovered the Federal presence. As Snead observed, "This was the first intimation that the State troops had that an enemy was in their front with intent to cut off their retreat."[23]

When Jackson and his officers learned of the Federal presence, Parsons urged an immediate attack. But Jackson decided against a hasty move. Instead, he ordered the army to advance against the Federals the next morning. At 4:00 a.m. on the morning of July 5, Jackson's army began its movement toward Carthage. At 7:00 a.m., having marched about five miles, the Guardsmen stopped to prepare breakfast. They learned from scouts that Sigel's force was advancing toward them from about three miles to the south. Sigel's scouts encountered Jackson's force at about the same time, locating the State Guard about nine miles north of Carthage on high ground that rose gradually northward from the heavily wooded banks of Coon Creek. As Sigel prepared to engage the State Guard, Jackson's adjutant recalled that the state troops watched the bayonets of the Federal soldiers "gleaming in the sunshine as they descended the opposite declivity in perfect order."[24]

Sigel knew that he faced a force numerically far larger than his own. As he examined the enemy battle line, he estimated that the enemy force numbered about 3,500 men "besides a strong reserve in the rear." Sigel's determination to attack Jackson suited his aggressive temperament but he also sensed vulnerability in Jackson's force. Sigel knew that Jackson lacked military training. The German veteran also knew how rapidly the State Guard had been driven into the southwestern corner of the state. Sigel knew that Jackson had not had time to arm and train an effective military force. Sigel's force of about 950 men was badly outnumbered, but they were well armed with long range military rifles. By contrast, many of Jackson's men were unarmed and many more were armed with shotguns and hunting rifles brought from home.[25]

Sigel sent forward two companies of the Third Regiment with two pieces of artillery to support his skirmishers as they advanced out of the wooded area bordering Coon Creek. To the south he posted one piece of artillery and one company of the Third below Dry Fork Creek to protect his rear and his supply train. As the Federal troops began to cross Coon Creek, General Rains of the State Guard directed Jo Shelby's mounted rangers (about forty men) to engage the Federals and halt their advance. Shelby's assault successfully diverted fire from Sigel's artillery and allowed Jackson to complete the formation of his defensive line at the crest of the hill. Following his feint, Shelby rejoined Rains who then sent him with a larger mounted force through the wooded area on the rebels' right in search of an undefended crossing of Coon Creek that would permit a movement to turn Sigel's left flank. The Battle of Carthage had begun. It was Shelby's first military engagement of the Civil War.[26]

Jackson formed his battle line by deploying Bledsoe's battery of three guns in the center with Weightman's brigade on the right and Slack's infantry on the left. Guibor's battery of four guns unlimbered to the left of Slack. To the left of Guibor was Parsons's infantry under Colonel Kelly. Clark's infantry under Burbridge took up positions to the left of Kelly. Mounted troops under Brown and Rives held the left flank. Mounted troops under Rains held the right flank. In all, Jackson deployed twenty-six hundred infantry and fifteen hundred mounted troops. Sigel had estimated the size of Jackson's force rather accurately. What Sigel did not know was that the "strong reserve" that he had seen to the rear of Jackson's

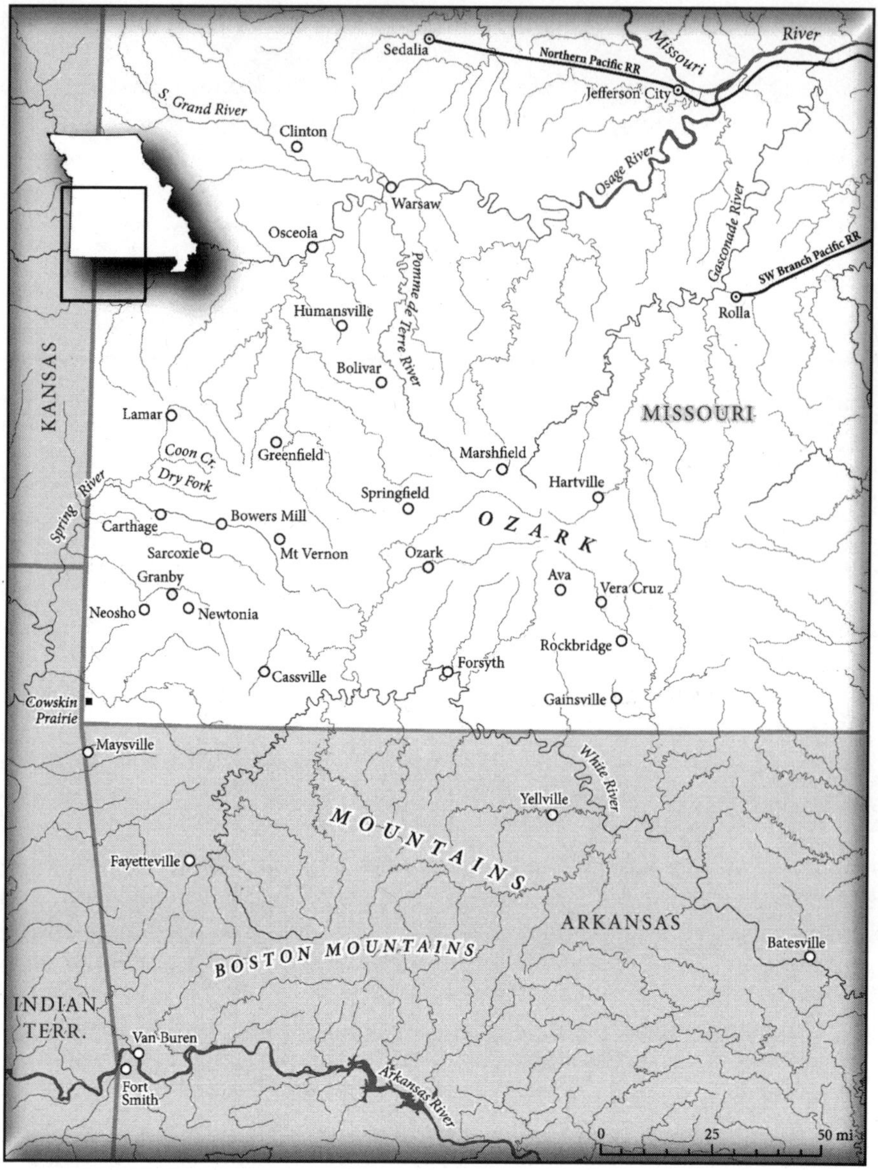

line consisted of an additional two thousand unarmed mounted men. Jackson's adjutant recalled that the Guardsmen looked on with "intense curiosity" as the Federals crossed Coon Creek and emerged from the woods to form their battle line "with the precision of veterans."[27]

After crossing Coon Creek, Sigel positioned elements of the Third Regiment on either flank with three artillery pieces to the right and four to the left. The

Fifth Regiment held the center of the line. About nine hundred yards separated Sigel from Jackson's line on the crest of the hill. Sigel opened fire with all seven of his artillery pieces and the State Guard gunners promptly returned fire. What one of Jackson's men described as an "ineffective artillery practice" continued for about an hour. Sigel then strengthened his left flank with all of his artillery pieces and made it known to his commanders and men that he intended to attack the rebel right flank held by Rains.[28]

Before Sigel could begin his attack, Jackson directed Brown and Rains's mounted men to advance against Sigel's right and left flanks. At the same time, Jackson sent the two thousand unarmed mounted men to find shelter in the heavily wooded area beyond his right flank. As Rains advanced against the Federal left, he faced "well-directed fire of grape and spherical-case shot." Nevertheless, Sigel felt compelled to retreat. As the Guardsmen advanced against both of his flanks, Sigel saw Jackson's reserves riding into the woods on the rebel right flank. Interpreting the movement as an effort to turn his left flank and block his retreat, Sigel withdrew south of Coon Creek and positioned an artillery battery on high ground to cover the ford and the approaches to it. At the same time, Sigel sent his infantry to the rear to defend his supply train from an expected attack. The Federals engaged some mounted State Guard (presumably Shelby's men) who had crossed Coon Creek upstream from the battlefield. But the main fight took place at the ford where accurate artillery fire from the Federal battery badly damaged the rebels as Weightman advanced his brigade and Slack's toward Coon Creek. Bledsoe's battery provided some cover for the State Guard but the Federal artillery fire scattered them rather badly.

Sigel continued a well-executed retreat across Dry Fork Creek and took up another defensive position. "This point," Rains reported, "was severely contested and the loss great." The fighting at Dry Fork Creek continued for about two hours. But Sigel's outnumbered force failed to halt the rebel advance. Throughout the afternoon, Sigel continued his retreat across the five miles of prairie that separated Dry Fork Creek from the Spring River. Rains's cavalry attempted to cut off the Federal retreat, but they were scattered repeatedly by "a heavy and destructive fire" from Sigel's artillery.[29]

Sigel and his men acquitted themselves well throughout the day. In the account of Jackson's adjutant, the discipline of the Federal forces contrasted sharply with the disorganized State Guard: "Sigel continued his retreat in good order, closely followed by a rabble of State troops and harassed on all sides by their mounted men, who did not, however, dare to attack his compact ranks."[30]

During the retreat through Carthage, Sigel's men made good use of the protection provided by houses and fences in the town and held off the advancing rebels until the Union supply train was safely on the road to Springfield. As his troops fell back to the Springfield road, Sigel placed artillery on a small bluff on the east edge of town and continued to hold back the State Guard as he completed his retreat. In the fighting at Carthage, Brigadier General Parsons, commanding the Sixth Division of State Guards, lamented the loss of "one of my bravest and best officer," a captain who had served as Parsons's orderly during the Mexican War. It was a painful personal loss for Parsons who commented bitterly that during the Mexican War he and the fallen captain had fought "to uphold the very flag which now floats at the head of the menials that attempt to oppress us." At sunset, Jackson's men went into camp on the outskirts of Carthage. Jackson savored the victory, but he had lost two hundred men in the battle, compared with forty-four dead on the Union side.[31]

Throughout the night, Sigel continued to retreat another fifteen miles to Sarcoxie. Arriving at that place about 3:00 a.m. on July 6, Sigel rested his men until daybreak and then pressed on to Mount Vernon. Finally realizing he was not being pursued, Sigel halted. For their part, the State Guard left Carthage on July 6 and marched south to Granby, just east of Neosho. At Neosho, the detachment left behind by Sigel surrendered without firing a shot when troops led by Confederate colonels Thomas J. Churchill and James M. McIntosh swept into town on July 5 with more than a thousand men. The Confederates released their Federal prisoners three days later after the German volunteers gave their "parole of honor not to serve any more against the Confederate States of America." A Confederate guard escorted the paroled troops about four miles outside of town before leaving them on their own to make their way back to Springfield. When they surrendered, the German troops needed the "security and protection" of the Confederates since "the people of Neosho and farmers of that vicinity . . . threatened to kill us in the streets." Without food and with their canteens confiscated by the southern troops, they walked eighty-five miles in fifty hours to reach the security of Springfield. The Federal surrender at Neosho buoyed the spirits of the Confederate troops as McCulloch led his men north with Pearce's Arkansas militia and Price's Missouri State Guards to engage Sigel and Lyon at Springfield.[32]

July 5 had been a grueling day for Sigel and his men. They had marched ten miles in the hot sun to engage Jackson's force north of Coon Creek. They had fought well against a force four times larger than their own and then retreated in order the ten miles back to Carthage before proceeding another fifteen miles to Sarcoxie without rest or food. When General Sigel submitted his report of the battle, Lyon expressed his "high appreciation of the generalship displayed" and the "high soldierly qualities exhibited by his officers and men."[33]

Sweeny, who had recently moved his headquarters from Rolla to Springfield, learned of Sigel's plight at Carthage and sent four hundred reinforcements to strengthen the retreating Federal force. With Sigel back in Springfield, Sweeny had twenty-six hundred men and officers under his command. Although Jackson had successfully joined Price, McCulloch, and Pearce, Sweeny believed he could hold his position at Springfield until Lyon arrived in about two or three days.[34]

Lyon joined Sturgis at Clinton on July 7. With some difficulty the Federal force crossed the flooded South Grand River and moved on to the Osage River. Here Lyon learned that Jackson had driven Sigel from his path and had met up with Price, McCulloch, and Pearce. Not knowing that Sigel had successfully retreated to Springfield and that Jackson had left him unmolested, Lyon pressed on with all possible speed. In one exceedingly hot day, July 11, Lyon moved his army fifty miles. Learning that Sigel was not in danger, Lyon then marched more leisurely to Springfield. On July 14, Lyon rode with an escort ahead of his army into Springfield to confer with Sigel.

The day after the Battle of Carthage, Jackson went back into camp at Cowskin Prairie with the newly united Missouri State Guard while McCulloch and Pearce returned to Arkansas. The lull in fighting gave Shelby the opportunity to embark on a recruiting raid into Lafayette County. He left Cowskin Prairie in late July with a full company of one hundred mounted men. Returning to Waverly, he captured the steamboat *Sunshine* loaded with supplies bound for Fort Leavenworth. For another week, Shelby continued his raid but met with little success in recruiting troops. By August 8 he was back with Rains's division as McCulloch and Pearce rejoined Price and prepared to advance against Lyon at Springfield. Within a few days after the Battle of Carthage, the contending forces were in place for a major military confrontation in southwest Missouri. After considerable discussion between McCulloch and Price, and amid significant ill will between the two generals, McCulloch assumed overall command of the Western Army, consisting of his own Confederate Brigade (now commanded by James M. McIntosh), Pearce's Arkansas state troops, and Price's Missouri State Guard.[35]

Although McCulloch was not a West Point–trained soldier, some of his commanders in the Confederate Brigade had attended the Academy. Although he ranked last in his class James McIntosh, now commanding the Confederate Brigade, had graduated from West Point in 1849. McIntosh had been born in Florida in 1828 where his father (a native of Georgia) served in the army. Stationed at Fort Smith, Arkansas, when the southern states began to secede, McIntosh promptly resigned his US Army commission and took command of a battalion in McCulloch's Confederate Brigade.[36]

Colonel Louis Hebert, who commanded the Third Louisiana Infantry in the Confederate Brigade, was also a West Point graduate. In his early forties when the war began, he was a native of Iberville Parish, Louisiana. Hebert graduated from West Point in 1845 but resigned his commission in 1847 to manage his family's plantation. He served as chief engineer for the state of Louisiana from 1855 to 1860.[37]

Elkanah Greer commanded the Third Texas Cavalry in the Confederate Brigade. Born in Paris, Tennessee, in 1825, he joined the First Mississippi Rifles commanded by Jefferson Davis and fought in the Mexican War. After the Mexican War, Greer moved to Marshall, Texas, where he made his living as a merchant, planter, and lawyer. A delegate to the Democratic Party Convention in Charleston in 1860, he joined the advocates of Southern Rights who opposed the nomination of Stephen A. Douglas. In May 1861, he joined the Confederate army and raised a cavalry regiment that was assigned to McCulloch's command.[38]

Thomas J. Churchill, like McCulloch, was a veteran of the Mexican War. Born on his family's farm near Louisville, Kentucky, in 1824, Churchill graduated from college and studied law before enlisting as a lieutenant in the First Kentucky Mounted Rifles to fight in the Mexican War. He later moved to Little Rock, Arkansas. He purchased a nearby plantation and served as postmaster at Little Rock from 1857 until 1861 when he took command of the First Arkansas Mounted Rifles in the Confederate Brigade.[39]

With no military experience, thirty-two-year-old Colonel Dandridge McRae commanded the Arkansas Infantry in the Confederate Brigade. An Alabama native, McRae graduated from South Carolina College in 1848 and later moved to Searcy, White County, Arkansas. There he studied law and was admitted to the bar in 1854. As the southern states seceded, McRae recruited and commanded the Arkansas Volunteers.[40]

Most of the Arkansas troops in McCulloch's Western Army were state militiamen commanded by Nicholas Bartlett Pearce (commonly known as N. Bart Pearce). Born in Caldwell County, Kentucky, in 1828, Pearce graduated from West Point in 1850. Stationed in Arkansas, he resigned his commission in 1858 to join his father-in-law in business in Osage Mills, Arkansas. Pearce opposed secession, but he became a brigadier general in the state militia. In June 1861 he assumed command of Fort Smith.[41]

Serving under Pearce was Colonel John Rene Gratiot. Born in St. Louis in 1820, Gratiot graduated from West Point in 1837 and served in the Mexican War with Missouri Volunteers under Major Meriwether Lewis Clark. Gratiot resigned from the army after the Mexican War and settled in Hempstead County, Arkansas, in 1848. There he commanded the Hempstead Rifles, a militia unit that became the core of his Third Arkansas Infantry.

Also serving under Pearce was Colonel James David Walker of the Fourth Infantry of Arkansas Troops. Walker was known as "Little Dave" to distinguish him from his prominent uncle, David Walker. The uncle served twice as a justice on the Arkansas Supreme Court and presided over the Arkansas secession convention. "Little Dave" Walker was born in Logan County, Kentucky, and moved to Arkansas in 1847. Admitted to the bar in 1850, he practiced law in Fayetteville and served as judge of the Fayetteville Circuit Court when the war began.[42]

Also under Pearce was Colonel Thomas Pleasant Dockery, who commanded the Fifth Infantry Regiment of Arkansas State Troops. He was born in North Carolina in 1833, and his family moved to Columbia County, Arkansas, where his father purchased a large plantation. Two cavalry units filled out Pearce's command. Captain Charles A. Carroll had raised a volunteer mounted force of about

40 men at Van Buren known as Carroll's Arkansas Cavalry. Colonel DeRosey Carroll commanded a cavalry force of 350 men. Born in Maryland, DeRosey Carroll settled in Huntsville, Alabama, before moving to Arkansas. Described as "a planter advanced in years and an ardent Southerner," DeRosey Carrol became commandant at Fort Smith for the seceded state of Arkansas after the Federal commander Samuel D. Sturgis (now with Lyon in Springfield) led loyal Federal troops to Fort Leavenworth, Kansas, in April 1861.[43]

Of Pearce's artillery commanders, little is known of Captain John G. Reid who commanded the Fort Smith Light Battery. More is known about Captain William E. Woodruff, commander of the Pulaski Light Battery. In 1860 Woodruff formed an artillery company, originally called Totten Artillery in honor of Dr. William Totten who commanded the US Arsenal at Little Rock and his son, Captain James Totten, who became its commander shortly before the Civil War began. Later, when James Totten joined Federal forces in St. Louis and went into the field with Lyon against the Missouri State Guard, Woodruff changed the unit's name.[44]

In Springfield, Lyon organized his Federal army into four brigades. Major Sturgis commanded the First Brigade, which included three companies of regular US troops commanded by Captain Joseph B. Plummer, a forty-five-year-old West Point graduate and Massachusetts native. German-born Major Peter Joseph Osterhaus commanded those elements of Boernstein's Second Regiment of US Volunteers that Lyon assigned to Sturgis's brigade. Born in Coblentz in 1823, Osterhaus had served as an officer in the Prussian army before joining the failed revolution and fleeing to the United States. He had settled first in Bellville, Illinois, and later in St. Louis.[45]

Also assigned to Sturgis's brigade was Samuel N. Wood who commanded the Kansas Rangers, a mounted company of the Second Kansas Infantry. Born in Mount Gilead, Ohio, in 1815, Wood was the son of Quaker parents with New England roots. After being admitted to the bar in 1854, he migrated to Kansas and soon emerged as a leader of the Free State movement. Wood was a delegate from Kansas to the first Republican Party convention in 1856, and he served in the Territorial Legislature in 1860 and 1861.[46]

Fighting with the Kansas Rangers in Sturgis's Brigade was Company D of the First US Cavalry. Originally, Captain David S. Stanley commanded Companies C and D of the First Cavalry. He was born in Ohio in 1828 and graduated from West Point in 1852. Stationed at Fort Smith, Arkansas, during the secession crisis, Stanley led his men to Kansas. Lyon assigned Stanley with Company C to the defenses of Springfield and placed Lieutenant Charles W. Canfield in command of Company D, now assigned to Sturgis's Brigade. Canfield was a native of New Jersey who entered West Point in 1853. A poor student, he withdrew from the academy. On May 14, 1861, immediately following the fall of Fort Sumter, Canfield received a commission as a lieutenant in the Second Regiment of US Cavalry. This regiment trained at Jefferson Barracks and then dispersed to garrisons throughout the West. Company C of the Second Cavalry (later assigned to Sigel's Brigade) moved east from Fort Leavenworth on June 11, 1861, and joined General Lyon at Springfield on August 6. Presumably Canfield arrived in Springfield with this company before being assigned to command Company D of the First Cavalry. Completing Sturgis's brigade was artillery commander James Totten, a figure well known to his counterpart, William Woodruff, fighting with McCulloch.[47]

The Second Brigade, commanded by Franz Sigel, included Charles E. Solomon's Fifth Missouri Infantry and Sigel's Third Missouri Infantry, now commanded by Lieutenant Colonel Anslem Albert. A native of Hungary, Albert served in the Austrian army. Albert later fought for Hungarian independence and joined the "men of 1848" who fled to the United States after the failed revolutions of that year. Albert eventually settled in St. Louis where the 1860 city directory listed him as a reporter for *Handels Zeitung*.[48]

Two companies of regular US Cavalry filled out Sigel's Brigade. Captain Eugene A. Carr commanded Company I of the First Cavalry. Born in New York in 1830, Carr graduated from West Point in 1850. Commissioned a second lieutenant of cavalry in June 1851, he was stationed at Jefferson Barracks, then Fort Leavenworth, and in the Indian Territory. During 1857, he served as aide-de-camp to Governor R. J. Walker in the Kansas Territory. In June 1858, he was promoted to captain of the First Cavalry and in 1859 was again posted in the Indian Territory. In July1861, he received orders to move into Missouri to support Nathanial Lyon.[49]

Another New Yorker, Lieutenant Charles E. Farrand, commanded Company C of the Second US Dragoons. Farrand graduated from West Point in 1857 and served first in the infantry before rising to take command of this cavalry company as it made its way from Fort Leavenworth to Springfield. Lyon assigned Farrand to Sigel's Brigade. Franz Backof with his six-gun battery continued under Sigel's command.[50]

Colonel George L. Andrews took command of the First Missouri Regiment when Frank Blair left Missouri after the skirmish at Boonville to attend the special session of Congress. A native of Rhode Island, Andrews moved to St. Louis. He now commanded the Third Brigade in Lyon's army.[51] Major Frederick Steele commanded a battalion of regular US troops in Andrews's Brigade. Born in New York State in 1819, Steele graduated from West Point in 1843 and served meritoriously in the Mexican War.[52] Lieutenant John V. DuBois's battery of four guns completed Andrews's Brigade. DuBois was another native of New York, a West Point graduate and veteran of the Mexican War. When the Civil War began, DuBois was at Carlisle Barracks, Pennsylvania, and he escorted new recruits west to Fort Leavenworth. There, DuBois assembled a field battery and accompanied Sturgis as he joined Lyon in Missouri.[53]

Lieutenant Colonel George W. Deitzler, who came into Missouri with the First Kansas Regiment, became commander of the Fourth Brigade of Lyon's army. Dietzler was born in Pennsylvania in 1826. In his late twenties, he joined the northern migration to Kansas and became one of the leading Free State fighters. With the beginning of the Civil War he raised the First Kansas Infantry, which he led as colonel. Colonel William H. Merritt commanded the First Iowa Regiment in Deitzler's Brigade. Merritt was born in New York City in 1820 and migrated to Iowa in 1838. He joined the gold rush to California in 1849 but returned to Iowa in the early 1850s. Elected lieutenant colonel of the First Iowa Regiment of Volunteers, he reinforced Lyon at Boonville. When the regiment's commander, Colonel John Bates, fell ill, Merritt took command of the Iowa troops.[54]

Another Free State partisan, Ohio-born Colonel Robert B. Mitchell commanded the Second Kansas Infantry. A veteran of the Mexican War, Mitchell moved to Kansas where he became active in the Free State movement. Mitchell joined Deitzler's Brigade. Lyon also assigned Lieutenant James Beardsley to Deitzler's brigade. Beardsley raised a company of the Thirteenth Illinois Regiment at Rock Island and reinforced Sweeny at Rolla. Most of Beardsley's regiment remained in Rolla, but Beardsley moved on to Springfield with a force of twenty men detached from his regiment to guard a Federal supply train. Beardsley commanded these Illinois men in the Fourth Brigade.[55]

Once Jackson had pushed past Sigel at Carthage and Lyon had successfully moved his army from Boonville to Springfield, no one doubted that a major battle loomed on the horizon. But, exactly how the battle would take shape remained uncertain, and commanders on both sides displayed a great deal of caution. During the last two weeks of July, both sides focused on reconnaissance as they tried to determine the size and disposition of the opposing army.

Chapter Three

"In the Valley of Wilson's Creek"

On the morning of July 6, Sterling Price and Ben McCulloch continued their advance into Missouri. They were well on their way from Neosho to Carthage when they received word that Claiborne Jackson had pushed aside Franz Sigel the previous day and was quickly approaching them. With Jackson no longer in danger, McCulloch and Bart Pearce returned to Maysville, Arkansas. The Missourians, in easy marches, proceeded to Cowskin Prairie. There, about thirty miles southwest of Neosho, they were about twelve miles north of Maysville. Price joined Jackson at Cowskin Prairie on July 9 and continued the difficult job of organizing his ungainly force. Price's adjutant, Thomas Snead, had taken note of the Missourians' shortcomings at the Battle of Carthage. The Missourians were not only untrained, they were also either poorly armed or entirely unarmed. Jackson's men succeeded in forcing Sigel to retreat, but they could not bring their superior numbers to bear in order to defeat him. The men who brought weapons with them from home fought with shotguns and hunting rifles. Only a few hundred stands of infantry weapons—long-range rifled muskets—had fallen into the hands of the State Guard. At least two thousand men came into Price's camp at Cowskin Prairie with no weapons at all.

Price's army was also desperately short of ammunition. Fortunately, the nearby Granby mines provided an abundant supply of lead. The gunpowder that Jackson had procured from St. Louis served Price well. Many of the men were experienced in molding their own bullets and shot, and with some practice Captain Henry Guibor and his men fashioned effective canister and shells for the artillery. By the end of July, Price had fashioned an army that he was eager to take into the field. He hoped to reunite with McCulloch to attack Lyon at Springfield.[1]

Shortly after Price set up camp at Cowskin Prairie, Jackson traveled to Memphis to confer with Major General Leonidas Polk of the Confederate army. Jackson hoped that Polk would coordinate an invasion of Missouri that would allow the deposed governor to reclaim his office. Much to Jackson's delight, Polk unveiled a plan to assemble a grand army of twenty-five thousand men. Composed of Confederate troops under Polk's command and the elements of the Missouri State Guard commanded by Price, this force would drive Federal troops from the state, oust the pro-Unionist provisional state government, and reinstall the duly elected (and pro-Confederate) government of Claiborne Jackson. Not surprisingly, Polk convinced Jackson to postpone his planned trip to Richmond and to accompany the Confederate and Missouri forces as they took control of Missouri.

Polk took his plan almost entirely from Gideon Pillow who had been eager for some time to lead his Tennessee troops into Missouri to support the flamboyant and ambitious Jeff Thompson. Thompson had met with Pillow in Memphis in June. At the time, Pillow was commander of the Provisional Army of Tennessee with the rank of major general. In July, when Tennessee joined the Confederacy, Pillow (with some displeasure) accepted a commission as brigadier general in the Confederate army. But Pillow's plan to invade Missouri gained support, first from Claiborne Jackson when he arrived in Memphis and then from Brigadier General William Hardee who arrived in Memphis on his way to raise troops in his semi-independent command in northern Arkansas. Polk, who arrived in Memphis in mid-June to command Confederate troops, adopted most of Pillow's plan as his own.[2]

In Polk's plan, Pillow would cross the Mississippi and enter Missouri at New Madrid with his command of six thousand troops. Once in Missouri, Pillow would be supported by Jeff Thompson's First Division of the Missouri State Guard, a force of about three thousand men. Pillow and Thompson would move north to take control of the railhead at Ironton. Pillow's advance would be supported by Brigadier General William Hardee whom Polk directed to move into Missouri from Pocahontas, Arkansas. Hardee would bring another seven thousand men to join Pillow at Ironton. From Ironton, the army of Confederates and Missourians would advance against the Federal stronghold of St. Louis.

Pillow and his new commander, Polk, knew that Lyon had concentrated his forces in Springfield. This deployment, they believed, opened opportunities for Confederate operations in eastern Missouri. Polk seemed confident that with an army of sixteen thousand men he could overcome the defenses of St. Louis. Once in the city he would resupply his army and move his troops by riverboats up the Missouri River into central Missouri (presumably installing Governor Jackson in Jefferson City along the way). Leaving the Missouri River (probably at Boonville), Polk planned to march southward and "pass in behind Lyon's [army] by land." As Polk's army advanced toward Lyon's rear, McCulloch would move north from Maysville, Arkansas, with six thousand men and join forces with Price's twelve thousand Missouri Guardsmen at Cowskin Prarie. In Polk's plan, Lyon's force of fifty-five hundred in Springfield would soon face eighteen thousand men commanded by McCulloch and Price advancing against him from the south and another sixteen thousand men under Polk's command advancing against the Federals from the north. With Lyon defeated and Jackson restored to office in Jefferson City, Polk proposed to return to Tennessee through Illinois "and take Cairo in the rear on my return."[3]

Polk embraced Pillow's ambitious plan but soon discovered that he could not effectively coordinate the activities of Pillow, Hardee, and Thompson. Part of Polk's difficulties stemmed from the facts that Pillow was not a loyal subordinate and that Hardee was not directly under his command. An Episcopal bishop turned general, Polk lacked military experience and soon demonstrated that he was not adept at directing and sustaining coordinated military activities.

Polk had graduated from West Point in 1827 but he resigned his commission later that year to study for the ministry. He owed his generalship to his personal friendship with Confederate president Jefferson Davis. Polk outranked Pillow and Hardee, although the latter were West Point graduates who had fought in the Mexican War. Pillow had been assigned to Polk's command, and he enthusiastically followed Polk's directive to enter Missouri. Hardee had been assigned to raise Confederate troops in Arkansas and although he supported Pillow's move into Missouri he found ample reasons not to form a junction with him.

As planned, Pillow crossed the Mississippi at New Madrid on July 28 commanding the short-lived Confederate Army of Liberation. The Confederate force arrived in New Madrid about 4:00 p.m. aboard eight steamboats. The move into southeast Missouri buoyed Pillow's spirits and the spirits of his men. "The whole population of New Madrid and the country around met me with a thousand cheers," he reported to Polk. As one of his soldiers wrote, "Gen. Pillow enters the state to lead us to St. Louis and we confidently believe that ere November, the Confederate flag will wave over the ruins of that city." Greeted as a liberator, Pillow did, indeed, expect to move quickly against the Federal forces at Ironton, the Fourth Regiment of Missouri Volunteers commanded by B. Gratz Brown. With only these German troops standing between his army and St. Louis, Pillow reported that his "whole force is full of enthusiasm and eager for the '*Dutch hunt*'."[4]

At first the invasion plan developed well. Jeff Thompson visited Pillow and Governor Jackson in New Madrid eager to coordinate the movement of his Guardsmen with the Confederates. On July 31, Hardee moved into Missouri, and by August 4 he had reached Greenville with about fifteen hundred men. But here the plan began to falter as Pillow and Hardee competed with each other for the support of Thompson, and Polk grew cautious and indecisive. Once in New Madrid, Pillow decided against attacking Ironton directly. He deemed the Union force at Cape Girardeau too large to leave in his rear, and he had concluded that a march directly to Ironton would take his army over land that "does not furnish subsistence." Pillows urged Hardee to join him in a movement against Cape Girardeau. Hardee responded by urging Pillow to move inland and join him. Claiborne Jackson, still in New Madrid, supported Pillow. Polk vacillated and then supported Hardee. Pillow became increasingly insubordinate as he resisted Polk's directions to support Hardee and the new Confederate defensive position at Island Number Ten.[5]

The large army envisioned by Polk never took shape. Hardee found it easy to recruit Confederate soldiers in northern Arkansas but it was difficult to arm them and time-consuming to train them. He reported to Polk that he had recruited about five thousand men but that this force was "badly equipped and wanting in discipline and instruction." Hardee kept most of his force in Arkansas, although he was "organizing my force with the greatest energy," he assured Polk. "I shall strain every nerve to move in a week," he continued. "My opinion," he advised, "is that General Pillow ought not to move upon Ironton until I am in readiness to support him." Pillow in the meantime had decided to attack Cape Girardeau before moving against Ironton. As the Confederate offensive stalled with the absence of a single plan and Polk's indecisive leadership, the new Federal commander, John C. Fremont, reinforced Federal forces. Pillow's movement into Missouri convinced Fremont that he could not reinforce Lyon at Springfield. Instead he organized an expedition to reinforce Federal forces at Cairo. At the same time, Ulysses S. Grant, the newly appointed brigadier general in the US army, brought fresh troops to Ironton. At Ironton, B. Gratz Brown's Germans had served their ninety-day term of enlistment and returned to St. Louis to be mustered out. Grant commanded about three thousand men at Ironton and eyed Hardee warily as the Confederate commander moved into Missouri. Leading Hardee's expedition into Missouri was a mounted force led by the St. Louis secessionist Basil Duke. Hardee advanced to Greenville, about twenty-five miles south of Ironton. There matters rested, however. Fremont's reinforcements caused Polk to become cautious. With most of Hardee's forces in Arkansas and with Pillow insistent that the Confederates take Cape Girardeau before moving on Ironton, the invasion of southeast Missouri fell flat. As McCulloch and Price prepared for a major battle in southwest Missouri, they did so without a coordinated Confederate advance in the east.[6]

Lyon set up his headquarters in Springfield, and he soon learned from Fremont that he would not receive reinforcements. Jackson and Price's State Guard now formed a junction with McCulloch, and Lyon also knew that he was badly outnumbered. Moreover, Lyon's overland line of supply to the railhead at Rolla was vulnerable to attack. If Lyon felt threatened by the enemy forces in southwest Missouri, Fremont suggested that he should avoid a major confrontation and withdraw to the railhead at Rolla. But Lyon was in no mood to retreat. He had moved a large number of men and supplies over long distances and in a short amount of time and remained determined to do all he could to disrupt the organization of the Missouri State Guard. Moreover, Lyon knew that he had under his command an experienced and disciplined force and he knew from his experience at Boonville how vulnerable to panic the Missouri Guardsmen had been. Finally, a retreat to Rolla was not without risks. A retreat would require Lyon to move his men over one hundred and fifty miles of difficult terrain. With a large enemy force nearby this could be dangerous, even disastrous. Lyon decided to meet the enemy with all of the force he could muster. At the very least he hoped to disrupt the enemy before beginning his retreat to Rolla.

Once the decision to fight had been made, Lyon focused his attention on reconnaissance. An early point of concern was the town of Forsyth, southeast of

Springfield on the White River. On July 20, Lyon dispatched Thomas Sweeny with twelve hundred men to clear any enemy forces from that location. The White River was navigable below Forsyth, and Lyon feared that a Confederate force at that location could easily be supplied and reinforced by river from Arkansas. At this point, Lyon planned to move against Price at Cowskin Prairie. An enemy presence at Forsyth could threaten his left flank. Sweeny's force advanced toward Forsyth in very hot weather and made slow progress. Once they reached the town of Ozark, moreover, they encountered the rugged terrain of the Ozark Mountains. On July 22, Sweeny's force arrived at Forsyth and approached the town cautiously expecting to confront a significant enemy force. Instead, he found only seventy-five poorly armed Guardsmen. A few of the rebels took up positions on the bluffs across the White River. Sweeny moved against this defensive line carefully. Despite the caution displayed by the Federal troops, it took them less than an hour to drive the enemy from the town and its environs.[7]

At this point, Sweeny inexplicably failed to maintain the discipline of his troops. The men had expected to engage in a battle and after experiencing little more than a skirmish, emotions undoubtedly ran high. Combined with the hostile attitude of some of the citizens of Forsyth, this apparently led to the arrest of about one hundred civilians for disloyal behavior. Looting ensued. When Sweeny returned to Springfield on July 25, Lyon expressed his displeasure with the reports he received about the conduct of Sweeny's men. Lyon directed his adjutant general to issue general orders to all of his commanders. Lyon refrained from reprimanding Sweeny, but he described as "disgraceful to our troops" the reports that had come to him regarding "cases of plundering, wanton destruction of property, and disregard for personal rights." Lyon ordered, "The persons and property of all law-abiding citizens will not be molested." This protection extended "to all persons, whatever may be their private opinions." Regarding individuals who actively resisted the authority of the United States, they would be dealt with by the proper Federal authorities. In cases of necessity, "where private property is seized or pressed into the use of the Army," orders must come from commanding officers and the property must either be paid for or the owner must be issued a certificate documenting the confiscation of property.[8]

Lyon no longer worried about his left flank and focused instead on the potential threat to his front. If the enemy moved against him, they would probably follow the road leading from Fayetteville, Arkansas, through Cassville, Missouri, to Springfield. It was locally known as the Telegraph Road or the Wire Road. Lyon soon received reports that Price had left Cowskin Prairie and had formed a junction with McCulloch at Cassville. The reports were correct. After more than two weeks of training and supplying his men at Cowskin Prairie, Price marched east to reach the Wire Road at Cassville on July 28, the same day that Pillow crossed into Missouri at New Madrid. At Cassville, Brigadier General James H. McBride joined Price with the 650 men he had recruited in the sparsely populated Seventh Military District east of Cassville. With McBride's arrival, Price's army now numbered more than 5,000 armed men and another 2,000 unarmed men. McCulloch arrived in Cassville on July 29 with his 2,700 Confederates. Arriving with McCulloch, Nicholas Pearce contributed another 2,200 Arkansas volunteers. The combined force advancing against Lyon had grown to about 10,000 effective troops plus Price's unarmed Missourians. On July 31, this army began to move northeast along the Wire Road. Springfield and Lyon's Federals lay about fifty miles ahead.[9]

With his army of about 5,400 men, Lyon began to move southwest on the Wire Road on August 1. He went into camp where the Wire Road crossed Wilson's Creek, a few miles southwest of Springfield. Lyon knew that he faced a superior force. But the reports that he now received greatly exaggerated the enemy's strength. Federal scouts estimated that McCulloch and Price commanded a combined force of more than 20,000 men. The faulty reports may have arisen from the fact that McCulloch, Pearce, and Price advanced from Cassville in three columns. In advance rode six companies of cavalry serving as scouts. The rebel commanders united again on August 1 where the Wire Road crossed Crane Creek. In two days, the Confederates, the Arkansas volunteers, and the Missourians had covered more than twenty-five miles and were about halfway between Cassville and Springfield. On August 2, McCulloch and Lyon both sent cavalry forward to reconnoiter: they clashed briefly with Lyon's scouts near Dug Springs, midway between the two camps.[10]

The late July days in southwest Missouri were extremely hot. Although the region was traversed by numerous creeks and graced with many springs, men and animals on both sides of the sectional struggle suffered mightily from thirst and dehydration. Thomas W. Knox, a reporter with the *New York Herald*, rode with Lyon's cavalry as they reconnoitered south of Wilson's Creek. After leaving the Wilson's Creek camp, Knox and the mounted troops made their way to Dug Springs. There they intended to water their horses and refill their canteens before continuing their search for McCulloch and Price. In the extreme heat, the men emptied their canteens far more quickly than they had anticipated and by the time they reached Dug Springs they were desperately thirsty. Knox was no stranger to heat and thirst. His earlier travels across parched sections of Kansas had exposed him to considerable suffering. But nothing in Kansas prepared him for the desperate thirst he experienced in Missouri. As he and the advanced elements of Lyon's column arrived at Dug Spring, the men broke ranks and scrambled for a drink. Knox found the springhouse thronged with frenzied soldiers. After considerable effort, he managed to get a single cupful of water. Knox and a growing number of soldiers continued to struggle for access to the spring. As more troops arrived, the disorder intensified. Some officers tried to break up the struggling mass of men, but while commands were given none were heeded. Knox watched as "officers and men were mingled without regard to rank, all struggling for the same object." The regular army men, who had remained aloof from the volunteers during their march south from Boonville and who took pride in their higher standards of discipline, now joined the mob. "On this occasion," observed Knox, "the superiority was not apparent." About twenty yards below the spring was a shallow pond used by cattle and hogs. Finding access to the spring cut off by the crowding, desperate soldiers turned to this "scum-covered pool." "In subsequent campaigns," concluded Knox, "I witnessed many scenes of hunger and thirst, but none to equal those of the day at Dug Springs."[11]

The two mounted forces clashed briefly near Dug Springs. Involved in the skirmish were Missouri State Guard troops commanded by James Rains and a combined force of regular Federal cavalry and Iowa volunteers led by Frederick Steele. Rains had been directed to probe the Federal positions north of Crane Creek.[12] While doing so, Rains hoped to induce a Federal force to engage him and, as he retreated, to lure the Federals into an attack on McCulloch's defensive position at Crane Creek. If the ruse worked, McCulloch could inflict significant damage on the enemy before launching his own attack. The plan failed, however, in part because Steele had established a defensive position of his own across the Wire Road south of Dug Springs. Along this line, with Captain James Totten's artillery battery deployed, Steele intended to intercept any approaching enemy force before it could get near Lyon's camp in the valley of Wilson's Creek.

From his defensive position, Steele observed the cloud of dust raised by Rains's six companies of approaching troops. Steele brought up his reserves and easily repulsed Rains's initial assault. The clash was a minor one. Only six of Rains's men were wounded in the initial exchange. A second assault by Rains produced more dramatic results. With greater accuracy, Totten directed canister and shell into the ranks of Rains's men. Four attacking soldiers fell dead and another six sustained wounds. More important, the artillery fire instilled panic among the Missourians and they fled in disarray back to Crane Creek. The terror that overcame Rains's troops was apparent to all. The fleeing Missourians reinforced the belief among Lyon's regulars that Price's Missouri State Guard was not an effective fighting force. The inability of Rains's men to engage the Federal force effectively and draw it into McCulloch's trap caused the Confederate commander (in the words of Price's adjutant) "to lose all confidence in the Missouri troops." Moreover, the "scare" of Rains's men "laid the foundation for that distrust and ill-feeling which eventually separated the combined armies." McCulloch conveyed his displeasure to Price and the already tense relationship between the two commanders became openly antagonistic.[13]

The armies were now within six miles of each other. The skirmish near Dug Springs might have been the prelude to a major battle. The fact that it was not reflected Lyon's decision to avoid a major engagement at this point. The principal reason for his caution was his uncertainty about the size and location of the enemy forces. Reports about the large number of mounted men leading the enemy advance left Lyon fearful that McCulloch and Price might sweep past his smaller force and cut him off from Springfield. Lyon decided to return to his Springfield camps. On August 4 and 5, Rains's troops harassed Lyon's rear guard, but Lyon successfully regained his old encampments.

As Lyon retreated to Springfield, McCulloch also became cautious. Lyon's retreat left him somewhat confused. McCulloch had moved his infantry forward quickly into what he expected to be a major battle. To facilitate this movement, McCulloch left his supply wagons in the rear and his soldiers carried only one day's supply of rations. Now, as McCulloch followed a retreating enemy, he separated his army even farther from its supplies. Both armies suffered severe thirst and exhaustion in the extreme heat, and added to this stress, McCulloch's troops had subsisted for ten days on what they could gather from the countryside. On August 6, McCulloch moved his army into camp at Wilson's Creek. There his men and horses slaked their thirst, rested from days of marching, and awaited the arrival of their supplies.[14]

By the morning of August 7, all of Price and McCulloch's twelve thousand men had arrived at Wilson's Creek. That evening they were positioned near the creek on either side of the Wire Road prepared to advance against Lyon's army at Springfield. Old disagreements flared once more as McCulloch and Price prepared their men for battle. The "scare" of Rains's men at Dug Springs reminded McCulloch he had never been comfortable operating with Price and the Missourians. Two intertwined issues generated antagonism between the two commanders. Basically, McCulloch distrusted the Missouri State Guard and Sterling Price's ability to command it. In McCulloch's view, Price was first and foremost a politician. McCulloch's attitude angered Price. Price had been governor of Missouri, to be sure, but he was quick to point out to McCulloch that he, Price, had outranked the Texan when both men served in the regular army during the Mexican War. But McCulloch now held the rank of brigadier general in the Confederate army, and Price owed his commission as major general of the State Guard to Governor Claiborne Jackson. Price learned early on that McCulloch would not defer to him as the senior commander. The bigger issue now was whether McCulloch would take command of the State Guard.

McCulloch felt some pressure from the Confederate War Department and from General Leonidas Polk to support the Missouri secessionists. But he remained extremely cautious as he moved into Missouri and began operating with Price. McCulloch very much wanted to keep the fate of his command separate from the fate of the secessionist movement in Missouri. Adding to the problems of command, McCulloch had developed a personal dislike for James Rains, and the disgraceful performance of Rains's men at Dug Springs deepened his fear that the Missourians could not rise from a rabble to become an army. McCulloch was particularly uncomfortable with the fact that Price insisted on bringing his two thousand unarmed mounted men into the field. McCulloch viewed them as camp followers and an encumbrance. He wanted Price to dismiss these men and send them home. Failing this, he at least expected Price to leave them behind at Cowskin Prairie. He thought Price had agreed to do just that. But when McCulloch joined Price at Cassville, the unarmed men were there foraging in the countryside and soon helping themselves to the supplies of the Confederate army. If the decision had been his alone to make, McCulloch would have remained in western Arkansas, prepared to defend that region and the adjacent Indian Territory from Federal invasion. Nevertheless, McCulloch had agreed to cooperate with Price, and now that he was in the field with Price he recognized the danger of a divided command when confronting a united and well-disciplined enemy. Accordingly, when McCulloch received a letter from Leonidas Polk informing him that Gideon Pillow had crossed into southeast Missouri at New Madrid, he informed the War Department that he immediately "consented to take the command and to march upon the enemy."[15]

McCulloch's decision to command the Missourians solved one major issue, but tensions between Price and McCulloch persisted. McCulloch expected Price's men to use their knowledge of the countryside effectively to scout Lyon's positions. Again the Missourians fell short in their commander's eyes. By August 8, McCulloch threatened to retreat to Cassville rather than continue to work with Price and make what McCulloch regarded as "a blind attack upon Springfield." Frustrated, McCulloch himself led several scouting forays and remained cautious —too cautious in Price's view. Far more than Price, McCulloch respected Lyon as a regular army officer. He also respected Lyon's successes in the field and feared falling into a trap. As McCulloch delayed, it was Price's turn to deliver an ultimatum. Unless McCulloch moved immediately against Lyon, Price would resume command of the State Guard and lead them into battle by himself. McCulloch acquiesced and on August 9 prepared to advance against Springfield. McCulloch's officers called in their pickets and prepared their men to march. That evening a light rain fell, and McCulloch and Price agreed that an immediate movement would not be prudent. Because many of the men lacked cartridge boxes, the rain would render their ammunition worthless. The rain ended before dawn on August 10, and McCulloch ordered his army to advance in four columns toward Springfield.[16]

In Springfield, Lyon also reviewed his options. Without reinforcements, he faced an enemy force twice the size of his army (and one that he believed to be three times larger than his own). He and his commanders had rejected Fremont's suggestion of an immediate retreat to Rolla. They recognized that their soldiers would be slowed by the inevitable throngs of fleeing civilians and would be easy prey for pursuing mounted troops. It would be better to strike the enemy, disrupt him, and retreat in order. Lyon would attack Price and McCulloch. How he would do so remained to be determined.

Lyon met with his commanders on the evening of August 8, and he found them still fully in agreement on the necessity of attacking. Lyon outlined a plan to move the army down the Wire Road the next night and attack the rebel camp at daybreak. Consulting privately with Franz Sigel late on the afternoon of August 9, however, Lyon changed his plan. Federal success against the larger enemy force required surprise. Sigel convinced Lyon that the element of surprise would be greatly enhanced if Lyon divided his army and attacked McCulloch and Price simultaneously on both flanks. Lyon then informed his commanders of his revised plan of attack. Some were apprehensive about the unorthodox nature of the tactic, but Lyon held to the plan. The Union army would begin its march toward Wilson's Creek that evening at 6:00 p.m. in two columns. Sigel took command of the Third and Fifth Regiments of the Missouri Volunteers with six field guns and two companies of regular cavalry (about twelve hundred men in all). His force would advance in darkness to the south end of the enemy camp. Sigel would attack at dawn in an attempt to turn the enemy's right flank. Lyon commanded the remaining forty-two hundred men. He too would advance in darkness to the north end of the enemy camp. Lyon would also attack at dawn in an attempt to turn the enemy's left flank. Having delivered his orders, Lyon reminded his commanders that Springfield was a center of Unionist support in southwest Missouri. "To abandon Springfield without a struggle would be a sad blow to our cause, and would greatly encourage the Rebels," observed Lyon. "We will fight," he concluded, "and hope for the best."[17]

In the days leading up to the Battle of Wilson's Creek, both McCulloch and Lyon displayed caution and uncertainty. They had good reason to do so. Both commanders had moved far from a secure line of supply. McCulloch had left his supply base at Fort Smith on the Arkansas River. Lyon was well beyond his old base of supply at Boonville on the Missouri River, and he was equally far from the railhead at Rolla linking him to St. Louis. Not only did Lyon's and McCulloch's armies face mounting supply problems, but they also faced the danger of being outflanked and cut off from retreat. Lyon overestimated the size of the Confederate force, but he correctly concluded that he faced a vastly superior force. McCulloch knew that as he moved further into Missouri he faced an increased threat on his left flank from Federal forces in Kansas. McCulloch and Lyon were committed to engaging the enemy, but they approached the battle with a degree of trepidation.

In the valley of Wilson's Creek, both armies gained relief from the heat and thirst that plagued their movements through southwest Missouri. The creek flowed southwest out of Springfield and then, where it flowed over the ford of the Wire Road a few miles outside of town, directly south to the James River, a tributary to the White River. The creek etched a narrow valley though the countryside. Trees lined its banks and clear water flowed over its gravel bed. As McCulloch's and Price's men approached the valley along the Wire Road from the south, they descended a gently sloping hill and passed the farm and home of Joseph Sharp. There the road crossed Skegg's Branch, which fed into nearby Wilson's Creek. For some distance, the road ran along the west bank of the creek. As the road passed

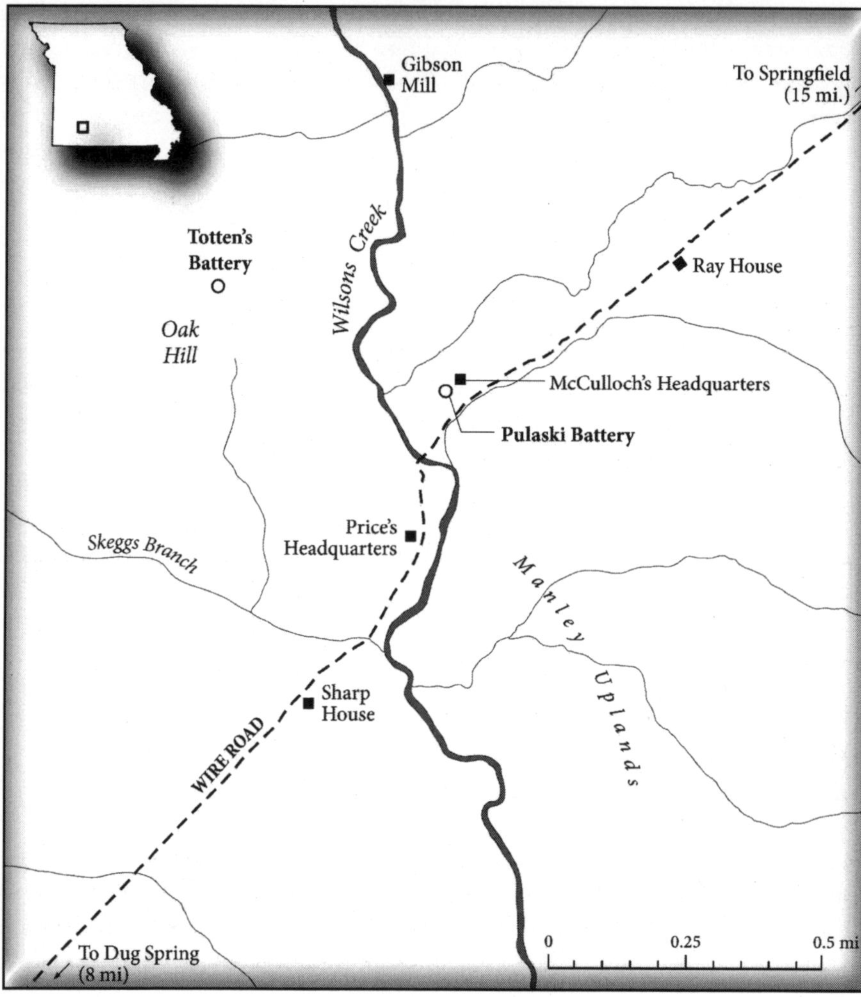

the Sharp House, the creek banks gradually receded to reveal a natural ford. Near the ford, on the west side of the creek, the ground rose about one hundred feet to the crest of Oak Hill. Burr oak and underbrush covered the countryside where the land had not been cleared for farming.

Beyond the ford, on the east side of the creek, the Wire Road curved and ascended from the valley. The road passed the farm and home of Larkin Winn and continued on to Springfield. As the road left the valley, it passed the farm and home of John Ray. The Ray house served as the post office for the cluster of farm families in the region. From its porch an unobstructed view opened to the west. Looking to the southwest, the Wire Road could be seen rising from the ford over Wilson's Creek. Directly to the west, Ray's cornfield sloped down to the wooded bank of the creek. Closer to the creek and somewhat further north, on a steep bank, John Gibson had constructed a mill trace and a mill, locating his family's home nearby. To the west beyond the creek rose the crest of Oak Hill.

As Price's and McCulloch's men entered the valley, their officers settled them in camps on both sides of the Wire Road and on both banks of the creek. Their camps stretched up and down the valley for about two miles from the Sharp farm to the south to Gibson's Mill to the north. Many of the Arkansas mounted men went into camp on the Sharp farm where there was ample forage for their horses. McCulloch and Pearce, however, located their headquarters farther north, on the rising ground east of the creek. Price and the Missouri State Guard went into camp on the west side of the creek, on the sloping fields across the creek from Gibson's Mill and along the southern slopes of Oak Hill. The location of their camps indicated the position they would hold as the army advanced against Lyon at Springfield. The mounted Arkansas troops held the right flank. Pearce and McCulloch's infantry held the center. Price's men (many of them mounted) held the left flank. At Wilson's Creek, Price located Guibor's battery of four guns on the high ground commanding the Wire Road where it crossed both Skegg's Branch and Wilson's Creek. McCulloch located four guns on high ground overlooking the ford from the northeast and located another four guns on the bluff directly across Wilson's Creek from Skegg's Branch. The commanders positioned their artillery to fend off any attack from the Wire Road and to control the ford over Wilson's Creek. When Lyon and Sigel attacked these positions at dawn on August 10, the focus of military concern shifted abruptly.[18]

The light rain that began to fall on the evening of August 9 effectively immobilized McCulloch and Price and allowed Lyon and Sigel to strike the first blow. At about 5:00 p.m. on August 9, Lyon began moving his troops down the Wire Road with Sturgis's First Brigade in the lead. After some initial exuberant shouting and singing, the Federal soldiers advanced silently into the darkness. Civilian guides led them about five miles down the road to a prairie, which they crossed in order to position themselves in the rear of the rebel's left flank. At 1:00 a.m. they halted about two miles from the Wilson's Creek camp and within sight of the enemy campfires near Gibson's Mill. Here they rested, sheltered themselves as best they could from the rain, and waited to attack at dawn.[19]

Unable to communicate with Lyon, Sigel began a sweeping march around the Wilson Creek camp to a position just to the south. Also led by civilian guides, Sigel left Springfield at 6:30 p.m. At 11:00 p.m. he rested his men for a few hours and then resumed his march at 2:00 a.m. As dawn approached, Sigel's brigade took up positions as planned, on high ground just south of the Confederate camp.[20]

Shortly before dawn, Lyon led his men from their fireless camps across the remaining stretch of prairie to the location of the enemy campfires they had watched during the night. This was the camp of the Missouri State Guard directly across Wilson's Creek from Gibson's Mill. The final advance of about two miles began undetected because Price and McCulloch had called in their pickets in preparation for their advance toward Springfield.

At dawn in the State Guard camp, Colonel James Cawthorn (with Rains's Eighth Division) prepared his cavalry to advance on McCulloch's left flank in the anticipated march to Springfield. He sent a squad of mounted men forward to scout the area northeast of Gibson's Mill through which he expected to advance. These troopers immediately detected Lyon's movement across the prairie west of the Wire Road and sent word back to Cawthorn, who dispatched a messenger to relay the report to General Price.

At dawn Price sent his adjutant, Thomas Snead, to McCulloch's quarters to discern the commander's final plans for the days' march to Springfield. At about 5:00 a.m. Snead returned to Price's quarters with McCulloch and Colonel James McIntosh, who would command the Confederate Brigade now that McCulloch assumed overall command of the army. The group prepared to confer over a breakfast of cornbread, beef, and coffee. Soon they received the first report that their troops were under attack. The agitated messenger sent by Rains reported that the Federal force advanced against them in strength, "their soldiers and cannon covering the whole prairie" northeast of Gibson's Mill. By this time, the disorderly retreat of the State Guard over the crest of Oak Hill was visible from Price's quarters. As Snead described the scene: "Looking up, we could ourselves see a great crowd of men on horseback, some armed, and other unarmed, mixed in with wagons and teams . . . horses, all in dreadful confusion, scampering over the hill and rushing down toward us—a panic stricken drove."[21]

Soon Price and McCulloch saw the flash and heard the report of Totten's guns firing into the fleeing rebels from the crest of Oak Hill. Almost immediately the commanders also heard Sigel's guns as they opened fire on the mounted men of the Confederate Brigade, driving them out of their valley camps on the Sharp farm and into the thick woods on either side of Skegg's Branch. McCulloch and McIntosh quickly rode off to take command of their Confederate troops on the east side of the creek. Price also rode off to investigate the status of his State Guard. It was 5:30 a.m.

Meanwhile, acting on his own authority, Cawthorn sent forward three companies of his cavalry with instructions to probe the enemy force and determine its strength. Lyon responded to the probe by forming his column into a battle line. Lyon located Osterhaus's Second Missouri on his right flank and Plummer's regulars on his left. He sent both forward as skirmishers. The First Missouri protected Totten's battery as its guns opened fire on the mounted Missouri Guardsmen. The Guardsmen quickly fell back to the crest of Oak Hill where they joined another six hundred men and formed the right wing of what Cawthorn hoped would be a defensive line. That piece of high ground, soon to be known as Bloody

Hill, became the epicenter of the Battle of Wilson's Creek. Before Cawthorn could finish his preparations, Lyon attacked him with more than twenty-five hundred men: the First Iowa, Frederick Steele's battalion of regulars, the First Kansas, and the First Missouri. The State Guard (which lost only two dead in the attack) quickly gave way amid what one colonel described as a "tremendous shower of case-shot, grape, and minie ball."[22] As in the earlier skirmishes at Boonville and Dug Springs, many of Rains's men fled in panic and disorder. It was now 5:30 a.m., and Lyon had gained the crest of Bloody Hill. Elements of the Federal force stretched about a mile to the rear, and Lyon halted his advance to bring his full army forward. By this time Price had joined his men, who were scattered across the southern and eastern slope of Bloody Hill.[23]

For Thomas Knox, the *New York Herald* reporter who accompanied Lyon's army, the fighting on Bloody Hill was his first battlefield experience. This was the case as well for many of Price's guardsmen and Lyon's volunteers. Knox described a sense of disorientation in space and time that may have been characteristic for inexperienced troops. When the Federals advanced against Cawthorn on Bloody Hill, Knox stood with Totten's battery. As Totten directed artillery fire into the ranks of the State Guard, Knox asked how far away the enemy was. The captain replied, "about eight hundred yards; not over that." Knox was surprised. As he looked toward Bloody Hill he would have judged the distance to be closer to a mile. Time, too, seemed to expand. As the fighting grew more intense, Knox glanced at his watch. Only five minutes had elapsed in a period of time that he had thought to be a half hour or more. These were common experiences, Knox learned, and in later battles he found his estimates of time and distance became less distorted.[24]

To the south, Sigel also met with initial success. Sigel's guides led him to a hill on the east side of Wilson's Creek, overlooking the camp of the mounted troops of the Confederate Brigade. As the sun rose, the enemy forces came into view across the creek. Sigel positioned four guns on the hill overlooking the camp. At 5:30 a.m., Sigel heard Totten's guns to the north and directed his own artillery to open fire. The Federal bombardment produced panic and prolonged disorder among the Confederates. Amid the shelling Sigel moved his main force across Wilson's Creek to the Wire Road to block the anticipated enemy retreat. As they moved north along the Wire Road, Sigel's men met virtually no resistance. Some Confederates fled to the south, away from their camp. The Federals took about one hundred prisoners. By 7:00 a.m. Sigel had consolidated his forces along the Wire Road and opened a new artillery barrage against the Confederates who had begun to form defensive lines on the west side of the creek. After a half hour of shelling, Sigel's advancing troops easily drove the remaining Confederates from the field.

Panic now engulfed both flanks of the rebel army. On the crest of Bloody Hill, Lyon saw the Missouri Guardsmen scattered before him seeking shelter on the lower slope of the hill and in the wooded west bank of Wilson's Creek. Seizing the moment, he quickly advanced his left flank to the east side of the creek. Lyon sent forward a company of his regulars as skirmishers, followed by the rest of Captain Joseph Plummer's battalion. Plummer tried to cross the creek upstream from Gibson's Mill but found his skirmishers stuck there in "a deep jungle" on the west bank of the creek. For a time the Federals also found themselves "checked by an impassable lagoon." Eventually, they made their way through the thicket and across the creek. By 6:30 a.m. they had "finally emerged in good order and all present." They now advanced with relative ease through the Ray farm cornfield toward the Wire Road. In front of them they could see the smoke from the guns of the Pulaski Battery as Captain William Woodruff directed fire across Wilson's Creek into Lyon's troops on Bloody Hill. Plummer intended to storm the battery and silence it.[25]

From Bloody Hill, Totten directed his gunners to return the Confederate artillery fire. From Totten's perspective, the Pulaski Battery was "masked" by trees, but his gunners gave "direction to their pieces by the flash and smoke of the opposing artillery." Totten could not know it, but the Federal fire was effective. One of Woodruff's gunners was struck by solid shot in the first hour of the battle. The cannonball broke his right arm and crushed his chest. He died before the battle ended. A second gunner was also hit by solid shot above the knee. He, too, died of his wounds. A third gunner fell wounded with a Minie ball in his leg.[26]

Plummer's advance in the Ray cornfield coincided with Sigel's attack at the Sharp farm and created a crisis for McCulloch and the Confederate Brigade on the east side of Wilson's Creek. McCulloch had just begun to respond to Sigel's attack when Woodruff reported that the advancing Federal left flank threatened his Pulaski Battery. McCulloch sent Colonel James McIntosh with his Arkansas Confederates north on the Wire Road to the Ray house where they soon faced Plummer's Federals emerging from a thicket near the Ray orchard. McIntosh's men took up positions behind a rail fence but absorbed considerable damage from the Federals. Supported by Colonel Louis Hebert's Louisianans, McIntosh took advantage of his superior numbers and led a charge. The Confederates drove Plummer back down the Ray cornfield and soon back across Wilson's Creek. Plummer reported that his retreat proceeded "steadily and without confusion." It also proceeded very rapidly, and Plummer himself sustained a serious wound that required him to transfer command to a fellow officer.[27]

Suddenly, with Plummer's hasty retreat, Lyon feared the collapse of his left flank. Fortunately for Plummer's battalion and for Lyon's command, Lieutenant John V. DuBois's battery, which was deployed east of Totten on the crest of Bloody Hill, saw Plummer's men retreating from a superior Confederate force. His gunners turned their cannon to the east and fired into the Confederates with speed and accuracy. It was now approaching 8:00 a.m. and the tide of battle shifted to favor the retreating Federals on the Ray cornfield. Under artillery attack, frightened Confederates scrambled for cover, and McIntosh and Hebert withdrew from the field. Although seriously wounded, Plummer and his men made good their retreat to the west side of Wilson's Creek. The Confederates had driven back Plummer's advance, but they paid a heavy price for their victory. The Confederates lost about one hundred men in the fight. Plummer reported nineteen dead, fifty-two wounded, and nine missing. Nevertheless, with Plummer's retreat, McCulloch could now concentrate fully on Sigel to the south. "Slowly but inevitably," as the historian Albert Castel observed, the numerical superiority of the rebel forces became evident in the continuing Battle of Wilson's Creek.[28]

During Plummer's withdrawal from the east side of Wilson's Creek, Sigel continued to hold his blocking position across the Wire Road south of Skegg's Branch. He had no way of knowing how Federal forces fared to the north, but he hoped that Lyon's troops would soon form a junction with him. That, of course, was the desired outcome of the plan he had proposed when he suggested dividing the Army of the West and attacking the enemy on both flanks. Eager to know what was transpiring to the north, Sigel's officers ventured to the south bank of Skegg's Branch from time to time. From that position, they could see the smoke of the fighting on Bloody Hill and discern some troop movements near the Wilson's Creek ford. When they saw a gray-clad regiment advancing rapidly down the Wire Road from the ford toward Skegg's Branch, they assumed it was the gray-clad First Iowa and reported that information to Sigel. When these advancing troops emerged from the thicket of the ravine formed by Skegg's Branch, they were in close range of Sigel's line. Sigel's decision to position his force so close to the ravine, combined with his confusion about the identity of the advancing troops produced devastating results. Sigel ordered his men not to fire. When four hundred men from the Third Louisiana rushed out of the brush of the ravine, they shattered Sigel's startled line. "It is impossible for me to describe the consternation and frightful confusion which was occasioned by this unfortunate event," Sigel reported after the battle. There was no confusion on the part of the Louisianans who opened fire on Sigel's line from close range. "The enemy arrived within ten paces from the mouth of our cannon, killed the horses, turned the flank of the infantry, and forced them to retire." Sigel's force was routed. They scattered frantically seeking shelter from their attackers where they could or fled in disorder south on the Wire Road. "The troops were throwing themselves into the bushes and by-roads," Sigel reported. The Federals retreated "as well as they could," Sigel continued, "followed and attacked incessantly by large bodies of Arkansas and Texas cavalry."[29]

Sigel's defeat was complete, and for those Federal officers who had opposed dividing the Army of the West (notably John M. Schofield), defeat was the consequence of Sigel's failures as a commander. In February 1862 when Sigel was being considered for promotion, Schofield—supported by John DuBois, James Totten, and seven other officers who had been present at the Battle of Wilson's

Creek—submitted a sharply critical account of Sigel's performance. Although Lyon commended Sigel for a skillful retreat at the battle of Carthage, Schofield scoffed that although Sigel faced an enemy force twice his size it was an enemy poorly armed "and entirely without organization and discipline." Schofield wrote, "Sigel retreated all day before this miserable rabble." Lyon had originally sent Sigel to Springfield in mid-June 1861 to prevent the Missouri State Guard from joining McCulloch's Confederates. Sigel had utterly failed to accomplish this objective, and the rebel forces had united—in Schofield's characterization—"absolutely without opposition." Schofield also insisted that it was Sigel's self-aggrandizing desire for a separate command that led him to "advocate the plan of a divided attack" at Wilson's Creek. Every other commander, according to Schofield, opposed dividing the outnumbered Federal force. Perhaps Schofield's most telling critique was that Sigel made no effort to rally his troops after they were driven from Skegg's Branch during the Battle of Wilson's Creek or to bring them to support Lyon: "No effort was made by Sigel or any of his officers to rally their men and join Lyon's division, although the battle raged furiously for hours after Sigel's rout, and most of his men in their retreat *passed in rear of Lyon's line of battle*."[30]

To be sure, Sigel may have been unable to rally his scattered force. But his failure even to attempt to report his defeat to Lyon is difficult to fathom. And failure in this instance was not without consequences. In a report submitted immediately after the Battle of Wilson's Creek, Lieutenant DuBois complained that not knowing Sigel position "embarrassed" him "during the entire engagement." DuBois reported, "On several occasions, I did not fire upon their [the enemy] troops until they had formed within a few hundred yards of our line, fearing they might be our own men advancing to form a junction with us."[31]

With Sigel's defeat, McCulloch had secured his right flank, but the fighting on Bloody Hill raged on. Lyon had taken control of the crest of Bloody Hill at 6:30 a.m. and pressed forward against the camps of the Missouri State Guard on the west side of Wilson's Creek. As Federal forces moved down the hill, they encountered stiffening resistance. Price succeeded in bringing a degree of order to his scattered troops and formed them into a defensive line. Over the next hour, Lyon's and Price's troops fought at close range, typically in company-sized engagements at various points along the Federal line.[32]

At this point in the battle, the close-range fighting offered an advantage to Price's men. Largely armed with hunting rifles and shotguns, the Missourians needed to fire at close range to be effective. Price formed his defensive line and awaited the Federal advance. When Lyon's men tramped through the scrub oak and underbrush to within fifty yards of Price's line, the Guardsmen opened fire and drove the Federals back into the underbrush. Out of sight, Lyon's men reloaded and reformed their line for a new attack. During these lulls in the fighting, Thomas Snead was struck by the "deep silence" that prevailed. Silence "fell upon" the battlefield "and rested undisturbed for many minutes, while the two armies, unseen of each other, lay but a few yards apart!"[33]

By 7:30 a.m. Price had gathered together a sufficiently large force of Guardsmen to launch a counterattack and push Lyon back to the crest of Bloody Hill. To regain the offensive, Lyon called up the Second Kansas, which he had held in reserve, and ordered the First Kansas to charge the enemy with fixed bayonets. This Federal charge drove Price's men back down the slope of Bloody Hill. But Lyon did not press further. Fearing that the Kansans might be engulfed by the superior numbers of the enemy, Lyon quickly called them back and reformed a defensive line at the crest of the hill.

From this defensive position, the well-armed Federal troops enjoyed an advantage. William Woodruff observed the fighting on Bloody Hill from the bluff occupied by his Pulaski Battery. He thought the Guardsmen made the best use they could of their "old [smoothbore] muskets, squirrel rifles and shot-guns." But when the Missourians fought in the open field, the Federals' "long range guns," their rifled muskets, took a heavy toll. The Federal soldiers often fought from positions that put them beyond the reach of the Guardsmen's short-range weapons. Toward the end of the battle, when Colonel John Gratiot deployed his Arkansas troops on Bloody Hill, their rifled muskets stopped a Federal advance well before the Union troops expected to receive return fire. Woodruff concluded that it was the "difference in arms" that accounted for the heavy losses suffered by the rebels, particularly by Price's men.[34]

As Price prepared for a second assault of Bloody Hill, he did not know what had become of McCulloch and dispatched his adjutant, Thomas Snead, to find the Texan. At about 8:45 a.m., Snead located McCulloch at the Sharp farm and learned that Sigel's forces had been driven from the field. McCulloch, in turn, learned that the Federal presence to the north remained formidable. McCulloch led the Third Louisiana up the Wire Road to join Price. As part of the second assault on Bloody Hill, McCulloch directed Colonel Elkanah Greer of the South Kansas–Texas Cavalry and Captain Charles of the Arkansas state troops to lead a cavalry attack on the Federal right. Greer led the charge gallantly but precipitously. He did not pause to give clear direction to subordinates and fewer than half the force of 750 men joined the charge. Fortunate for the Federals, Lyon had just completed positioning a company of the Second Kansas on the right flank as skirmishers, and they received the brunt of the uncoordinated Confederate cavalry charge. Lyon, wounded in the leg but unwilling to leave the field, directed Totten's artillery to support the Kansans. When Greer's men galloped toward the Federal line, they met effective infantry and artillery fire. As Snead noted, "the ground was ill-adapted to the operations of cavalry." With the cavalry hobbled by thick underbrush and steep ravines, the Kansas troops and Totten's gunners easily drove them back. In his report, Totten dismissed the enemy cavalry in general as "utterly worthless on the battlefield." Undoubtedly aware that Greer and his horsemen envisioned a heroic charge, Totten denigrated their effort as "so *effete* and ineffectual in its force and character as to deserve only the appellation of child's play."[35]

The second attack on the Federal line, supported by Greer's charge, came at 9:00 a.m., and fighting lasted for about an hour. Much of the fighting at the center of the Federal line took place at very close range. Despite his wound, Lyon continued to direct the Federal line. However, a glancing blow from a bullet to his skull sent him briefly to the rear. As aides bandaged his wounds, Lyon confided to his chief of staff, John Schofield, that he feared defeat was inevitable. Schofield urged the general to press on, and Lyon returned to the front line to organize what would be the last Federal advance. With a fresh mount, Lyon rode to the front of his troops, waved his hat, and urged them forward. Almost immediately an enemy bullet struck Lyon in the ribs and tore through his lungs and heart. Breathless, he fell to the ground and died.[36]

Most of the Federal soldiers knew nothing of Lyon's death until after the battle. Despite the ferocity of the enemy assault, the Federal line held, and Price's and McCulloch's men retreated for a second time down the slope of Bloody Hill. As the rebels withdrew, Schofield informed Sturgis of Lyon's death. Sturgis now assumed command of the Army of the West. Sturgis adjusted the Federal line in preparation for the third Confederate attack. It came about 10:30 a.m. with Gratiot's Arkansas troops now bolstering Price's line on its right flank. But it was the Federal center, held by the Kansans and supported by Totten's battery, that again faced the full force of the enemy assault. Rebels advanced to within twenty feet of Totten's artillery, but blasts of canister prevented a break of the Federal line.[37]

For the third time, the rebels disengaged and retreated to the protected base of Bloody Hill. It was about 11:30 a.m. According to *New York Herald* reporter Thomas Knox, Sweeny thought that the third Confederate assault on Bloody Hill would be their last and that the Federals could hold their current position.[38] But, with the heat of the day mounting and his men short of water and ammunition, Sturgis decided to withdraw. Steele's Regulars, supported by companies detached from the First Iowa, the First Kansas, and the First Missouri, remained on Bloody Hill to cover the Federal retreat. They drove off a final enemy probe of their position. When as many of the wounded as possible had been removed, Steele joined the retreating column. As he left the battlefield, Steele "saw nothing of the enemy; it was evident that he had been severely punished." Sturgis halted his retreating troops at Ross's Spring, about two miles north of Bloody Hill. As his men rested and quenched their thirst, they also eagerly consumed wagonloads of bread that had been sent to them from Springfield. Here, too, Sturgis first learned of Sigel's fate.[39]

The Federals retreated with many of their dead and wounded, but they also left many behind. The correspondent Thomas Knox heard reports that the rebels cared for their own wounded but not for the Federals. Indeed, he reported, some of the Federal wounded were "shot or bayoneted" by the rebels. Two days after the battle, Price and McCulloch allowed wagons from Springfield to collect the Federal wounded. The party from Springfield found clusters of wounded men. "One party of four built a shelter of branches of trees as a protection against the sun," reported Knox. Another group "crawled to the bank of the creek, and lay day and night at the water's edge."[40] Some of the dead men and horses were not found, and they rotted in the field. Eleven weeks after the battle, Knox accompanied General Samuel Curtis's army to Springfield. This Federal advance prompted Price to retreat toward Arkansas and gave Knox the opportunity to revisit the Wilson's Creek battlefield. He found the silence of the place striking. He also found scattered graves and the skeletons of horses and men. "It well illustrated the desolation of war," he concluded.[41]

The retreating Federal troops arrived in Springfield at 5:00 p.m. Sigel was already there, and Sturgis called a meeting of his officers. Undaunted by defeat, Sigel convinced Sturgis to cede to him command of the Army of the West. Sigel had been with the army since its inception, he argued. Accordingly, the responsibility of commanding the army following Lyon's death properly fell to him. It was a brazenly self-serving argument that ignored the fact that Sturgis, like Lyon, came into the field commanding regular US troops. But Sturgis deferred to Sigel much as Lyon had done. In both cases, a sense of deference probably arose from the fact that Sigel was the undisputed leader of the German troops. Neither Lyon nor Sturgis spoke German. Because of the language barrier, as well as Sigel's popularity with the German troops, Sturgis relied on Sigel to command the German-speaking troops. With this leverage, Colonel Sigel of the Missouri Volunteers displaced Colonel Sturgis of the US Army as commander of the Army of the West. Expecting that McCulloch and Price might attack Springfield at dawn, Sigel ordered the army to begin its retreat to Rolla at 2:00 a.m. the next morning. Sigel overslept, however, and the march to Rolla did not begin until 4:00 a.m. The last of the Federal troops moved out of Springfield at 6:00 a.m. It was fortunate for the retreating Union army that McCulloch was eager to return to Arkansas, and Price's army, weary from battle and poorly supplied, did not attack.

The Army of the West reached Rolla on August 19 with Sturgis again in command. During the march, Sigel angered and alienated the English-speaking troops and their commanders. Three days into the march, Schofield reported that "almost total anarchy reigned in the command." The problems stemmed from Sigel's marching orders and from what appeared to be his blatant favoritism toward the German troops. Each day, Sigel's brigade led the march and rested several hours in the middle of the day. The rest of the army followed. Each night, Sigel's men arrived in camp in daylight with time to set up camp and cook a meal. The rear guard arrived well after dark. On the third day, when Sigel and his men stopped to slaughter beef for a late breakfast, accumulated tensions reached mutinous levels. "At length," reported Schofield, "after numerous entreaties from officers of the command," Sturgis resumed command. Sturgis acknowledged that Sigel had been with the Army of the West for a long time, but the German commander had not yet received an "appointment from any competent authority" in the regular US army.[42]

Internal dissention also divided the rebel camp. Although Price's Missourians had taken the brunt of the Federal blow at Wilson's Creek and, after their initial panic, had displayed resilience and fought well, they did not overcome McCulloch's negative view of them. McCulloch continued to view Price's army as a disorderly rabble without proper military leadership. "We have little to hope or expect from the people of this State," McCulloch wrote from his camp near Springfield on August 24. "The force now in the field is undisciplined and led by men who are mere politicians; not a soldier among them to control and organize this mass of humanity." The Missourians were "in no condition to meet an organized army," McCulloch continued, "nor will they ever be whilst under the present leaders."[43]

It is not entirely clear what it was that so deeply troubled McCulloch. It was true that neither Price nor his commanders had been trained at West Point. They had all followed careers in law and politics first and served as Missouri militiamen second. But McCulloch was not a West Pointer, either, and Price—together with John B. Clark and Mosby Parsons—could plausibly argue that their military experience in the Mexican War gave them standing as soldiers in rough parity with McCulloch's service as a Texas Ranger. What seemed to trouble McCulloch so fundamentally was the demeanor of the commanders and troops of the Missouri State Guard. McCulloch had accepted a commission in the Confederate army, and he intended to defend the interests of the Confederate nation in the West. It was not clear to McCulloch what cause Price and his men intended to serve. The marauding behavior of the Missouri Guardsmen threatened to demoralize McCulloch's men as surely as it angered the civilian population. "They are not making friends where they go," McCulloch reported shortly after the battle, "and from all I can see we had as well be in Boston as far as the friendly feelings of the inhabitants are concerned." Woodruff of the Pulaski Light Battery also noted that Price's Missourians were hampered in their movements by "unwieldy private trains" of wagons carrying the supplies and equipment they had brought from home or pilfered along the way. Again the presence of large numbers of unarmed camp followers provoked complaint. "The foraging of so large a number of unarmed men," Woodruff concluded, "was grievous to the country and injured the cause."[44]

Franz Sigel characterized Price's Missourians somewhat differently. Sigel pointed to the "ever-changing" nature of the Missouri State Guard. They were, as Sigel noted, "without stability of quarters and security of resources." In important respects they lacked the characteristics of a disciplined military force. Armed and unarmed men came and went from camp at will. On the morning after the

Battle of Wilson's Creek, McCulloch sent Lieutenant Colonel Walter P. Lane with four companies of the Third Texas Cavalry to investigate the status of Federal forces in and around Springfield. At the edge of town, Lane encountered a soldier walking toward him with a rifle on his shoulder eating a loaf of bread. Lane ordered the man to identify himself. He was with Price's army, he said. He had been on picket duty the previous night, he explained, but he had gotten hungry and went to town to find something to eat.[45]

McCulloch was clearly uncomfortable to be associated with Price's army. Well after the Battle of Wilson's Creek, McCulloch continued to express his anger at Price's lax discipline, particularly in regard to the thousands of unarmed men Price permitted to accompany his army. They were "straggling camp followers" in McCulloch's view who epitomized the "unorganized condition of the Missouri forces."[46] In December 1861, when complaints reached the Confederate War Department that McCulloch "was not willing to assist Missouri," the outraged Texan repeated his complaint that Price's unarmed camp followers were an undisciplined, thieving lot. During the Battle of Wilson's Creek, they had "robbed our dead and wounded on the battlefield."[47] It did not impress McCulloch that these Missourians took up arms and equipment in order to join the fight against Lyon. He had earlier complained that Price's camp followers had stolen at least three hundred stands of arms "from my killed and wounded." The Missourians had also stolen Confederate tents (left behind at Cassville to hasten McCulloch's march north), and they refused to return the six hundred muskets loaned to them before the battle by General Pearce. The Missourians were stealing from Confederate and Arkansas forces to advance their own cause in Missouri. McCulloch feared a contaminating effect: "the fighting men of the army" could become demoralized "by having such material among them."[48]

McCulloch had reason to believe that his worst fears might soon be realized if he did not separate himself quickly from the Missourians. Shortly after the battle, Jo Shelby returned to "recruitment" raids in and around Lafayette County. Price, too, was eager to return to the Missouri valley to gather more recruits and supplies. McCulloch wanted to distance his Confederate army from the Missourians. McCulloch had been directed to defend Arkansas and the Indian Territory; Price seemed more interested in extending the fighting into the Missouri valley.[49]

Not surprisingly, the collaboration between McCulloch and Price ended shortly after the Battle of Wilson's Creek. Price resumed command of his Missouri State Guard on August 14. McCulloch returned to Arkansas, leaving Price with the recommendation that he fortify Springfield. Price ignored the advice. Instead he headed north for the Missouri valley. Price sent Rains forward with a mounted force to drive Kansas Jayhawkers from western Missouri. On August 25, Price led his entire army toward Fort Scott, Kansas, with the intention of joining Rains. After defeating Jayhawkers in western Missouri and eastern Kansas, Price intended to continue recruiting men and gathering supplies in central Missouri.[50]

The Battle of Wilson's Creek reverberated across the North in several significant ways. Coming just weeks after the Federal defeat at the First Battle of Bull Run, the retreat of Federal forces from the fighting at Wilson's Creek served as a painful reminder that the fight to preserve the Union would not be easily won. The death of Nathaniel Lyon, moreover, added to the sense of crisis that came with the Federal defeat. But Lyon, in death, also strengthened the Union cause. From the struggle with General Harney and the meeting with Price and Jackson at the Planters House Hotel to the Battle of Wilson's Creek, Lyon had made himself known across the land as a great champion of the Union cause. His death while leading his men in battle transformed him, for a time, into an inspirational figure of heroic proportions: the qualities displayed by Lyon—determination, decisiveness, and courage—were perceived as qualities that would carry the North to victory.

Another commander's reputation gained national prominence after the Battle of Wilson's Creek. Among Germans across the North, Franz Sigel remained extremely popular, notwithstanding his disastrous defeat on the enemy's right flank at Wilson's Creek. Detractors like John M. Schofield continued to emphasize Sigel's errors of judgment and his limitations as a military tactician. But Sigel's popularity in the German community made him an indispensable commander, and he continued to rise in stature despite his shortcomings.[51]

In the aftermath of the Battle of Wilson's Creek, the strategic balance in the state shifted significantly. It had been the purpose of Lyon's frenetic and ultimately fatal attacks against the Missouri State Guard to scatter those forces before they could be effectively organized. This campaign had met with initial success as Lyon drove Claiborne Jackson from Jefferson City and routed the State Guard camp at Boonville. M. Jeff Thompson wrote Confederate president Jefferson Davis early in July 1861 that "there is no system or plan of campaign for the people to go by." Thompson himself had fled from St. Joseph to join "exiled Missourians" in Pocahontas, Arkansas. The state government had been dispersed, and the revenues it had appropriated to fund the State Guard had been confiscated by the Federal government. State funds, explained Thompson, "are locked up in banks, and every town in the state in which there is a bank is now in the possession of Federal troops." Moreover, the rail and telegraph lines and the mails were all controlled by Federal forces. With Governor Claiborne Jackson in exile and Sterling Price's headquarters "unknown to any one in this portion of the country," Thompson put himself forward as the champion of the Southern Confederacy in Missouri. Within a few days, however, the fortunes of Jackson and Price brightened considerably as Franz Sigel at the Battle of Carthage failed to prevent Jackson from forming a junction with Price and McCulloch in the southwest and as Pillow and Hardee entered southeastern Missouri. Now, in the wake of the Federal retreat at Wilson's Creek, Price acted quickly to consolidate as much of the State Guard as possible.[52]

In northeast Missouri, Thomas Harris and Martin E. Green continued to raise State Guard forces in the Second Military District. Taking the field against them with the specific goal of protecting the Hannibal and St. Joseph Railroad were two West Point graduates and veterans of the Mexican War, Ulysses S. Grant and John Pope. A career soldier, Pope had been appointed brigadier general in June 1861 and assigned to raise troops in Illinois. On July 4, George B. McClellan, commanding Federal troops in the West from his headquarters in Ohio, directed Pope to take command of six regiments of Illinois volunteers and move from Springfield to Alton, Illinois. Grant, who had resigned from the army and had recently settled in Galena, Illinois, resumed his military career as a colonel of a regiment of Illinois volunteers. On July 3, Grant moved his regiment from Springfield to Quincy, Illinois, and then across the Mississippi to Palmyra, Missouri. The nearby Salt River bridge of the Hannibal and St. Joseph Railroad had been destroyed by rebels, and Grant's first assignment in Missouri was to provide protection for the workers rebuilding it. By July 17, Pope also moved into Missouri, intending to protect the North Missouri Railroad, which led from St. Louis, northwest through St. Charles, to a junction at Macon with the Hannibal and St. Joseph Railroad.

This was an enormous task, and Pope soon realized it would be an impossible task unless rebels could be driven from the countryside and nominally loyal citizens could be engaged to report guerrilla movements. In Pope's view, the decision of Claiborne Jackson to flee from Jefferson City "furnished an evil example to all the minor officials" in the state. The result was that much of the state had no functioning civil government. Pope's plan was to establish committees of safety in local communities and hold them responsible, through military acts of reprisal, for maintaining the peace. In this manner Pope thought that the hard hand of war could strengthen civil government. From his headquarters in St. Louis, however, commanding general John C. Fremont decided to declare martial law. Pope believed that the growing bureaucracy of provost marshals further weakened civil government.[53]

To protect the rail line connecting St. Louis to the Free State settlements in Kansas, Pope established his headquarters at Mexico, Missouri, where Grant soon joined him. After overseeing the reconstruction of the Salt River bridge, Grant moved west to Florida, Missouri, where he expected to find the camp of Thomas Harris's Guardsmen. Harris had abandoned the camp, however, and Grant proceeded further west to Mexico. While in Mexico, Grant imposed a degree of discipline on the newly recruited northern troops camped there. Some soldiers had been in the habit of leaving camp with their weapons and entering private homes seeking food and drink. Soldiers also accosted civilians on the streets and required them to recite the Federal loyalty oath. Grant brought an end to both practices and believed that he gained the goodwill of the local citizens in the process.[54]

In Mexico, Grant continued to train his troops and realized that his previous military experience had been with flintlock muskets and with Winfield Scott's guide on infantry tactics. The infantrymen's weapons had changed since the Mexican War with the introduction of the rifled musket and percussion caps. Tactics had changed too. Scott's *Tactics* were no longer in use. In 1855, at the request of Secretary of War Jefferson Davis, William Joseph Hardee published *Rifle and Light Infantry Tactics*. Jefferson Davis was now president of the Confederate States of America, and Hardee, a brigadier general in the Confederate army, was busy raising a brigade of regiments in northern Arkansas. Grant obtained a copy of Hardee's *Tactics* but soon lay the volume aside, concluding that he could better rely on his own experience and intuition to adapt tactics appropriate for the new weaponry of the Civil War. Grant ignored Hardee's *Tactics*, but he could not ignore Hardee, who now threatened a coordinated attack with Gideon Pillow's Confederate forces at New Madrid and Jeff Thompson's Missouri State Guard at nearby Bloomfield.[55]

Late in July, Grant was appointed brigadier general and took command of Federal troops at the railhead of Ironton. At Ironton, Grant prepared to confront Hardee, whose troops had taken Fredrickstown while Pillow and Thompson had taken Sikeston and moved north to within a few miles of Benton. Along the way, Thompson took control of the river town of Commerce, Missouri, a few miles south of Cape Girardeau. A cavalry force commanded by Basil Duke led Hardee's advance. Duke had returned to Missouri from Kentucky and, initially, tried to reach Sterling Price's command at Springfield. But the Federal presence in eastern Missouri was too dense to penetrate safely, and Duke made his way south to Pocahontas, Arkansas, where James S. Marmaduke and other exiled Missourians had joined Hardee's brigade. Duke had wanted to lead a raid north of Ironton to burn the Meramec River rail bridge near St. Louis. This would cut the line of supply to the Federal force at Ironton and perhaps promote a Confederate movement toward St. Louis. But as Duke recalled, the colonels in Hardee's command did not support the idea. The Confederates in southeast Missouri would soon assume a defensive demeanor.

At the same time, Grant's plan to move against Hardee at Greenville died, as well, when he was called to Jefferson City to help deal with the mounting crisis created by Price's move north after the Battle of Wilson's Creek. At Jefferson City, Grant was initially directed to lead an expedition to Boonville, Chillicothe, and Lexington to remove the bank deposits from these towns and move them to St. Louis. Before he could begin that action, however, Colonel Jefferson C. Davis arrived to relieve him. Grant took command of the "territory south of St. Louis," in the states of Missouri and Illinois. Grant soon moved his headquarters from Ironton to Cape Girardeau. By early September he had established his headquarters at Cairo, Illinois, at the confluence of the Ohio and Mississippi Rivers. Pillow left New Madrid on September 3 and occupied Columbus, Kentucky. Three days later, Grant occupied Paducah, Kentucky. With these moves, Grant sidestepped Jeff Thompson who was now threatened by Federal forces advancing out of Ironton to retake Fredericktown.[56]

In northeast Missouri, Thomas Harris and Martin Green made their way south of the Missouri River. On August 26, Price directed Harris to form a junction with him at Lexington. Price repeated the order on September 13 adding a sense of urgency: Harris should move "*as rapidly as possible, night and day*."[57] Early in September, Fremont directed Pope to locate and destroy Martin Green's three thousand mounted troops before they could make their way south of the Missouri River and join Harris. On September 10, Pope located Green at Hunnewell, west of Hannibal, chased him from his camp, and pursued him westward with two regiments of infantry. Pope knew he would not catch Green's mounted men with his infantry, but he hoped he had scattered the Guardsmen sufficiently to give his troops time to advance to Glasgow, where he hoped to prevent Green from crossing the Missouri River. But Green's force crossed at Arrow Rock, downstream and several miles south of Glasgow. With Harris and Green now south of the Missouri River, Price had succeeded in drawing several regiments of troops out of northeastern Missouri as his army advanced from Springfield north to the Missouri River.[58]

By September, as Price advanced in strength through Warrensburg toward the Missouri valley, Jeff Thompson and the Confederate commanders Gideon Pillow and William Hardee menaced southeast Missouri. Now it was the Federal forces and not the Missouri State Guard that seemed scattered and vulnerable. After Wilson's Creek, Sigel's Germans guarded the railhead at Rolla while Sturgis's Kansas troops relocated to Palmyra, where they operated in conjunction with the troops commanded by Grant and Pope. For Federal troops north of the Missouri River, the principal tasks were to protect the rail line across the state, disrupt the State Guard, and keep the state's bank deposits out of the hands of Price's advancing army. Colonel Jefferson C. Davis now commanded Federal forces at Jefferson City. He had served as an artillery commander at Fort Sumter when it surrendered in April. By May 1, Davis had returned to Indianapolis in his home state to raise troops. A captain in the regular army, Davis was appointed colonel of the Twenty-Second Indiana Volunteer Infantry regiment and by late August had joined Fremont's command in the Department of the West. At Jefferson City, Davis was joined by Colonel James A. Mulligan and the Twenty-Third Illinois, a regiment raised in Chicago and locally known as the Irish Brigade. Davis assigned Milligan's regiment the task of defending Lexington and keeping the bank deposits there out of the hands of the Missouri State Guard.[59]

Daniel Frost

Basil Duke

William S. Harney

Francis P. Blair, Jr.

Thomas Sweeny

Nathaniel Lyon

Henry Halleck

Rufus Saxton

JOHN M. SCHOFIELD

Franz Sigel

John S. Bowen

John Knapp

George G. Stifel

STERLING PRICE

JAMES H. MCBRIDE

John S. Marmaduke

BEN MCCULLOCH

HENRY GUIBOR

John Q. Burbridge

Richard Hanson Weightman

HIRAM BLEDSOE

BENJAMIN ALLEN RIVES

Samuel D. Sturgis

PETER JOSEPH OSTERHAUS

DAVID S. STANLEY

EUGENE A. CARR

FREDERICK STEELE

LEONIDAS POLK

WILLIAM H. MERRITT

GIDEON PILLOW

WILLIAM HARDEE

Chapter Four

"Tell My Wife that I Died like a Brave Man for Missouri"

For Price, the march north from Springfield was triumphal. McCulloch's disdain continued to rankle, but the Texas Ranger was now back in Arkansas, and Price returned to the heartland of Missouri with State Guardsmen who had fought well at Wilson's Creek. With Lyon dead and Lyon's army in retreat, Price now hoped to secure much of the state for Governor Jackson. A first priority was to punish the Kansas Jayhawkers who had been emboldened by the Federal pursuit of Jackson and Price. Many of Price's men were veterans of the fight against the Free State forces in Kansas. Although Price's border foes had emerged victorious when Kansas became a free state under the Topeka constitution in January 1861, Price was determined to keep Jayhawkers and any taint of abolitionism out of Missouri. A particular point of concern for Price was Fort Scott, Kansas, where a Free State community had grown up a few miles from the Missouri border around an abandoned Federal army post. Price received reports that Kansas militiamen were gathering in large numbers at that location. Indeed, James H. Lane had assembled a force of about twelve hundred mounted men at Fort Scott. Moreover, Lane was well aware of Price's movements. As Price marched slowly north through Vernon County, Missouri, he was about a dozen miles east of Fort Scott. Lane seized the opportunity to strike the Missourians before they could reach the Missouri valley. Hoping to catch Price off guard, Lane led his Kansas Brigade into Missouri and lay in ambush as Price's column approached Dry Wood Creek.

The road Price followed north passed for several miles through a landscape of rolling prairie covered with grasses rising five or six feet high. Through this landscape, Dry Wood Creek carved a ravine running northeast to the Marmaton River. Densely wooded forest covered each bank. Lane set up his ambush on the southern edge of the woods. Late in the afternoon of September 2, Price's advance guard, commanded by Alexander Steen, fell victim to Lane's trap. Lane had succeeded in catching the Missourians by surprise, but if he had also expected to instill panic in his enemy he failed. Price's column continued to move forward, and the Missourians' advantage in numbers steadily took hold. Price was pleased with the relative calm displayed by his men as they responded to the ambush. The humiliations at Boonville and Dug Springs were now faint memories. Price believed the fierce fighting at Wilson's Creek had "converted" his men "into veteran soldiers." At Dry Wood Creek, Price's officers and men moved confidently into line to fight the Jayhawkers. Price believed his men now regarded these field maneuvers and the ensuing fight as "but trifles."[1]

Nevertheless, a brisk fire fight continued for about two hours. Lane's skirmishers fell back into the wooded banks of the creek, and there the Kansans held their ground for a time. As the Missourians pressed their attack, Lane's men retreated across Dry Wood Creek, regained their mounts, and rode west across the prairie to the relative security of Fort Scott. To facilitate what became a hasty retreat, Lane left his mules and the supplies they carried to the advancing Missourians. Price had earlier proposed to attack Fort Scott, but Governor Jackson evidently discouraged the idea. Perhaps, too, the victory at Dry Wood Creek accomplished what Price had intended. In any case, Price did not pursue the retreating Kansans. "It is my earnest desire to keep my army within Missouri," Price reported to Jackson. But if raiders like Lane committed "renewed outrages upon the people of this state," Price vowed to cross into Kansas and "lay waste to the farms and utterly destroy the cities and villages of that State."[2]

After "chastising the marauding armies of Lane and Montgomery," Price moved north into central Missouri where new recruits flocked to his army. His command increased "hourly in numbers and enthusiasm," he reported. On September 10, Price prepared to encamp a few miles west of Rose Hill in southwest Johnson County. There he received reports that a Federal force was advancing from Lexington toward Warrensburg intending "to rob the bank in that place and plunder and arrest the citizens of Johnson County." Although his troops were tired by several days of steady marching, Price pressed forward until 2:00 a.m. the next morning. Leaving the infantry to rest several miles south of Warrensburg, Price rode forward with his mounted troops and came within view of the town by dawn. He discovered that the Federal forces had withdrawn about midnight and burned bridges to cover their retreat.[3]

The retreating Federal troops were the Thirteenth Regiment of Missouri Volunteers commanded by Colonel Everett Peabody. A native of Massachusetts and the son of a prominent Unitarian minister, Peabody had settled in St. Joseph, Missouri, in the late 1850s as an engineer for the Hannibal and St. Joseph Railroad. He had graduated from Harvard in 1849, and he joined the Thirteenth Missouri as a major when the Civil War began. He had been appointed colonel of the regiment on September 1. As the Federal forces at Lexington labored to fortify their position, Peabody had been sent south to support Lane.[4]

Peabody probably also had instructions to remove funds from the bank at Warrensburg. One of the purposes of sending Federal troops to Lexington had been to remove the deposits from the bank there. Peabody probably intended to do the same at Warrensburg. Price knew very well what was at stake. He and other leaders of the state's central slaveholding clique had won the passage of a new banking law in Missouri in 1857. The law expanded the banking system in the state in a way that secured the interests of wealthy slave owners. Price was a state bank commissioner when the Civil War began, and the banking law that he helped to administer required the establishment of new banks in the state's largest slaveholding counties. To create these new banks, the bank commissioners shifted capital out of St. Louis and into central Missouri. It was a Faustian bargain that St. Louis merchants and manufacturers were willing to enter into in order to overcome the state's severe restrictions on banking. In the secession crisis, as pro-southern Missourians began to form the Missouri State Guard, leading slave owners helped to fund the state's military forces with promissory notes, which were readily accepted by the pro-southern bankers in central Missouri. Later in the war Unionists took full control of the banks and began to file civil suits to recover the debt created by the promissory notes. But in 1861 the newly formed banks held funds that Price intended to draw upon to supply his army and defend the government of Claiborne Jackson.[5]

Peabody did not get a chance to visit the bank in Warrensburg. Approaching the town from the north, he learned that Lane had been swept aside and that Price was advancing toward Warrensburg from the south with more than 10,000 men. With a single regiment of 900 infantry reinforced with 350 cavalry and two six-pound field guns, Peabody conceded Warrensburg and its bank to Price and returned to the Federal defenses at Lexington.[6] For his part, Price did not attempt to attack the retreating Federal troops. It had begun to rain, and he decided to rest his men and continue his advance under more favorable conditions. At Warrensburg, Price took time to regroup. His infantry and artillery rejoined the mounted force, and the entire army enjoyed the town's hospitality as its citizens "vied with each other in feeding my almost famished soldiers."[7]

On September 12, Price prepared to leave Warrensburg and continue his advance into the Missouri valley with a specific focus on Lexington and the bank deposits confiscated there by Federal forces. A storm delayed the departure, but by mid-morning the march of about thirty miles began. With General William Slack wounded at Wilson's Creek, Benjamin Rives assumed command of the Fourth Division. Rives's troops and Mosby Parson's Sixth Division led the advance. About 3:00 p.m. that afternoon the lead elements of Price's column approached the outskirts of Lexington and encountered Federal skirmishers concealed in cornfields and behind hedges and fences. Colonel Robert T. Van Horn commanded this first line of the Federal defenses. Van Horn was determined to blunt Price's advance and forestall an immediate assault on the Federal earthworks, which were still being constructed around the Masonic College. As one of Price's officers recalled, the Federal troops "stood their ground," although they eventually fell back when Price brought his artillery forward. Van Horn's efforts succeeded. Rives lost three men killed and several wounded in the fighting. One of the dead Guardsmen was Rufus Chadwick of Daviess County, whose dying words were quoted in his commander's official report: "Tell my wife that I died like a brave man for Missouri and only regret that I had not another to give her."[8]

As Parson's division moved forward, the Missourians flushed the Federal skirmishers from their hiding places and into the earthworks around the Masonic College on the bluff above the Missouri River. Gradually, the rebel army of about twelve thousand men arrived in force. By that time, the Federal garrison of about twenty-seven hundred men had consolidated within what Price described as their "strongly fortified" defensive position. Price positioned his artillery "within easy range of the college," the fortified buildings. During the initial bombardment, Hiram Bledsoe's battery was commanded "gallantly," as Price reported, by Captain Emmett MacDonald of St. Louis. Bledsoe had been wounded at Dry Wood Creek and resumed command a few days later. Henry Guibor's battery also participated in the shelling. But the Federal defenses remained strong, and as evening approached, Price withdrew from the town and encamped at the fairgrounds. Here, Price waited for reinforcements and his supply wagons.[9]

For the most part, the Federal forces in Lexington had prepared their defenses well. The senior officer and garrison commander was Colonel James A. Mulligan. He and his fellow officers were confident they could defend themselves effectively within their earthen fortifications. Although a New Yorker by birth, Mulligan was a prominent member of the Chicago Irish American community. Both of his parents were natives of Ireland, and when his widowed mother moved to Chicago in the late 1830s Mulligan became active in the city's Irish community. In the late 1850s he was elected captain of the Chicago Shield Guards, an Irish militia company. When war broke out, Mulligan presided over a meeting of Irish militia companies that soon formed the Twenty-Third Illinois Regiment of Volunteers to which he was elected colonel. Thin and over six feet tall Mulligan was a devout Catholic and a strict temperance man. With considerable skill and industry he directed his troops to fortify the high ground around the Masonic College, including the three-story brick building of the college itself. Around this structure, Mulligan's soldiers threw up an earthen rampart twelve feet high and twelve feet thick. Behind the rampart were rifle pits. Mulligan could easily have escaped from Price on the two steamboats he had at his disposal on the Missouri River wharf north of town. But he was confident of his defenses and confident, too, that his commanding general, John C. Fremont, would send the requested reinforcements. As Price approached Lexington with a force more than four times the size of his own, Mulligan decided to hold his ground.[10]

It took some time for all of Price's men and supplies to arrive in Lexington. For the next several days, the rebels left the Federal garrison largely unmolested. One of Price's officers later recalled these days were marked by "desultory skirmishes with pickets and foraging parities." But no serious fighting took place. Mulligan took advantage of the lull to strengthen his defenses. In doing so, he authorized the destruction of two private homes. One was the Wallace House, which stood near the college and the Federal earthworks and provided shelter for rebel sharpshooters. A squad of Federal troops succeeded in burning it to the ground. The second home destroyed was the Fleming House, which helped to shelter Price's artillery. Federal gunners set it ablaze with red-hot shot. Price's gunners also fired red-hot shot into the Masonic College but without much effect. A local boy of thirteen who had joined the Federal garrison took on the responsibility of removing these shots with a shovel and dousing any flames.[11]

As Price prepared to lay siege to the Federal fort, he sought reinforcements. One of the principal goals of moving into the Missouri valley was to recruit troops. On the evening of September 15, Price directed General David Rice Atchison of the Missouri State Guard to make his way west to Liberty, Missouri, upstream from Lexington on the north bank of the Missouri River. At this location a substantial number of recruits were preparing to cross the Missouri and join Price's army. It was Atchison's task to take command of these men and guide their crossing. Atchison knew the place well. Born in Kentucky in 1807, he had moved to Liberty in 1830 where he practiced law and became active in state politics as a proslavery Democrat. Atchison entered the US Senate by appointment in 1843 and won election in 1849. Fiercely hostile to the Free State movement in Kansas, Atchison led five thousand Missourians into Kansas to secure the election of a proslavery legislature in 1855. Atchison initially declined an appointment as a brigadier general in the Missouri State Guard, but early in July 1861 after Lyon had attacked Governor Claiborne Jackson and the Missouri State Guard at Boonville, he joined the governor's entourage and served as Jackson's aide while the governor remained in Missouri. Atchison had been with Jackson at the battle of Carthage. He then accompanied Jackson when he conferred with Confederate general Leonidas Polk in Memphis and with Confederate president Jefferson Davis in Richmond. The two men returned to Springfield on September 7 and learned that Price had moved north. They joined Price at Warrensburg and moved with the army to Lexington.[12]

The rebel troops massing at Liberty had been recruited in Alexander Steen's Fifth Military District. Steen had been ill for some time, however, and it was Atchinson's job to rendezvous with the nearly four thousand new troops at Liberty and guide them across the Missouri River to reinforce Price at Lexington. Atchison located the recruits at Liberty at about 4:00 p.m. on September 16. On the same day that Atchison left Lexington for Liberty, General Samuel Sturgis at Fort Leavenworth, Kansas, learned of the rebel activity near Liberty and directed Lieutenant Colonel John Scott to lead a detachment of the Third Iowa Infantry from Cameron, Missouri (where they guarded the Hannibal and St. Joseph Railroad in the northeast corner of Clinton County), south to Liberty in an effort to prevent the rebel recruits from crossing the Missouri River. Scott's detachment of five hundred Iowa volunteers was reinforced with about seventy Home Guard and a squad of German artillerists operating a single six-pound gun. Heavy rain slowed Scott's progress from Cameron to Liberty. Scott's main force arrived in Liberty about 7:00 a.m. on September 17. By 11:00 a.m. Scott's scouts encountered Atchison's skirmishers a few miles south of Liberty on the road to Blue Mills Landing. By this time, Atchison had his crossing well in hand. He had begun crossing troops and supplies the previous evening. It was a slow operation, however, and it continued all night and into the next day. Utilizing three small flatboats, Atchison painstakingly guided the crossing of nearly four thousand men and a hundred supply wagons. The skirmishers that Scott's advance force met south of Liberty had been deployed by Atchison as a defensive line about two miles north of the landing.[13]

Atchison faced a competent adversary in Colonel John Scott. Born in Ohio in 1824, Scott was a veteran of the Mexican War. Like Atchison, he was active in politics. Admitted to the bar in Steubenville before moving to Kentucky, Scott joined a Kentucky regiment to fight in the Mexican War. He returned to Kentucky where he edited a Whig newspaper. Scott's antislavery views made his residence in Kentucky increasingly uncomfortable, however, and in 1856 he moved north to Nevada, Iowa. When the Civil War began, Scott left his Iowa state senate seat to become captain of Company E of the Third Iowa Infantry. The regiment was mustered in at Keokuk in June 1861. In the Third Iowa, Scott soon rose to the rank of lieutenant colonel.[14]

On the morning of September 17, Scott established his camp on high ground north of Liberty. He soon learned that the State Guard recruits had passed through the town the previous afternoon and that they had taken the road leading to Blue Mills Landing. Scott's advance troops discovered Atchison's defensive line concealed in brush on both sides of the road leading south to the landing. Atchison had deployed nine hundred men to protect the crossing. As the Federal troops advanced against the Guardsmen, Atchison's men concentrated their fire on the artillerists at the center of the enemy line. The German gunners were badly hit and only managed to fire their cannon twice in the hour-long fight. More important, Scott reported that "some of the gunners abandoned the piece, carrying off the matches and primer, and could not be rallied." With his artillery silenced, Scott began to retreat. The Iowans brought the cannon off the field by hand, but their ammunition wagon was stuck between a tree and a log on the side of the road and Scott decided to abandon it, convinced that his men would sustain serious losses if they tried to retrieve it.[15]

The Federal force retreated from the field quickly but in order. Several times they formed a battle line and fired a volley or two at the pursuing rebel recruits. Atchison's men sustained significant losses (probably about seventy were killed or severely wounded compared to about sixty dead and severely wounded on the

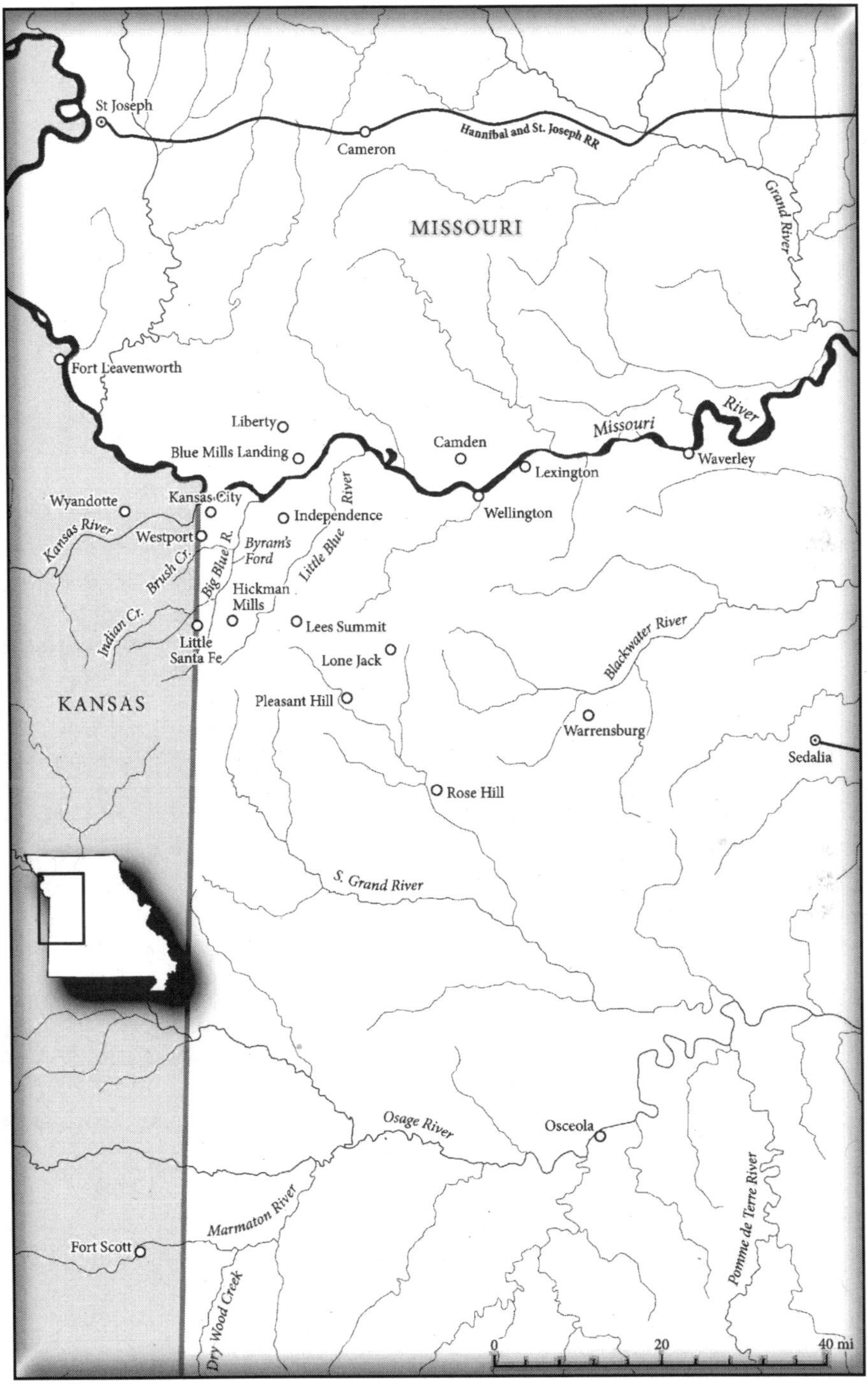
St Joseph
Cameron
Hannibal and St. Joseph RR
Grand River
MISSOURI
Fort Leavenworth
Liberty
Blue Mills Landing
Camden
Missouri
River
Waverley
Lexington
Wellington
Wyandotte
Kansas City
Independence
Kansas River
Westport
Byram's Ford
Little Blue River
Brush Cr.
Big Blue R.
Hickman Mills
Indian Cr.
Little Santa Fe
Lees Summit
Lone Jack
Blackwater River
KANSAS
Pleasant Hill
Warrensburg
Sedalia
Rose Hill
S. Grand River
Osage River
Osceola
Pomme de Terre River
Marmaton River
Fort Scott
Dry Wood Creek
0
20
40 mi

Federal side). But Atchison was elated with his victory. The Guardsmen, Atchison reported, pursued the Federals "until they annihilated the rear of their army." The Missourians followed the retreating Iowans "like hounds on a wolf chase, strewing the road with the dead and wounded." Describing the weather as "very warm," Atchison reported that his men gave up the chase "from exhaustion" as evening approached. Atchison completed his crossing and soon joined Price at the siege of Lexington.[16]

On the morning of September 18, with his full force assembled, Price advanced in force against the Federal entrenchments at Lexington. As one of Price's officers recalled, the rebel army marched out of their fairgrounds camp with colors flying and "a full band of field music in front." Price established his headquarters in a building on Main Street near Tenth. Price directed Rives, with the Fourth Division, to take up positions on the west side of the Federal earthworks. In doing so, Rives routed Federal soldiers concealed in buildings and behind lumber piles along the river. Other Union soldiers put up stiff resistance at the iron foundry and steam mill near the river, and also from the "richly freighted" steamboat *Clara Bell*. The rebels soon captured the steamboat. Among the riches they acquired was a large supply of sugar and the Guardsmen enjoyed a double ration of sugar for several days after the battle. After clearing Union troops from the landing, the Guardsmen pursued the enemy up the bluff to their entrenchments.[17]

The fighting on the west side of the Federal earthworks now focused on the Anderson House. Price later reported that Rives's men drew "heavy fire" from the house, although he acknowledged that the Federal forces used the building "as a hospital" and that they identified it as such with a "white flag." But Rives understood the military importance of the Anderson House, and he probably regarded enemy fire coming from the vicinity of the building as sufficient justification for attacking it. Several companies of Harris's Second Division joined "the gallant soldiers of the Fourth Division" to storm the building. The Guardsmen now controlled what Price described as an "important position" just over one hundred yards from the Federal entrenchments.[18]

When Rives entered the Anderson House, he discovered in the cellar a group of escaped slaves who had made their way to Federal lines, some from as far north as Utica, near Chillicothe. Rives had the fugitives placed under guard to be returned to their owners.[19] The Federal hospital now became a valuable military asset for Rives. From the building, Rives's sharpshooters fired directly into the fort. The rebel sharpshooters "annoyed" the Federal forces sufficiently that Mulligan's men determined to retake the building. Assigned to this task was one company from Mulligan's Twenty-Third Illinois regiment. They were joined by a detachment from Peabody's Saint Joseph regiment known as the German Company. Rives reported that the Federal assault was "bravely accomplished" and "would have elicited our admiration had not the act been tarnished by the murder of three of my men." Price, too, reported that the Federal assault would have

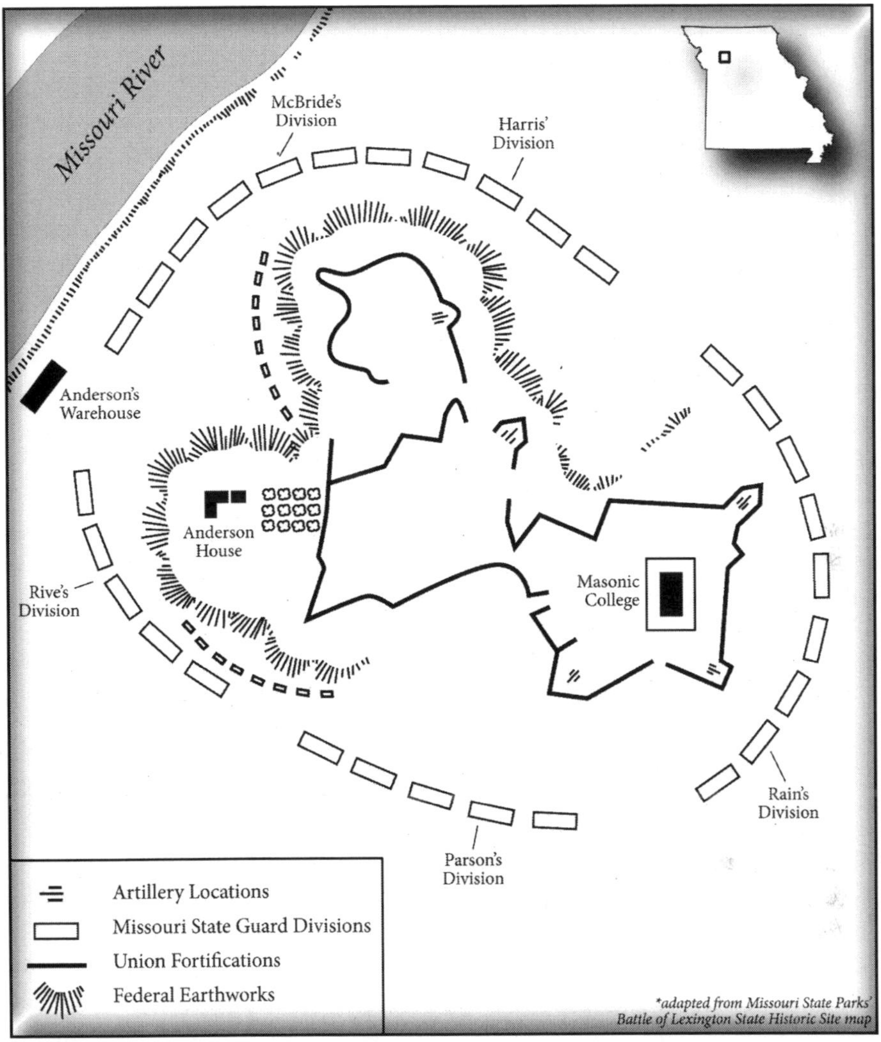

been "honorable" had it not been followed "by an act of savage barbarity." The Federal troops regarded the Guardsmen's military use of the hospital as a violation of the laws of war. Several Federal soldiers had been killed by Rives's sharpshooters and some of Mulligan's and Peabody's men took their revenge when they recaptured the Anderson House. Price reported the executions that followed the Federal assault as the "cowardly murder of three defenseless men, who had laid down their arms and surrendered themselves as prisoners." A fourth Guardsman escaped through what Rives described as the "kindheartedness" of an ill Federal soldier, an Illinois cavalryman, "who kindly furnished him a place on his bed and a portion of his blanket, by which he escaped the observation of the bloodthirsty soldiers whose bayonets were reeking with the blood of defenseless men." The Federal occupation of the hospital was brief. Rives's men retook the building later that day and held it against several Federal attacks during the night of September 18. Several "citizens and amateur fighters" joined Rives's troops and "rendered efficient service with their rifles and double-barreled shotguns." At 5:00 p.m. on the evening of September 19, the status of the Anderson House as a hospital ended. Price agreed to a truce, and the sick and wounded men in the Anderson House were removed from the battlefield. The Anderson House now became the military stronghold from which Price launched his final assault on the Federal garrison.[20]

On the morning of September 19, Price captured a messenger carrying news to Mulligan that Samuel Sturgis would advance from Fort Leavenworth with one thousand men to try to relieve the siege. Price directed Parsons to move three thousand men across the Missouri to block any Federal advance toward Lexington from that direction. Parsons sent Colonel Congreve Jackson, commanding Clark's Third Division, across the river for this purpose. Jackson advanced about a mile and half north of the river but soon learned there was no Federal force advancing toward Lexington and rejoined the siege.[21]

The inability of John C. Fremont to deal at all effectively with the growing danger at Lexington hastened the erosion of confidence within the Lincoln administration concerning his capacity to command the Department of the West. Fremont's response to the defeat at Wilson's Creek had been largely passive. To be sure, he did not receive good information from commanders in the field about Price's movements after Wilson's Creek, but neither did he direct scouting activities to follow Price. By contrast, Fremont had a much more detailed sense of Federal resources and enemy movements on the Mississippi River south of St. Louis. Central Missouri did not seem to concern him. By the time he recognized the significance of Price's move north it was September 15, and Price was already in Lexington. Three more days passed before Fremont acted to concentrate Federal forces in central Missouri. By then it was too late. Mulligan's men were in desperate shape and surrender was inevitable.[22]

If Mulligan had known that he would face Price without reinforcements, he might have deployed his forces differently. In retrospect it was an error not to move Colonel Thomas A. Marshall's seven hundred cavalrymen and their horses north of the Missouri River. This was the opinion of Colonel Van Horn who published his recollection of the battle in 1903. Van Horn, a native of Pennsylvania, was editor of the *Kansas City Journal.* He later served as a mayor of Kansas City. According to Van Horn, Marshall's cavalrymen had not yet been issued rifles. They were armed with sabers and pistols, which was the standard for cavalrymen, but these weapons were of little use defending the fortifications around the college. Protecting these men and their mounts increased the burden on the

Federal defenses. Most important, the horses hastened the depletion of the supply of cistern water inside the college. Once Price's siege cut Mulligan off from the river and State Guard sharpshooters threatened death to any man who ventured out of the fortifications seeking water, thirst quickly ravaged the Federal garrison. As the Federal garrison drained the cistern, attention focused on a spring in the wooded area to the east of the fort and on a well and nearby spring at the Anderson House on the west side of the fort. At the Anderson House alone, over thirty Federal soldiers were killed or captured trying to get water, particularly during the night of September 19.[23]

On the morning of September 19, the Guardsmen began deploying hemp bales to create movable breastworks on either side of the Anderson House. According to one account, the Guardsmen approached the Federal entrenchments "under cover of bales of hemp, rolling them before us." One of Price's officers later recalled that "two or three men would get behind a bale, roll it awhile, then stop and shoot awhile." A second line of bales would be similarly advanced and then stacked on top of the first row.[24] On the morning of September 20, Price had hemp bales brought up from the wharf. General Harris initially directed that the bales be soaked in the river "to protect them against the casualties of fire of our troops and of the enemy." But it quickly became evident that the bales became too heavy for the men to roll them up from the river. Instead, the men positioned the bales and wetted them in the field. On the morning of September 20, Harris directed that the line of hemp bales on both sides of the Anderson House "be used as portable breastworks, to be pushed forward towards the enemy's lines in parallel approaches." Advancing behind these shields, Price's men nullified the Federal defenses and Mulligan surrendered.[25]

Shortly after noon on September 20, Mulligan offered his surrender. By 2:00 p.m. the surrender was complete. It was a one-sided victory for Price who lost one hundred of his men whereas Mulligan lost half of his garrison in the fighting (more than seventeen hundred men) and surrendered the rest. Mulligan's Irish Brigade surrendered with a flourish, however. They marched around the inside of the fort as their band played. Before them flew their brigade flag bearing the image of a gold harp of Erin on a green field. Mulligan's men then furled their banner and stacked their arms. Price required the defeated Union troops to listen to a speech delivered by Governor Claiborne Jackson. Price then paroled the soldiers and dismissed them. Mulligan himself refused parole, insisting that Price had no authority over a Federal officer. Mulligan remained with Price until October 30. By Mulligan's account, Price treated him well and even permitted Mulligan's young wife (who had accompanied him to Lexington) to join him. Mulligan was eventually exchanged for the paroled commander of Camp Jackson, Daniel M. Frost.[26]

During the week following the battle, Price remained in Lexington, gathering new recruits and distributing more than three thousand captured rifles. He also took the opportunity to return the Federally confiscated funds ceremoniously to the Farmers' Bank in Lexington. With the defeated Colonel Mulligan at his side, Price restored the funds, confident that the bank's director would continue the practice of funding the promissory notes that men of southern principles had issued to arm and supply the rebel army.[27]

While Price savored his victory at Lexington, Jim Lane and his Kansas Brigade reentered Missouri ostensibly to disrupt Price's line of supply. After being pushed aside by Price at Dry Wood Creek, Lane had returned to Fort Scott and requested reinforcements from Fort Leavenworth. If properly reinforced, Lane promised to return to Missouri and stop Price before he could cross the Osage River. No reinforcements came, however, and Lane contented himself with raiding in Price's rear. On September 23, Lane claimed to have been ambushed outside of the town of Osceola, Missouri, on the southern bank of the Osage River. According to Lane, the Missourians who attacked him fled into the town and took refuge in its buildings. "We were compelled to shell them out," Lane reported, "and in doing so the place was burned to ashes, with an immense amount of stores of all descriptions."[28]

Price's victories at Wilson's Creek, Dry Wood Creek, and Lexington proved inspirational to young men of southern sympathies. Price now took full advantage of the rich recruiting fields available to him in central Missouri. His army grew to eighteen thousand men, an increase of 50 percent since leaving Springfield.[29]

Price's victories had shaken Fremont. Humiliated by the defeats at Wilson's Creek and Lexington, and with Lincoln's doubts growing about his competence as a commander, Fremont belatedly prepared to lead an expedition to drive Price from central Missouri. Price's victories also emboldened Confederates to expand their control of the state. If rebel forces in southeast Missouri could coordinate their movements with Price and McCulloch in southwest Missouri, Confederates could hope to secure a northern border across the state. For a time the prospect for such coordination seemed bright. General William Hardee supported Thompson with Confederate troops from Arkansas. Basil Duke, the former leader of the St. Louis Minute Men, joined Hardee in this movement and hoped to fight his way to western Missouri to join Price. Duke found Hardee overly cautious, however. Without a significant infusion of Confederate troops, Duke realized, Thompson lacked the resources to advance north beyond the swamps that separated Missouri's Boot Heel from the rest of the state. When Hardee withdrew from Missouri late in August, Duke concluded that his fight in Missouri was over. He returned east to Lexington, Kentucky, and fought the rest of the war with John Hunt Morgan's cavalry.[30]

Hardee's cautious efforts to coordinate with Jeff Thompson took place in the context of wider Confederate maneuvering in the Mississippi valley below Cairo, Illinois. On September 3, 1861, Gideon Pillow, on orders from Leonidas Polk, occupied Columbus, Kentucky, and began to fortify the town. Polk soon made

Columbus his headquarters and took command of what he intended to be the anchor of Confederate defenses on the Mississippi. Artillery batteries on the river bluffs north of Columbus commanded the river. Across the river, just upstream from the Missouri town of Belmont, Polk positioned a regiment of infantry, supported by an artillery battery and cavalry. Polk had the heavily wooded river bank cleared. This brought the Confederate garrison at Belmont under the protection of the artillery at Columbus. It also provided the materials for the construction of an abatis to help defend the camp from attack by land.[31]

On September 4, Grant moved his headquarters from Cape Girardeau, Missouri, to Cairo, Illinois. He positioned Federal garrisons at Cape Girardeau, on the Mississippi north of Cairo, and at Ironton, which was the terminus of the Iron Mountain Railroad linking the mining region of southeast Missouri to St. Louis. Commanding at Ironton was Colonel William P. Carlin, an Illinois native and an 1850 graduate of West Point. Commanding at Cape Girardeau was another West Pointer, the Massachusetts-born Joseph B. Plummer. Plummer was a veteran of the Battle of Wilson's Creek and had recuperated from a wound he received in that fight.[32]

On September 5, Grant received news from a Federal scout that Polk planned to send four thousand Confederate troops from Columbus to occupy Paducah, on the Ohio River at the mouth of the Tennessee River. Grant surprised Polk (and the alarmed citizens of Paducah) by occupying the town with Federal troops on September 6. No knowing that Grant had initially arrived in Paducah with only two regiments, Polk's Confederate force returned to Columbus, and Grant brought reinforcements into Paducah as quickly as he could.[33]

In mid-September 1861, Albert Sidney Johnston took command of the Confederate Western Department. This command brought with it responsibility for creating a long defensive line from the Appalachian Mountains to the Mississippi valley and beyond his command westward through Missouri and Arkansas to the Indian Territory. Governor Claiborne Jackson and his military commander Sterling Price wanted the northern border of the Confederacy to include as much of Missouri as possible. Jackson and David Atchison met with Leonidas Polk in Memphis for discussion. It seemed clear to Jackson and Atchison that Price's successes in southwest Missouri (and the potential for Thompson's success in southeast Missouri) should encourage the Confederates to move aggressively into Missouri. Jackson and Atchison found Polk supportive, but Johnston, the new Confederate commander in the West, concluded that he lacked the resources to launch such an offensive. Polk and Pillow had established Columbus as a strong defensive position on the Mississippi, but General Johnston was preoccupied with strengthening Confederate positions on the Tennessee and Cumberland Rivers. Forts to protect these rivers had not yet been completed. (Work on them resumed in earnest in December, with much of the labor being supplied by slaves from Alabama.) Rather than reinforce Confederate positions in the Mississippi valley to support an advance into Missouri, Johnston wanted to shift resources from Columbus to the Tennessee valley.

From Johnston's perspective, the fighting in Missouri was significant to the extent that it distracted Federal forces and gave him time to define and defend a Confederate border east of the Mississippi. Claiborne Jackson feared as much, but he and Price continued to advocate boldly a decisive Confederate movement into Missouri. With no intention of shifting resources into Missouri, Johnston acted to keep these hopes alive. In October, he and Polk gave their blessing to Jeff Thompson's plan to lead a Missouri expedition north of Cape Girardeau. Thompson began the operation with high hopes. He would disrupt Federal forces, recruit soldiers, and capture supplies. Of particular interest were the lead supplies at the smelters near Fredericktown. If fortune favored him, Thompson would capture weapons and ammunition from the Federal garrison at Ironton. Beyond Ironton, Thompson imagined an even wider campaign. In a dispatch sent to the Confederate quartermaster in Memphis, Thompson expressed his desire to form a junction with Sterling Price. "If I succeed in the adventure," wrote Thompson, "I will completely relieve General Price, or be near enough to operate with him." All of this required Confederate support, which Thompson requested but which Johnston was not eager to provide.[34]

As Jeff Thompson's expedition began, he directed his infantry commander Lieutenant Colonel Aden Lowe to occupy Fredericktown. This move threatened the Federal garrisons at Ironton to the west and Cape Girardeau to the east. Lowe arrived at Fredericktown early in the afternoon of October 16 and his presence had the desired effect of worrying the commanders of the nearby Federal garrisons. With a mounted force, Thompson probed farther north. At Blackwell, Missouri, where the Iron Mountain Railroad crossed the Big River, Thompson defeated a detachment of Federal troops and burned the bridge. Thompson reported that his men were particularly adept in "bushwhacking fights." After the fight at the Big River bridge, Thompson lingered with some of his men at the Blackwell Station to collect and distribute captured Federal equipment. They were surprised by an attack by a previously undetected company of Federal troops. Unable to form a battle line, Thompson directed his men to "go in on their own hook." They did so with alacrity. "Each man dashed at them," Thompson reported, and in about ten minutes they had driven the Union troops away.[35]

Jeff Thompson's raiders had penetrated into Jefferson County, less than fifty miles south of St. Louis. "I have them terribly frightened," Thompson reported. At the same time, Thompson regretted that he had not managed to capture a train during the raid. A train freighted with supplies for Ironton would have been a great prize. Also, he hoped to use an engine "as a catapult on Ironton," evidently intending to drive it through the Federal defenses. Rather than attack Ironton, Thompson moved his men "back into the hills to rest their horses." Despite his success at the Big River, Thompson's adventure was not fulfilling his highest hopes. He admitted that he was "sadly disappointed in recruiting my army." Throughout the region, he found the population friendly and supportive. From New Madrid to the Big River, Thompson reported that "we have been welcomed in the most flattering and encouraging manner." The problem was that he had no weapons to distribute to new recruits, and "the people will not go without they know when and where they are to receive them." Thompson needed—and evidently still hoped to receive—Confederate support. After testing Federal defenses near St. Louis, he prepared to join his infantry at Fredericktown and then "fall back to the swamps" to await reinforcements. With Confederate support he promised to take Ironton and complete the destruction of the Iron Mountain Railroad.[36] Thompson and his raiding party approached his main force at Fredericktown at about 10:00 a.m. on October 17. He and his men approached the town from the north, preparing to enter it from the west on the Ironton road, which passed over the Little St. Francis River bridge. Near the bridge Thompson discovered a Federal cavalry detachment. The Federal troops were evidently probing Lowe's positions in Fredericktown. Thompson's mounted troops charged the bridge at full gallop, "yelling like Indians." The Federal troops gave way and Thompson entered Fredericktown unscathed, but he was beginning to recognize how vulnerable his position had become. "I am in a damned tight place," he wrote the Missouri State Guard commandant at Bloomfield. "I believe I will get out safely," he continued, but he urged the commander to be prepared to support him if Federal troops followed him through the swamps.[37]

From his headquarters at Cairo, Grant directed the movement of Federal forces in response to Jeff Thompson's raid. On the afternoon of October 15, Carlin at Ironton learned that Thompson had captured the Big River bridge. Expecting to be attacked, Carlin consolidated his forces. At the same time, Grant reinforced Plummer at Cape Girardeau with one regiment of infantry and supporting cavalry. Grant directed Plummer to continue to protect the river town but also to organize an expedition to "meet Thompson." Thompson's elusiveness had already become legendary, and while Grant expected that the Federal movement he ordered would compel Thompson to withdraw, he also expressed to Plummer "little confidence in your even seeing" the Missourian. Grant also offered Plummer reassurance that he did not face a large Confederate invasion: Hardee and the Confederates had not been in Missouri for the past month. Grant assured Plummer that he only had to contend with Thompson and Lowe and about three thousand Guardsmen. Grant directed Plummer to coordinate his expedition with the Federal commander at Ironton. As directed, Plummer dispatched a messenger to Carlin with a letter explaining that he would advance from Cape Girardeau toward Fredericktown from the southeast with the intention of blocking Thompson's retreat. Inexplicably, the messenger followed the main road from Cape Girardeau to Ironton. That road passed through Fredericktown, and the messenger took insufficient precautious to evade the enemy forces there. On October 20,

Plummer's messenger fell into Thompson's hands. Thompson now knew that Plummer intended to attack him from the southeast. He did not yet know that Carlin also planned to attack him from the west.[38]

Plummer left Cape Girardeau on October 18 with fifteen hundred men, leaving about the same number of troops to guard the town. He marched northwest and reached Fredericktown about noon on October 21. Not knowing his message to Carlin had been intercepted, Plummer was not surprised to find Carlin had entered the town about 9:00 a.m. that morning with a force of about three thousand men. Carlin, too, hoped to trap Thompson. Carlin had learned from his scouts that Thompson's camp extended along the Ironton road from the bridge crossing the Little St. Francis River to the center of town, a distance of about three-quarters of a mile. Carlin planned to move his troops across the Little St. Francis River using a ford south of the bridge. He would then attack Thompson from the southwest intending to catch the enemy by surprise. When Plummer and Carlin joined forces at Fredericktown, they discovered that Thompson had retreated to the south.[39]

At Fredericktown, the two Federal commanders agreed that Plummer would take command. Carlin grumbled that he was "senior by commission," but he acknowledged that he had no battlefield experience and that Plummer did. Plummer took command of two of Carlin's regiments and elements of Major John M. Schofield's First Missouri Light Artillery. Carlin remained in Fredericktown with the reserve troops. Plummer learned from residents in town that Thompson and Lowe had moved south on the Greenville road. He proceeded in that direction to overtake what he believed to be a retreating enemy.[40]

Jeff Thompson hoped to ambush an unsuspecting Federal force. When Thompson captured Plummer's messenger, he quickly withdrew from Fredericktown about twelve miles south on the Greenville road. There he secured his supplies. Confident that he had secured his line of retreat as well, Thompson moved his infantry back toward Fredericktown and prepared to ambush the pursuing Federal troops. About two miles outside of Fredericktown, Thompson concealed his forces on high ground across the Greenville road. Thompson positioned Lowe's regiment of Guardsmen to his front. These troops were concealed in a cornfield and behind a rail fence and protected by an eight-pound field gun. It was Thompson's plan to have Lowe's men engage the Federals and entice them to attack in force. Once the Federals had committed themselves to the fight, Thompson instructed Lowe to fall back to the main defensive line, whereupon Thompson would open on the Federals with the main body of his infantry and his artillery. As it happened, Lowe bravely held his ground too long and fell dead with a bullet in his head.[41]

In pursuit of Thompson, Plummer's troops left Fredericktown about 1:00 p.m. on October 21. Two companies of cavalry and the Seventeenth Illinois led the column. About a mile out of town the Federal troops spotted Lowe's men and

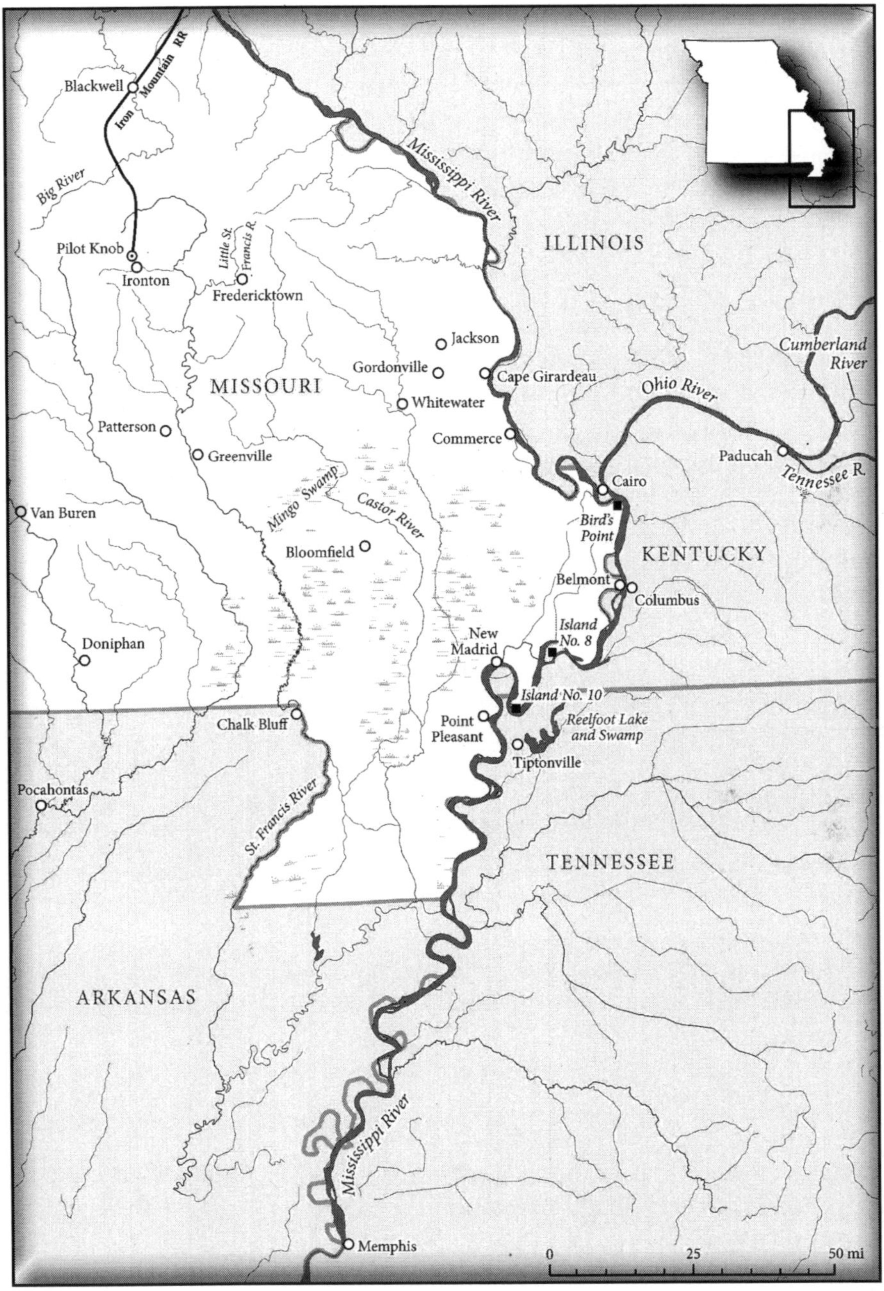

Blackwell
Iron Mountain RR
Big River
Pilot Knob
Ironton
Little St. Francis R.
Fredericktown
Mississippi River
ILLINOIS
Jackson
Gordonville
Cape Girardeau
MISSOURI
Whitewater
Ohio River
Cumberland River
Patterson
Greenville
Commerce
Paducah
Tennessee R.
Cairo
Mingo Swamp
Castor River
Van Buren
Bird's Point
Bloomfield
KENTUCKY
Belmont
Columbus
Island No. 8
New Madrid
Doniphan
Island No. 10
Chalk Bluff
Point Pleasant
Reelfoot Lake and Swamp
Tiptonville
Pocahontas
St. Francis River
TENNESSEE
ARKANSAS
Mississippi River
Memphis
0
25
50 mi

reported a suspected ambush. Colonel Leonard F. Ross, commanding the Seventeenth Illinois, sent three companies of his infantry forward as skirmishers. On the right side of the road the skirmishers met strong resistance from Thompson's main defensive line, and Ross deployed four more companies. On the left, Federal skirmishers encountered Lowe's intended ambush. Lowe's failure to withdraw struck Ross as heroic. He reported that Lowe fell dead "while bravely fighting at the head of his regiment." Lowe died in full view of Ross's line with "his pistol firmly clenched in his hands ready to fire." Notwithstanding Lowe's bravery, however, the rebel ambush failed. Ross lost one dead and twenty-seven were wounded in the encounter, but after Lowe's death his men began to flee from their hiding places. It was too late for them to do so safely and they made easy targets for the pursuing Federals. On Plummer's left, the Seventeenth Illinois, now supported by the Twentieth Illinois and the Eleventh Missouri, continued to advance, routing Lowe's men and turning Thompson's right flank.[42]

On Plummer's right flank, Thompson took direct command. He tried to rally his men to reform a battle line across the road where they could be supported by his artillery. To break up this effort, Plummer ordered his cavalry to charge the line and gain the battery. The charge failed. Several Federal horsemen were killed and many more fell wounded. Thompson reported that his men had emptied the saddles of the Federal force. Nevertheless, Thompson continued his retreat, hastily but in order. As evening approached, Plummer disengaged from battle and resumed a cautious pursuit the next morning (October 22). Plummer's cavalrymen advanced more than twenty miles south of Fredericktown and encountered only evidence that Thompson continued his retreat. The Federals found "dead bodies, arms, saddles, and clothing on the road as far as we pursued them." Reporting that the enemy was "apparently . . . in confusion," Plummer returned to Fredericktown. On October 23, he left about forty wounded prisoners there to be cared for by residents and returned to Cape Girardeau with another forty prisoners and captured weapons.[43]

After the battle at Fredericktown, Carlin ordered the destruction of two furnaces that had supplied the rebels with lead. Destructive reprisals quickly multiplied as Federal troops set fire to buildings owned by civilians they deemed to be sympathetic to the enemy. "Six or seven buildings were burned," Plummer reported. He and his officers finally stopped the "incendiarism" and restored order.[44]

Jeff Thompson's threat in southeast Missouri rose and fell as John C. Fremont launched his expedition to reassert Federal military dominance in central Missouri. After the Federal surrender at Lexington, Fremont assembled a large army. In contrast to his earlier timidity, Fremont now promised bold action. The Pathfinder of the West proposed to drive Sterling Price from Missouri, defeat the renowned Texas Ranger Ben McCulloch in Arkansas, and lead a triumphant Federal army down the Mississippi River to capture New Orleans. Few outside of Fremont's inner circle had much confidence in the plan, however, and the difficulties inherent in organizing a large military force and moving it across the Missouri and Osage Rivers quickly laid bare Fremont's weakness as a commander. Nevertheless, about a week after the surrender at Lexington, elements of Fremont's army began to gather at Georgetown, Missouri, near the Sedalia railhead. The massing of Federal forces in central Missouri once again put Price on the defensive.

Among the first Federal troops to arrive in Georgetown was a battalion of mounted men that had been assembled by Major Frank J. White in Jefferson City. White had begun the war fighting with a New York cavalry regiment. Before joining Fremont in the Department of the West, he had seen action near Fortress Monroe, Virginia. In Jefferson City he organized his mounted force as the "Prairie Scouts," combining two companies of the Third Illinois Cavalry with a company of Irish dragoons originally recruited to join Colonel James Mulligan at Lexington (Mulligan had surrendered at Lexington while these troops remained in Jefferson City).

The growing Federal presence at Georgetown convinced Price to withdraw from Lexington. With a large concentration of Federal troops also in Kansas City, Price "deemed it prudent not to risk being hemmed in." Again, he drifted southward from the Missouri valley. In "slow and easy marches," the State Guard moved through Greenfield in Dade County to Neosho, where Price went into camp a day's march away from Ben McCulloch. Price reached Neosho on October 20. Elements of the Missouri General Assembly gathered there and passed an ordinance of secession. On November 28, the Confederate Congress declared Missouri to be the twelfth state of the Confederate States of America. In short order, the regiments of the Missouri State Guard entered Confederate military service, although Price himself did not formally enter the Confederate command structure until Earl Van Dorn took command of the Military District of the Trans-Mississippi on January 29, 1862.[45]

Price moved south undisturbed—but not unobserved. Major White led the Prairie Scouts (about 130 in number) into the field to track the movement of the rebel force. The Scouts advanced first to Lexington where they drove off a small rebel garrison, freed a number of wounded Federal officers being held prisoner there, and reclaimed the steamboats captured by Price. From Lexington, White followed Price south, passing through Warrensburg to Warsaw on the Gasconade River. The Prairie Scouts now took the lead of Franz Sigel's column as it pressed on toward Springfield.[46]

By mid-October, Fremont had moved his army of forty thousand men south from Georgetown to a camp on the Pomme de Terre River about fifty miles north of Springfield. Fremont's movements had been slow and poorly organized, and a crescendo of complaints concerning the general's shortcomings reached the Federal War Department and President Lincoln. The president feared that Fremont's grandiosity combined with his ineptitude could be a formula for a major military disaster in the West. Unaware that he would soon be relieved of command, Fremont continued south with the vague hope of confronting Price and McCulloch and decisively defeating them. To place his signature indelibly on what he hoped would be a redeeming victory, Fremont sent forward his personal bodyguard to take command of the Prairie Scouts at the head of the Federal column. Fremont had fashioned this Body Guard as an elite cavalry unit. According to the newspaper correspondent Thomas Knox, the unit "was composed of the best class of the young men of St. Louis and Cincinnati." Commanding the Body Guard was Charles Zagonyi, a veteran of the failed Hungarian revolution and one of a group of flamboyant exiles who made up the inner circle of Fremont's command. Zagonyi had followed Fremont west from New York and impressed the commander with his horsemanship. Fremont lavished attention on the Body Guard. They were distinguished from ordinary Union troops by their plumed hats and dark blue uniforms. Zagonyi selected matching chestnut horses for the men. The Body Guard accompanied Fremont's movements with a showiness that led them to be ridiculed as a "kid glove" cavalry. Nearing Springfield, the Body Guard led the Federal army, and both Fremont and Zagonyi eagerly awaited an opportunity to demonstrate the unit's skill and bravery.[47]

Zagonyi left the Pomme de Terre camp on the night of October 24 and joined the Prairie Scouts at Bolivar the next day. There Zagonyi took command of the combined force of nearly three hundred men. Major White had fallen ill, and Zagonyi left him behind to rest and follow in a carriage. Zagonyi rode on toward Springfield where he believed a force of about two thousand State Guardsmen held the town. The rebels Zargonyi soon encountered in Springfield were newly recruited local men commanded by Colonel Julian Frazier. With Price's veteran troops in Neosho, Frazier had little hope of putting up much of a fight against Fremont's army with his untrained and poorly armed men whose effective strength was probably not much greater than one thousand. But Frazier's recruits vastly outnumbered Zagonyi's cavalry, and Frazier prepared to defend his command on the Mount Vernon road on the west side of town.

Zagonyi approached Springfield from the north on the afternoon of October 25. About eight miles out of town, the Federal troops captured five State Guardsmen in a foraging party. A sixth forager escaped and gave warning to Frazier. Zagonyi now expected the enemy to be prepared for an attack along the Bolivar road from the north. With the guidance of a local farmer, Zagonyi took a five-mile detour to enter the Mount Vernon road and approach Springfield from the west. Unaware of the detour, Major White continued by carriage down the Bolivar road and was soon captured by State Guardsmen (he would later be freed by his own men). It was now about 4:00 p.m. Zagonyi's cavalry advanced east on the Mount Vernon road and located Frazier's defensive line on high ground partly concealed by dense woods and underbrush.

Zagonyi's force was badly outnumbered, but the commander and his men were determined to strike a heroic blow. The Federal troops were magnificently mounted and armed with sabers and pistols. One company also carried carbines. For their part, the State Guardsmen were well positioned and they poured deadly fire into the Federals when the horsemen halted to dismount and dismantle a rail fence preparatory to organizing their charge. Zagonyi and the Body Guard led the charge. The Prairie Scouts, commanded by Captain Patrick Naughton in Major White's absence, followed. The charge was everything that Zagonyi (and Fremont) had hoped for. The Body Guard cut through the rebel line causing the infantry to flee into the woods while the rebel cavalry sought refuge in town. Wasting no time, Zagonyi rallied his men and continued to bear down on the enemy where they could be found in the streets of Springfield. As daylight faded, Zagonyi gathered his men in the center of town. Only eighty of the original three hundred remained mounted. Aware that he could not hold Springfield with such a small force, Zagonyi withdrew to the north. Little of military significance had been accomplished although Zagonyi may have prevented Frazier from delivering additional recruits to Price at Neosho. But news of the gallant charge thrilled a northern public eager for news of Federal victories.[48]

Zargonyi's exploits did not deter President Lincoln from moving forward to replace Fremont as the Federal commander of the Department of the West. Fremont continued to enjoy the support of Radical Republicans and Germans who shared his views on emancipation and were ecstatic about Zagonyi's exploits. Lincoln, however, had steadily lost confidence in Fremont's political judgment and in his capacity to succeed as a military commander. Federal troops occupied Springfield on October 27, but on November 2, Lincoln directed General David Hunter to serve as the interim commander of Federal forces in Missouri until the new commander, General Henry Halleck, arrived later in the month.

Hunter arrived in Fremont's camp near Springfield and assumed command at 10:00 p.m. on November 3. The next morning, Fremont departed for St. Louis. General John Pope had been part of the Federal advance toward Springfield and he had been one of Fremont's leading critics. He noted Fremont's flamboyant departure. The general and his entourage were preceded by a military band playing "The Red, White and Blue." A group of Shawnee and Delaware Indians also accompanied Fremont. Pope described them as dressed "in bright colors, yelling and dashing about in a manner more picturesque than alarming."[49] It was, Pope suggested, a fitting departure for a vainglorious commander.

In sharp contrast to Fremont's waning military career, the vigor displayed by Ulysses S. Grant at his new headquarters at Cairo, Illinois, attracted increasing attention. On November 7, Grant led Federal troops in a bold assault on the Confederate garrison at Belmont, Missouri, across the Mississippi River from Columbus, Kentucky, and just downstream from Cairo. The fight at Belmont began in the context of Fremont's advance against Price at Springfield but ended as part of a more complex series of military maneuvers involving Grant's and Albert Sidney Johnston's efforts to control western waterways. The earlier fighting against Thompson at Fredericktown (a few days before Zagonyi's charge at Springfield) had also underscored the importance of the western rivers to secessionist ambitions and to the Federal fight to restore the Union.

The large Confederate force assembled at Columbus, Kentucky, worried Fremont as he began his advance into southwest Missouri. After Lincoln removed Fremont from command, the Columbus garrison remained a major concern for David Hunter. Both Fremont and Hunter feared that Confederate troops and supplies could be transported from Columbus, down the Mississippi, to the mouth of the White River. From there, Confederate reinforcements could be sent to Price in southwest Missouri via the White River, which remained navigable as far north as Forsyth, Missouri. As Fremont moved away from his line of supply at the railheads of Sedalia and Rolla, he faced a foe potentially well supplied from the Mississippi valley. Until he could return Federal forces to Sedalia and Rolla, Hunter shared Fremont's concerns. Grant had removed the menace posed by Jeff Thompson in southeast Missouri, but Polk's presence at Columbus remained a significant threat. Shortly after Lincoln removed Fremont from command, Grant received orders to prevent any movement of Confederate troops out of Columbus. To accomplish this, he sent troops to Bird's Point, on the Missouri side of the Mississippi, a few miles south of Cairo. These troops joined the Federal forces earlier sent to Cape Girardeau. Following the Federal victory at Fredericktown, these troops marched south to occupy New Madrid, on the west bank of the Mississippi several miles below Columbus.

By this time, the Confederate garrison at Columbus had grown too strong for Grant to attack it directly. Instead, he planned to threaten the Confederates sufficiently to forestall any troop movements to the White River. Grant directed troops from Paducah to advance by land to within a few miles of Columbus. Grant himself took three thousand men aboard steamers from Cairo and dropped down the Mississippi to a point about six miles above Columbus. Grant found that his officers and men were extremely excited at the prospect of going into battle for the first time. Although Grant's troop movements were sufficient to prevent any reduction in the Confederate garrison at Columbus, he decided to engage his troops in combat before they returned to Cairo.[50]

Polk sent scouts north on the east bank of the Mississippi and learned that Federal gunboats and transports were approaching Columbus. It was early in the morning of November 7, four days after Lincoln had removed Fremont from command in southwest Missouri. Polk sent Pillow across the river with about twenty-seven hundred men. From this location Grant feared that the enemy could advance against the Federal garrison at New Madrid. By this time, Hunter's troops had been withdrawn from Springfield and the urgency of Grant's display at Columbus had greatly diminished. However, Grant feared that he could not "maintain discipline, or retain the confidence of my command" if his men failed to see combat. Grant decided to break up the enemy concentration at Belmont before returning to Cairo.[51]

The Mississippi River was low at Belmont when Grant approached early in the morning on November 7. The banks of the Mississippi River rose steeply to heavily wooded land, broken in places by cultivated fields and by marshy ground and sloughs. Grant landed with his force a few miles upstream from Belmont where a cornfield provided access to a river road leading to town. A short distance downstream from the landing point, Grant found a dry slough. Here he located a regiment concealed in the bordering forest. These troops and Grant's two gunboats would protect the troop transports as Grant led about two thousand men further downstream to attack the Confederate camp at Belmont. Grant also intended that the troops in the slough would form a defensive line to cover his retreat.

Grant landed above Belmont at about 8:00 a.m. Aware of Grant's movements, Pillow arrived in Belmont with Tennessee troops at about 9:00 a.m. Pillow decided to confront the Federals outside the defenses of the abitis. About a half mile north of the Confederate camp, Pillow formed a battle line across the road leading from Grant's point of landing to the Belmont camp. The terrain did not favor the Confederates. Many of Pillow's men were badly exposed in an open field. On either side of the road, the Federal infantry advanced through woods toward the Confederate line. The fighting began as Grant's skirmishers engaged the Confederate line, and the fighting grew heavier as the bulk of the Federal infantry came forward. The exposed Confederate line suffered badly. As one of Pillow's soldiers commented, he was forced into "fighting a duel with his enemy behind a tree and he in the open field."[52]

Grant's movements confused Polk at Columbus. Federal troops also menaced the Columbus garrison from the east by land. Polk concluded that Grant's movement at Belmont was a feint, intended to draw a large number of Confederate troops across the river and thereby render the Columbus garrison vulnerable to attack by land and by river. Consequently, Polk cautiously reinforced the camp at Belmont only sparingly. Grant sensed Polk's confusion and pressed his attack over the next four hours. Pillow's artillery, at the center of his defensive line north of Belmont, came under particularly heavy Federal attack. Soon the Confederate gunners ran out of ammunition, and Pillow directed them to retreat. Retreat in the open field proved dangerous, however, and disorder reigned as the Confederates abandoned their guns to flee, first from the field and then from the camp.

The Confederate infantry also ran low on ammunition and Pillow ordered a bayonet charge. Uncoordinated in its execution, the charge was fragmented further by the necessity of crossing a rail fence. Concealed in the woods, Grant's infantry poured a withering fire into the charging Confederates who were caught badly exposed in an open field. When Federal artillery opened fire, the Confederates' line disintegrated and the soldiers fled back through their camp to the protection of the riverbank. There they welcomed the arrival of about five hundred reinforcements from Columbus. Pillow began to rally his troops and mount a counterattack.

Grant had a horse shot from under him in the early fighting, but he found a fresh mount and continued to lead the Federal advance until it reached the rebel camp. During the first phase of the battle, Grant reported that his officers and men fought like veterans. When the Federals entered the rebel camp, however, discipline collapsed. With the Confederates out of sight, Grant's officers and men "became demoralized from their victory and failed to reap its full reward." At this point the Confederates cowered by the river, and Grant believed they would have quickly surrendered if they had been pressed to do so. Instead, many of the Union soldiers laid down their arms to pillage the rebel tents in search of souvenirs. The officers performed as poorly as their men. To Grant's dismay, some of the officers "galloped about" delivering to separate groups of men "a short eulogy upon the Union cause and the achievements of the command." In the meantime, Pillow's Confederates regrouped. Protected by the riverbank they began to make their way upriver and threatened to cut Grant off from his transports. Making matters worse, Grant saw two steamboats loaded with soldiers ("from boiler-deck to roof") making their way across the river from Columbus. Watching the fighting from Columbus, Polk now realized that the Federal attack had stalled, and he decided to join Pillow with substantial reinforcements. Polk took command at Belmont as the Confederates attempted to surround the Federals.[53]

When the Confederates began their counterattack, Grant managed to restore order among his troops. He stopped the pillaging by setting fire to the rebel camp. This and artillery fire from Columbus succeeded in refocusing the attention of his troops. The Federals reformed their battle line and began to fight their way back to their transports. Again they drove the Confederates over the riverbank. By now, however, Polk with his reinforcements had disembarked close to the transports. Closely pressed by the enemy, the Federal troops scrambled onboard. The defensive line that Grant had positioned in the dry slough abandoned their position and joined the rush to board the transports. Grant narrowly escaped been cut off during the retreat. As the transports backed into the river, he was very nearly left behind. Grant recalled that his horse seemed to understand the situation perfectly and negotiated the steep riverbank and narrow gangplank swiftly and effectively. From the riverbank, Confederates continued to fire into the upper decks of the boats. Bullets riddled the smokestacks of the transports and injured some of the men. But the Federal gunboats—the *Lexington* and the *Tyler*, both converted side-wheel steamboats commissioned at Cincinnati—opened an effective fire on the Missouri shore and prevented Polk and Pillow from concentrating their troops. The transports were soon out of range and Grant's expedition made its way without further incident back to Cairo.[54]

Grant acknowledged in his memoirs that he received press criticism for his action at Belmont. He had lost nearly five hundred men, a relatively high casualty rate at this point in the war. Grant had inflicted nearly one thousand Confederate casualties, however, and had captured a good deal of military supplies, but when he returned to Cairo it was not clear that he had in any way weakened Confederate defenses on the Mississippi. It could easily be concluded that Grant had accomplished nothing by attacking Belmont. But Grant's movements took place in a wider military context that exposed significant Confederate weaknesses and foretold Grant's emergence as one of the Union's great generals.

At the very least, the battle of Belmont displayed Grant's aggressiveness. His men were eager to fight. They had volunteered to fight the enemies of the Union, and Grant was pleased that he could offer them an opportunity to do so. Moreover, Grant and his men gained valuable experience in the battle, particularly in coordinating the movement of infantry, artillery, and cavalry with river transports supported by gunboats.

One Confederate weakness that Grant helped to expose when he attacked at Belmont was the difficulty rebel commanders experienced in coordinating their movements. After Fremont was relieved of command, Price continued to hope that Albert Sidney Johnston would coordinate military movements in southeast Missouri to strengthen Confederate positions in the trans-Mississippi West. Indeed, Price continued to aspire to extend Confederate control through southern Missouri and threaten St. Louis. On November 7, as Grant led the attack on Belmont, Price wrote to Johnston recommending a coordinated campaign in which Price and McCulloch would engage Hunter's Federal forces in the southwest while Johnston advanced to take St. Louis. Such a move would trap Hunter's army between two Confederate forces: "Your movement threatening St. Louis will of course compel the Federal commander to hasten to that point . . . when, having him between us, his capture will be certain."[55] Grant's aggressive move against Belmont doomed Price's plan and revealed to Johnston (and probably to Grant) just how difficult it would be for Confederates west of the Appalachians to defend their northern border.

Confederate forces in Missouri remained segmented but potent. In the southwest, Hunter left Springfield on November 8, and Federal forces retreated to the fortified railheads. McCulloch moved north to occupy Springfield while Price returned to recruiting south of the Osage River, moving his army north from Neosho to Osceola. Hunter did not oppose Price's move northward. On the south bank of the Osage River, Price continued to challenge Federal control of central Missouri. He sent detachments north into the Missouri valley to recruit troops and gather supplies. At Osceola, Price's principal adversary was John Pope, who had been assigned as commander of the newly formed Federal District of Central Missouri with specific responsibility for protecting the rail line from Sedalia to Jefferson City. Pope proposed to attack Price at Osceola. But Pope's new commander, Henry Halleck, was more directly concerned with preventing fresh recruits from reaching Price's army. Halleck directed Pope to move northwest toward Lexington to break up the bodies of recruits gathering in that region. Pope knew that his movements would be quickly reported to Price, and he requested and received permission from Halleck to feint in the direction of Osceola before advancing toward Lexington.[56]

From camps at Sedalia and Otterville, Pope organized two brigades under Colonel Jefferson C. Davis and Colonel Frederick Steele, a force of more than three thousand men. Expecting (and now desiring) southern sympathizers to inform Price of the Federal troop movements, Pope planned to send his adversary misleading information by marching out of Sedalia on December 15 following the road leading south to Warsaw. At Warsaw, on the north bank of the Osage, Pope would be just a few miles downstream from Price at Osceola. Pope wanted Price to expect an attack. To reinforce this expectation, Pope sent forward four companies of cavalry to probe the Confederate defenses. At the same time Pope moved his main force west to take control of the road that ran south from Warrensburg through Clinton to Osceola. Pope's troops encountered a group of rebel recruits at Chilhowee, a few miles west of the Warrensburg road. The Federals easily scattered them and proceeded north toward Warrensburg. As Pope moved out of Sedalia, he also sent scouts northwest to the Grand Pass region of the Missouri valley between Lexington and Arrow Rock. There he expected to find Price's most extensive recruitment activity. He was not disappointed. As Pope moved north toward Warrensburg, his scouts returned with reports that a large body of recruits was moving south from the Grand Pass region toward Warrensburg and Knob Noster. Pope located his main force along a line between Warrensburg and Knob Noster on the evening of December 18. The next day, Pope received reports that the enemy force had gone into camp just south of the town of Milford (now Valley City). Pope kept his main force in place to block any enemy movement to the south and sent Davis forward with a strong cavalry force to locate the Confederate recruits.[57]

Davis rode north with eight hundred mounted men supported by artillery. Late in the afternoon on December 19, he located the enemy as reported on the west bank of the Blackwater River just south of Milford. Davis had found elements of three Confederate regiments, more than a thousand men, encamped on a horseshoe bend. Pope later described the river as "deep and miry." The only crossing, located on the north side of the bend, was a covered bridge guarded by the enemy. Beyond the bridge, rebel officers hastily organized their men into a defensive line. Davis led a charge that drove the rebels off the bridge and continued into the line of defenders. The Federals took some casualties but the force of the cavalry charge quickly broke the Confederate line and the rebel officers promptly surrendered their commands.[58]

At the Blackwater River, Davis captured thirteen hundred men, including three colonels. One of the captured officers was Frank Robinson who had fought with Price at the battle of Carthage and served as a Confederate scout at the Battle of Wilson's Creek. Price commissioned Robinson a colonel in the State Guard before sending him to the Missouri valley to recruit his regiment.[59]

Another prominent prisoner was Ebenezer Magoffin, the brother of the pro-southern governor of Kentucky, Beriah Magoffin. Ebenezer had settled in Boone County, Missouri, in the mid-1850s and now supported the Confederate cause. He had been captured and paroled before the battle of Lexington. Now, in violation of the condition of his parole, he faced trial by a military commission in St. Louis. Sitting on the commission was Lieutenant Colonel John Scott of the Third Iowa Infantry, the Federal commander that State Guard forces had defeated at the battle of Liberty, Missouri, in September 1861. On February 20, 1862, the commission sentenced Magoffin to death. Beriah Magoffin, with the help of the venerable Kentucky moderate John J. Crittenden, sought Lincoln's intervention. On March 25, 1862, Lincoln suspended the death sentence pending a review of the case. On July 24, 1862, Ebenezer Magoffin escaped from the Alton military prison.[60]

Also captured with the Confederate recruits and their officers were five hundred horses and mules, seventy-three wagons loaded with equipment, gunpowder, and supplies, and a thousand stands of arms. Close to midnight on December 19, Davis brought his prisoners and their supply wagons into Pope's camp near Knob Noster. It was bitterly cold and at dawn it began to snow. All that day Pope's men, with their prisoners and captured supplies, made their way through the blowing snow back to Sedalia. Pope shipped the prisoners and supplies by rail to St. Louis.[61]

Pope's expedition, made memorable by Davis's vigorous charge, successfully broke up Price's recruiting activities in central Missouri. Shortly before Christmas, Price retreated from Osceola to Springfield, where his men built log cabins and prepared to go into winter quarters. McCulloch returned to Arkansas and also went into winter quarters. Jo Shelby detached his mounted men from Price's camp and led them in raids in and around his home in Lafayette County. Shelby operated with relative impunity for some time since low water made the Missouri River unnavigable and limited the movement of Federal troops. In February, when higher water brought the return of Federal patrols, Shelby moved south and rejoined Price at Springfield.[62]

When Halleck took command of Federal forces in Missouri, his principal concern was to maintain control of the railheads and rail lines. In addition to the railheads at Ironton, Rolla, and Sedalia, the North Missouri Railroad connected St. Louis to the Hannibal and St. Joseph line. Among the troops guarding these lines were those commanded by Brigadier General Benjamin M. Prentiss at Palmyra. A Virginia native, Prentiss had moved to Hannibal with his parents, and then as a young man he moved across the Mississippi and opened a rope-manufacturing company in Quincy, Illinois. Prentiss joined an Illinois volunteer regiment to fight in the Mexican War. When the Civil War broke out, he joined an Illinois regiment as a captain and quickly rose in rank to brigadier general. On December 23, 1861, he received orders to move from Palmyra southwest to Sturgeon to root out rebels who were destroying portions of the North Missouri Railroad.[63]

Prentiss left Palmyra for Sturgeon on December 24. At Sturgeon he took command of Colonel John M. Glover's Third Missouri Cavalry. Born in Kentucky in 1822, Glover moved to Missouri as a young man and was admitted to the bar in St. Louis. The gold rush lured him to California for a time, but he returned to St. Louis in 1855. He served as colonel of the Third Regiment of Missouri Cavalry from September 1861 until his resignation for reasons of health in February 1864.[64]

Also joining Prentiss at Sturgeon was Colonel John M. Birge's Fourteenth Regiment of Missouri Volunteers. Known as Birge's Western Sharpshooters, the under-sized regiment had been organized at Benton Barracks in September and October of 1861 with the enthusiastic support of John C. Fremont, who wanted the companies of Birge's regiment to draw sharpshooters from all of the loyal states of the trans-Appalachian West. Birge's men were armed with hunting rifles manufactured by H. E. Dimick and Company in St. Louis (and by other gunsmiths in the city). Birge's sharpshooters molded their own bullets and distinguished their attire with squirrel tails atop their hats. When Halleck took command in Missouri, he abandoned to project of building a full regiment of sharpshooters and directed Birge to disperse his men to protect the North Missouri Railroad. They now joined Glover's cavalry under Prentiss's command at Sturgeon.[65]

Prentiss arrived in Sturgeon in northern Boone County on the evening of December 26. The next morning he sent a company of Glover's cavalry southeast to Hallsville in search of a rebel force commanded by Colonel Caleb Dorsey. Dorsey had moved out of Pike County, and as he made his way south, he continued to recruit troops and lay waste where he could to the North Missouri Railroad. A few miles south of Hallsville, the Federal cavalry encountered Dorsey's rear guard as the main body of the rebel force advanced south intending to camp on high ground near the Mount Zion Church (located about fifteen miles northeast of Columbia). In the skirmish that took place on December 27, the captain commanding the Federal cavalry was wounded and captured. However, the rest of the company managed to break off their engagement and made their way back to Sturgeon.

Prentiss now knew the location of Dorsey's force, which he thought to number about nine hundred men. He moved quickly to engage the enemy at the Mount Zion Church. With his five companies of cavalry and five companies of sharpshooters, Prentiss advanced against the enemy with about five hundred men. Prentiss expected to encounter a force more than twice his size, but he knew that most of Dorsey's men were new recruits and that many were unarmed. Leaving Sturgeon at 2:00 a.m. on December 28, Prentiss located the rebel camp in a wooded area about a hundred yards from the church. Two companies of Birge's sharpshooters joined Glover's dismounted cavalry in the first assault, which failed to drive the rebels from their cover. As more of Birge's troops came

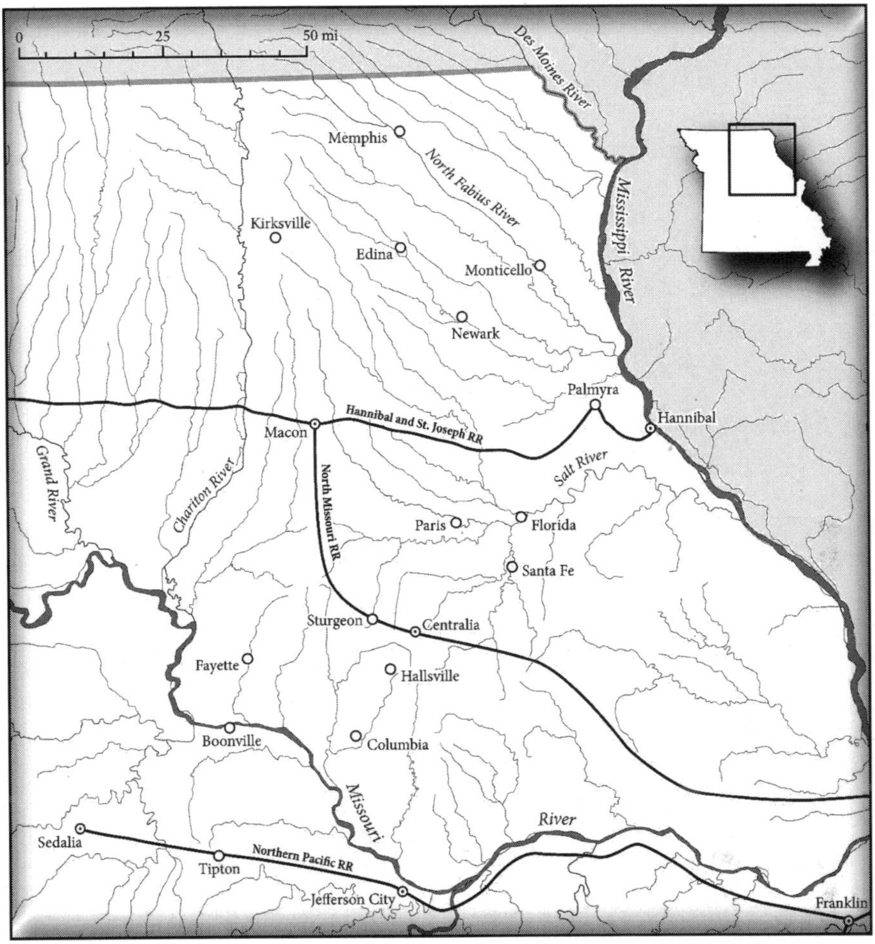

forward, however, the Federal attack intensified. Running low on ammunition, the rebel troops gave way and fled from their camp, leaving Prentiss to capture ninety horses and more than one hundred stands of arms. The entire engagement lasted about an hour with the most intense fighting lasting less than a half hour. The battle of Mount Zion Church was over by 11:00 a.m.

The rebels had used the Mount Zion Church as their hospital, and Prentiss located the wounded rebels there while he alerted nearby residents (presumably friends of the enemy) of their need for care. By 4:00 p.m. on the afternoon of December 28, Prentiss's column moved north and had returned to Sturgeon by 9:00 p.m. that night. After Dorsey's defeat at Mount Zion, Sterling Price directed the commander to scatter his men. Prentiss had succeeded in destroying Dorsey's regiment, although Dorsey and many of the men he had recruited acted on their own and in small groups to cross the Missouri and join Price's army in Springfield.[66]

After the defeat of Dorsey's rebel force at Mount Zion in Boone County, Federal forces focused on breaking up a similar body of Confederate recruits raised by Colonel John A. Poindexter in neighboring Howard and Randolph Counties. Major W. M. G. Torrence of Keokuk, Iowa, commanded a large Federal cavalry force assembled for this purpose. Torrence himself commanded the First Iowa Cavalry and was joined at Boonville by Major Charles B. Hunt who commanded a detachment of "Merrill's Horse." Torrence and Hunt crossed the Missouri River and camped near Fayette where they were joined by Major James M. Hubbard with the First Missouri Cavalry.[67]

Colonel Lewis Merrill, who raised the cavalry regiment that took his name, remained with much of his command at Columbia, wary of an attack on the Federal garrison at that location. Notwithstanding Dorsey's defeat at Mount Zion, reports of rebel activities in the region persisted. Merrill, a Pennsylvania native and an 1855 graduate of West Point, raised his regiment at Benton Barracks and now participated in the task of guarding rail lines in central Missouri. On the evening of January 5, Merrill received a report from Colonel Birge at Sturgeon that several hundred rebels were at Renick and were preparing to move to Roanoke and cross the Missouri River at Arrow Rock. Merrill dispatched Hunt to join the Federal cavalry force that would try to block this move, while Merrill remained in Columbia prepared for an attack by the remnants of Dorsey's command.[68]

On the morning of January 8, the Federal cavalry force, composed of about 450 well-equipped and well-armed men, gathered at Fayette and headed north in search of Poindexter. The rebel force they pursued was much larger than theirs, but the men were untrained and poorly armed. Torrence believed the enemy consisted of between 600 and 800 armed men accompanied by an equal number of unarmed "aiders and abettors of rebellion." The Federal horsemen passed through Roanoke (about fifteen miles north of Fayette) and then moved on to Silver Creek, where Poindexter was reported to be camped. Torrence located the rebels that afternoon at a place called Roan's Tan Yard. At about 4:00 p.m. he prepared to attack them.[69]

Torrence placed at the front of his column all of his men who were armed with carbines. They advanced as dismounted skirmishers with instructions to draw fire from the enemy and return it with as much vigor as possible. As the skirmishers poured fire into the rebel camp, Torrence and Hubbard planned to charge the camp with the cavalry armed with pistols and sabers. The Federal attack proceeded as Torrence had planned it. The enemy force proved to be about one thousand men strong, but it was quickly routed. It is not known how many of Poindexter's men were armed, but when they fled in the face of the cavalry charge they left behind significant military assets, including 80 kegs of gunpowder, 160 horses, and 200 rifles and shotguns. Torrence took twenty-eight prisoners and the horses back to his camp near Fayette, but he destroyed the rest of the captured supplies in the field. Gathering darkness and a dense fog prevented Torrence and Hubbard from pursuing the fleeing rebels. But the Federal victory effectively brought an end to Price's effort to continue recruiting in central Missouri. The Federal attack scattered what was meant to become Poindexter's regiment, although Poindexter himself (and presumably scattered groups of his men) crossed the Missouri and joined Price at Springfield.[70]

By mid-January 1862, Halleck began to realign Federal forces to confront Confederates throughout the state—Price and McCulloch in southwest Missouri and Polk and Pillow in southeast Missouri. This realignment brought an end to Pope's central Missouri command. Halleck called Pope to St. Louis and put him in charge of a new Federal force assembled to drive Confederates from New Madrid and Island Number Ten. General Samuel R. Curtis gathered a similar force at Rolla to confront Price at Springfield. Price saw the gathering danger and continued his retreat south through Cassville and into Arkansas, where he once again formed a junction with McCulloch. Curtis defeated Price and McCulloch in Arkansas at the Battle of Pea Ridge early in March 1862.[71]

The Federal advance into Arkansas returned many soldiers, including Franz Sigel, to the familiar landscape of the Battle of Wilson's Creek. Despite his failures at Wilson's Creek, Sigel remained popular with the German population across the country, and this popularity translated into a degree of political influence that Sigel was skillful in using to advance his military career. After Wilson's Creek, Fremont assigned Sigel the responsibility of protecting the Pacific Railroad. Sigel located his headquarters at Sedalia. In mid-October, Sigel brought his troops across the Osage River and joined Fremont at Springfield. After Fremont was relieved of command early in November, Sigel retreated to Rolla.[72]

Shortly before Halleck took command in Missouri in late November, Sigel became extremely ill and took a leave of absence to recuperate at his home in St. Louis. When Halleck took command, he placed Curtis in command of all of southwestern Missouri, including Rolla. When Sigel returned to duty on December 22, 1861, he found he was subordinate to Curtis. Angered by what he considered a demotion Sigel tendered his resignation to Halleck, claiming that he was being badly treated because he was German. For the most part, Halleck functioned effectively with the conflicting personalities and rival ambitions that constituted the politics of high command. With Franz Sigel, however, he was conspicuously unsuccessful.

Initially, Halleck tried to placate his temperamental subordinate. Sigel remained truculent and insisted that Halleck send his resignation forward. A few days later, however, Sigel changed course and told Halleck he would retain his command. This sparring and Sigel's threatened resignation attracted the attention of President Lincoln. Well aware of Sigel's popularity, Lincoln turned to

Illinois's leading German politician, Gustave P. Koerner, for advice. Koerner confirmed what Lincoln suspected. Sigel's enormous popularity made it politically imprudent for Halleck to displease his subordinate. Indeed, Koerner concluded, a promotion would give Germans everywhere "unbounded satisfaction."[73]

Halleck was incensed by rumors that reached him concerning a promotion for Sigel. He charged Sigel with political maneuverings that constituted insubordination bordering on mutiny. Halleck sought and found a friendly ear in his commander George B. McClellan. Both men were Democrats and hostile to the antislavery wing of the Republican Party, of which Sigel was a prominent part. Halleck sent McClellan extracts from the German press in St. Louis to warn him that the "German and Abolition press throughout the country" conspired to elevate Sigel and restore Fremont. Although Lincoln relied on Halleck for ever wider administrative responsibilities, the president took no heed of Halleck's critique of Sigel. On March 22, 1862, as a result of Lincoln's initiative, Sigel was promoted to major general.[74]

To Sigel's credit, he served well under Curtis as Federal forces returned to Springfield in February 1862. On his return to Springfield, Sigel found the city bleak and barren. Most of the Unionists had left when Sigel retreated to Rolla the previous November, and most of the Confederate supporters left with Price. As Curtis continued his pursuit of Price, Sigel led one column southwest via Little York, Marionsville, and Verona. Curtis moved the second column down the Wire Road. The two Federal columns formed a junction at McDowell, skirmished with Price at Cassville on February 17, and then crossed into Arkansas where they decisively defeated Price and McCulloch at the Battle of Pea Ridge early in March.[75]

Sigel's promotion to major general was dated to follow the Federal victory at Pea Ridge. His subsequent military career took him out of Missouri, but he remained a prominent figure until late in the war. In mid-May 1862, the War Department transferred him to Harpers Ferry where, under Nathaniel Banks's overall command, he rejoined Fremont. Lincoln's confidence in Fremont's military abilities remained low, but the president continued to bow to political pressure to retain the Pathfinder in a field command. At Harpers Ferry, it was Fremont's unenviable task to control Stonewall Jackson in the Shenandoah valley. His failure led to Fremont's final removal from the field. Sigel's corps then became part of the defenses of Washington. During Ambrose Burnside's Fredericksburg campaign, Sigel commanded a reserve division. Sigel's distaste for Burnside's replacement, Joe Hooker, led to another threatened resignation in March 1863. This time Sigel's querulous behavior infuriated Secretary of War Edwin Stanton as well as Sigel's old foe Halleck, now in command of all US forces. The War Department placed Sigel on leave. In July 1863, Halleck took his revenge and assigned Sigel to garrison duty in the Department of the Susquehanna in rural Pennsylvania.[76]

Wisely, Sigel did not openly support Fremont during his presidential challenge to Lincoln in 1864. This forbearance helped to convince Lincoln to offer Sigel another prominent field command. In March 1864, Sigel returned to the valley of Virginia. In May he led a Federal advance south, with the intention of drawing Confederate forces away from the defenses of Richmond. Harassed by guerillas and confronted by John C. Breckenridge at New Market, Sigel was decisively defeated. Grant, now commander of Federal forces in the East, removed Sigel from command. Sigel remained in the army, without a command, until May 1865. He then moved to New York City where he worked as an engineer and remained active in politics. He died in New York in 1902. In St. Louis, admirers dedicated an equestrian statue of Sigel in Forest Park in 1906.[77]

Chapter Five

"There Is No Rebel Flag Now Flying in Missouri"

If Ulysses Grant ever met James B. Eads he made no mention of it in his *Memoirs*. While Grant struggled to make a living in St. Louis in the 1850s, Eads lived in comfortable retirement in his city home on Compton Hill. But metaphorically (and probably physically), the paths of the two men frequently crossed as the ironclad gunboats constructed by Eads in Carondelet (a village south of St. Louis later annexed to the city) helped Grant take command of western rivers and, by July 1863, force the surrender of Vicksburg. In Missouri, Eads's gunboats played a pivotal role in the campaign to drive Confederates from defensive positions they had established at New Madrid and Island Number Ten.[1]

Although named for his successful cousin James Buchanan, Eads came to St. Louis from his Indiana home as a lad of thirteen with no financial resources and no formal education. He found work on steamboats, first as a clerk and later salvaging cargo from sunken boats. Eads's salvage business grew rapidly, and he retired a moderately wealthy man. Steamboat companies paid to have snags removed from the river, and merchants and their insurers paid to have goods recovered from wrecked boats. In this business Eads also became an experienced diver and boatman with an intimate knowledge of river currents and navigation.

In the secession crisis, Eads identified himself as an unconditional Unionist. He fully understood the strategic significance of western rivers to Confederate hopes of nationhood and his own determination to restore the Union. Following the fall of Fort Sumter, Eads contacted a friend, the St. Louis lawyer Edward Bates who was now Lincoln's attorney general. At Bates's request, Eads traveled to Washington, DC, to present to the War Department his ideas concerning the need for a strong river navy. The idea was not original to Eads, and while in Washington he soon learned that naval commander John Rodger and naval engineer Samuel Pook had already been authorized to construct armored gunboats for a river navy. Pook's design inspired the nickname Pook's Turtles for the gunboats. According to Pook's specifications, the gunboats were to draw no more than six feet of water and were to carry thirteen heavy guns, protected by two and a half inches of iron plating. To support the plating Pook designed a heavy oak frame with sloping sides to deflect enemy fire. The boats were powered by two steam engines located on either side of a single drive shaft that turned the rear paddle wheel. Twin smokestacks rose above the gun deck.

Pook also offered detailed instructions on how the iron plating should be manufactured and attached to the oak housing. The iron plates should be between one and two feet wide with a lip on each side that was half the thickness of the plates. The overlapping plates were bolted to the oak frame from one foot below the water line to the roof of the boat. Each boat carried thirteen guns: three in the bow, four on each side, and two at the stern. The bow guns provided the boats with their greatest firepower. They were initially rifled guns converted from older smoothbore cannon, but commanders, as quickly as they were able, replaced all of the boat's cannon with more advanced rifled weapons designed by John Dahlgren and Robert Parrott. The ironclads were most effective against artillery batteries and concentrations of troops close to the river. They fired repeated broadsides from their four side cannon as they steamed in a circle.

The cannons in the bow were used for long-range bombardment. Pilots soon learned that they had greater control over the boats when the bow cannon were in use when they steamed upstream into the current. It was far more difficult to fire against a target when heading downstream, backing against the current. When firing the bow guns from this position, commanders often lashed two or more boats together for stability. Alternatively they lashed the boats to trees on the shore. But commanders greatly preferred to approach their targets while powering upstream. In addition to improved stability, an upstream target meant that a disabled boat would float away from the enemy not toward him. On the Tennessee and Cumberland Rivers, which the Federal gunboats entered from the Ohio, the targets were upstream. As Federal forces made their way down the Mississippi, it proved far more difficult to achieve this advantage.

In August 1861 the Federal War Department began accepting bids for the construction of seven ironclads built according to Pook's design. Eads won the contract with the lowest bid and his Carondelet boatyard soon buzzed with activity. As construction began, Rodgers visited St. Louis to test the quality of the plating Eads would use. Using a ten-pound Parrott rifled gun on a sandy bank of the Mississippi, Rodgers fired a shell at a sheet of armor from eight hundred yards and then from five hundred and two hundred yards. The armor passed Rodgers's test, and Eads rushed his men to deliver the boats to Andrew H. Foote who, in September, replaced Rodgers as commander of the new river navy.

Eads constructed four of the gunboats, including the *Carondelet* which was the first to be launched (on October 12, 1861) at Carondelet. Each of the gunboats carried a crew of 159 sailors and several officers. A historical study of the crew of one gunboat revealed that most of the boatmen were seasoned rivermen but that nearly as many came from New York and other eastern cities. About a third of the crew was foreign-born, with Irishmen making up the largest contingent. When the gunboats moved south, runaway slaves also became members of the crew.

Eads also constructed the *Benton* in St. Louis. This was the largest and most powerful gunboat to be built, and in February 1862 it became Foote's flagship. The *Benton* was a converted snag boat. Eads had purchased the *Benton* from the Federal government in 1857, and for the next several years the 633-ton boat was known as Eads's *Submarine Number Seven*. It served as a floating platform upon which to hoist snags and sunken cargo. The vessel had two hulls outfitted with derricks. Divers descended to the river bottom between the hulls and attached lines to the material to be drawn out of the water. Eads removed the derricks to create a gun deck and built an armored superstructure similar to the design provided by Pook. The *Benton* was two hundred feet long and seventy-five feet wide. Its boiler powered a single rear paddle wheel and a single smokestack rose behind the pilothouse. The boat carried sixteen cannon: four at the bow, two aft, and five on each side. In a similar manner, Eads also converted a smaller snag boat, the *Essex*, into a gunboat carrying five guns. Early in December, at Foote's request, Eads accompanied the boats as they made their way from Carondelet to Cairo.

In January, Grant traveled to St. Louis to meet with Halleck hoping that the new commander would support a Federal attack against Confederate forces at Columbus or at the recently completed Forts Henry and Donelson on the Tennessee and Cumberland Rivers. Grant found Halleck cautious and returned to Cairo without the support he had hoped to get. But Grant still operated under orders from McClellan to support Don Carlos Buell at Louisville. This, Grant believed, provided him with the authority he needed to move against Forts Henry and Donelson on his own. Supported by Foote's flotilla of gunboats, he proceeded to do so.

On February 2, 1862, Grant transported about eight thousand troops by river steamers to the east bank of the Tennessee River about nine miles downstream from Fort Henry. Foote supported Grant's infantry with the *Essex* and three of Eads's "city class" gunboats. Three more timberclad gunboats joined the flotilla, escorting the troop transports. The landing was completed the night of February 5 and Grant began an attack on Fort Henry the next morning at 11:00 a.m. The ferocity of the bombardment unleashed by Eads's gunboats convinced the Confederate commander, General Lloyd Tilghman, to move his infantry to Fort Donelson before he surrendered his artillerists to Foote. As one Confederate officer reported, the bombardment from the Federal gunboats "exceeded in terror anything that the imagination had pictured of shot and shell, plowing roads through the earthworks and sandbags, dismantling guns . . . setting on fire and bringing down buildings within the fortification, and cutting in two, as with a scythe, large trees in the neighborhood."[2]

Fort Henry had been no match for the gunboats. Located close to the water, its gunners damaged two of the gunboats but quickly succumbed to the power of Foote's flotilla. Fort Donelson proved a more formidable challenge for Grant and Foote. Grant sent troops overland from Fort Henry to hold the Confederate garrison at Donelson in place, while Foote brought the gunboats up the Cumberland River. Foote began his bombardment of Fort Donelson at 3:00 p.m. on February 14. All of the gunboats were heavily damaged. Much of the damage came from the Confederate artillery firing from the bluffs down onto the top of the gun-deck housing where the shot could not be deflected as it was from the angled siding. The first day of fighting ended as the disabled gunboats floated away from the fort. The next morning Foote, injured in the fighting, met with Grant and explained the necessity of returning the gunboats to dry dock for repair. Foote promised to return in ten days, and Grant prepared to lay siege to Fort Donelson. A siege did not prove necessary. Fearing they would be trapped between the gunboats to the east and Grant's army to the west, the Confederates attacked the center of the Federal line. Grant responded by attacking the Confederate right flank where Federal troops overran the rebel rifle pits. That night, Gideon Pillow escaped with about three thousand infantry to Nashville. Nathan Bedford Forrest also escaped with about one thousand mounted men. On the morning of February 16, General Simon Bolivar Buckner surrendered to Grant.

The capture of Forts Henry and Donelson opened important invasion routes for Federal forces. For the Confederates, the defeats forced Albert Sidney Johnston to withdraw from central Tennessee. P. G. T. Beauregard, newly arrived from the East and charged with creating a defensive line in the West, concluded that it was necessary to evacuate Leonidas Polk's fortifications at Columbus.

Beauregard commanded Confederate forces between the Tennessee and Mississippi Rivers, and he immediately faced the consequences of the Federal victories at Forts Henry and Donelson. Polk glumly accepted his role as Beauregard's subordinate and complied with his commander's directive "to evacuate Columbus and take up less vulnerable positions on and in the vicinity of Island No. 10 and at New Madrid." As Polk moved his forces south about sixty miles, Beauregard solicited from the governors of Tennessee, Mississippi, and Alabama between five thousand and ten thousand men each. With the new fortifications at New Madrid Bend protecting his rear, Beauregard proposed to go into the field with an army of forty thousand men to retake Paducah, "assail" Cairo, and "threaten, if not indeed take, Saint Louis itself."[3]

The task of fortifying New Madrid Bend fell to Confederate general John P. McCown, a Tennessee native and West Point graduate. McCown was a veteran of the Mexican and Seminole Wars. When the Civil War began he was stationed in the Dakota Territory. He promptly resigned to join the Confederate army. He had been promoted to brigadier general in October 1861. He arrived at Island Number Ten of February 26 and hurried to fortify the island (a narrow piece of land about one mile long and 450 yards wide), the Tennessee bluffs to the east of it, and the nearby town of New Madrid, Missouri.[4]

Halleck was elated with Grant's victories and quickly realized that, with Federal forces advancing up the Tennessee River, a victory over the Confederates digging in at Island Number Ten opened the Mississippi River at least to Memphis. To move against New Madrid, Halleck summoned John Pope to St. Louis from his central Missouri command. The two men met on February 18 in the Planters House Hotel where Halleck had his headquarters. Halleck placed Pope in command of a new army, which would be assembled with troops from St. Louis, Cairo, and Cincinnati. On February 22, Pope arrived in the Mississippi River town of Commerce, a few miles south of Cape Girardeau, Missouri, with two companies of infantry and prepared to organize his "Army of the Mississippi." The regiments that poured into Commerce were largely fresh recruits. Pope quickly organized them in divisions and gave them what military training he could. By February 27, Pope deemed his men ready to move against the Confederate stronghold at New Madrid Bend.[5]

Pope selected Commerce as the location for assembling his army because, at that point on the river, bluffs rose above the Great Mingo Swamp that extended thirty miles south and west to New Madrid. The only road to New Madrid from the north began at Commerce. It was an ill-maintained corduroy road that often required the labors of Pope's engineers to rebuild sections that had been reclaimed by the swamp. New Madrid itself was located on a low bluff that rose above the swamp. Below the town the terrain again became swampy. The Confederates at New Madrid and Island Number Ten may have believed that they were protected by the swamp. But, as Pope noted, swamp land also surrounded Reel Foot Lake on the east side of the Mississippi. If Federal forces could take New Madrid and control the Mississippi below Island Number Ten, it would be exceedingly difficult for the Confederate forces on the island to receive supplies or, indeed, to escape. The march through the Great Mingo Swamp was exceedingly difficult: "We waded and trudged for three of the most disagreeable days I ever passed," recalled Pope. But the Federal army successfully made its way through the swamp and the Confederate forces at New Madrid Bend were quickly imperiled.[6]

As Pope arrayed his forces against the defenses of New Madrid, he commanded an army of twenty-five thousand men organized in five divisions. The First Division was commanded by Brigadier General David S. Stanley. Born in Ohio in 1818, Stanley graduated from West Point in 1852 and was serving in the Indian Territory when the Civil War broke out. He had participated in the skirmish at Dug Springs before the Battle of Wilson's Creek and later guarded the Federal supplies in Springfield during the battle. He was promoted to brigadier general in September 1861. In Pope's army, Stanley commanded thirty-three hundred Ohio troops. Brigadier General Schuyler Hamilton commanded the Second Division. From a prominent family in the Hudson valley, Hamilton was also a West Point graduate. He was the grandson of Alexander Hamilton and also Halleck's brother-in-law. Hamilton had earlier served as an aide to Halleck in St. Louis.

During the New Madrid campaign, Hamilton commanded three thousand Iowa, Indiana, and Missouri troops.[7]

What became the Third Division was commanded by Brigadier General John M. Palmer. Born in Kentucky in 1831, Palmer moved to Illinois as a boy and settled with his family in Alton. He was an antislavery Democrat who took an active role in the formation of the Republican Party, and his command consisted largely of Indiana troops. Another Illinois resident, Brigadier General Eleazor A. Paine, commanded over three thousand Illinois troops that made up Pope's Fourth Division. An Ohio native, West Point graduate, and veteran of the Mexican War, Paine was practicing law in Illinois when the Civil War began. He joined an Illinois regiment as colonel and in September 1861 rose to the rank of brigadier general. Pain's division included the Sixty-Fourth Illinois regiment known as Yates Sharpshooters in honor of Illinois governor Richard Yates. Pope formed the Fifth Division around Joseph B. Plummer, a West Point graduate who had been wounded the Battle of Wilson's Creek.[8]

During the march to New Madrid, Pope's men fought several skirmishes with Jeff Thompson's Confederates. At this point Thompson—the "Swamp Fox," as he had come to be known—commanded a few hundred men who had in their possession a few very small cannon. Thompson made an attempt to confront Pope in the swamp, but the Federals easily scattered his force, and Thompson's men abandoned their field guns as they fled. Thompson's command was shrinking steadily at this point. The period of enlistment for his troops had passed, and he commanded a band of about six hundred mounted men when Confederates began to fortify New Madrid Bend. Thompson could do little more than harass the Federal army. He continued to present himself as a gallant figure, but his men did not impress the new Confederate commanders at New Madrid Bend, one of whom described them as "a wretched, ragged, dispirited looking set of men; half armed, undisciplined, careless, and inattentive."[9]

As the lead elements of Pope's army arrived at the New Madrid fortifications, the Confederate defenders drove back two Federal probes on March 2 and 3. On March 4, while awaiting the arrival of siege guns, Pope sent a force of three thousand men commanded by Colonel Plummer further downstream, to Point Pleasant, Missouri, a location McCown had failed to protect. From Point Pleasant, Plummer intercepted Confederate supplies to New Madrid. At dawn on March 12, with his heavy guns freshly arrived from Cairo, Illinois, Pope began a daylong bombardment of the Confederate fortifications at New Madrid. Federals and rebels exchanged artillery fire all day. Pope concentrated his fire on the rebel gunboats and on the enemy artillery batteries. His gunners scored several hits, but one of Pope's siege guns was also disabled by enemy fire. Casualties on both sides were light, but McCown with thirty-five hundred men faced a vastly superior force. By nightfall on March 13, the Confederate commander concluded he could not hold the town and decided to evacuate under cover of darkness.

McCown planned to conduct an orderly withdrawal, as the Confederates had done at Columbus. Instead confusion and panic seized his troops. A heavy thunderstorm added to the disorder. Pope was uncertain about the Confederate activities. The fleeing troops and the transports that arrived to carry them away generated a good deal of noise, but Pope initially concluded the enemy was being resupplied and, perhaps, reinforced. Daylight revealed signs that the fort had been abandoned. Warily, Pope entered the Confederate bastion. He found a few stragglers sleeping but all around him lay evidence of the Confederates' disorderly retreat. In addition to abandoned clothing and half-finished meals, the Confederates left behind twenty-five artillery pieces, five hundred tents, two hundred horses and mules, and large amounts of ammunition. Federal forces quickly took control of the fortifications and the town. An exuberant Henry Halleck wired Secretary of War Stanton: "This was the last stronghold of the enemy in this state—there is no rebel flag now flying in Missouri."[10]

With the capture of New Madrid, the Confederate stronghold at Island Number Ten was left dangerously isolated. On the day New Madrid fell (March 14), Foote left Cairo with his flotilla of eight gunboats, ten mortar boats, and several troop transports. By mid-day on March 15, Foote's boats approached Island Number Ten. There the Mississippi River formed the New Madrid Bend: two sharp bends, first to the north and then to the south. Island Number Ten was located at the bottom of the first bend and New Madrid at the top of the second bend. Island Number Ten—the tenth island below the mouth of the Ohio River—controlled this section of the river. The Confederate fortifications on the island were strongly supported by batteries on the bluffs of the nearby Tennessee shore. Foote halted the advance of his flotilla about five miles southeast of New Madrid as the crow flies, but the Confederate fortifications kept his gunboats at least ten miles upstream from Pope's troops at New Madrid. The damage Foote had sustained at Fort Donelson caused him to be cautious, and he initially stayed well out of range of the Confederate guns. He deployed his mortar boats on the west bank where a point of land shielded them from the enemy's view. Aboard the *Benton* on the east bank of the river, Foote could see past the bend to the fortified island. From this vantage point Foote directed the mortar fire. The mortar shells arched over the point of land and crashed into the Confederate fortifications sending plumes of earth dozens of feet into the air. Some of the fused shells exploded above their targets sending a shower of iron over a large swath of earth below. The *Benton* contributed to the bombardment with its large bow guns. A half hour after the Federal bombardment began, the Confederates began to return the fire. It was a largely symbolic effort, however, since the rebel shot and shell fell at least a half mile short of Foote's gunboats. As night fell, Foote broke off the attack.[11]

The next morning, Foote brought more mortars into action and resumed the long-range shelling. That night the Federal mortar fire continued until dawn. The thunderous roar of the mortars could be heard for miles and the sight of the shells at night was spectacular. "We are throwing mortar shells into the forts at night," Foote wrote to his wife. With their burning fuses they made "a beautiful sight, like a shooting star in a parabola." On the morning of March 17, Foote attempted a direct assault with his gunboats. To increase the stability of the boats as they faced downstream, Foote had two of the city class gunboats lashed to each side of his flagship, the *Benton*. In this manner Foote advanced to within two hundred yards of the Confederates' forward battery. The three ironclads opened fire simultaneously and within fifteen minutes poured more than fifty rounds into the island's fortifications. Now, however, the rebel's return fire began to inflict damage. The *Benton* took four hits, and a rifled cannon on one of the smaller gunboats exploded leaving fifteen men killed or wounded. At nightfall, Foote again withdrew. He now had a good idea of the configuration of the fortifications he confronted. "This place is even stronger and better adapted for defense than Columbus has ever been," Foote wrote to Secretary of the Navy Gideon Welles. "[E]ach fortification commands the one above it," Foote explained. He counted nine separate batteries and guessed that the Confederates had deployed a hundred guns.[12]

By the evening of March 18, it was clear that Foote's offensive had stalled. The cautiousness instilled at Donelson was now amplified by his somber, listless demeanor. He continued to suffer from the wound he had received at Donelson. Painful as well was a letter from home reporting the death of his thirteen-year-old son. Pope thought Foote had lost his will to fight, and perhaps he had. For the rest of the month the stalemate continued. But Foote could not delay indefinitely. The Island Number Ten campaign had become a focus of attention for the nation. James Eads and Illinois congressman Elihu Washburne visited the *Benton* as did an assistant secretary of war. Fifteen northern newspapers sent reporters to the scene. The novelty of the siege soon dissipated, and the stalemate grew wearisome. "The siege of Island No. 10 has become as tedious as a twice told tale," complained a reporter from the *New York Times*. "Each day drags on its heavy length more wearily than the one before."[13]

Pope, with some help from Halleck and from Gideon Wells, pressed Foote to run some of his gunboats past Island Number Ten. Once he had taken control of New Madrid, Pope was eager to move his army across the Mississippi and attack the Confederate batteries on the Tennessee shore. He would thus trap the entire Confederate garrison at New Madrid Bend. Pope needed the protection of the gunboats to facilitate his crossing. The Confederate gunboats had been driven from New Madrid, but they remained in the area. They were no match for the Federal ironclads, but they could easily wreak havoc on Pope's unprotected troop transports. Moreover, anticipating a crossing, Confederate forces had constructed earthworks and deployed artillery and troops on the east bank of the Mississippi at possible points of crossing. Pope wanted to cross at Tiptonville, but he needed Foote's gunboats to silence the enemy artillery and protect him while he did. Repeatedly Pope asked Foote to have two or three of his gunboats run past the Confederate defenses. Foote declined to do so. On March 20, Foote solicited the advice of his gunboat commanders and found that only one officer thought it was possible to run successfully past the Confederate guns.

At the suggestion of General Schuyler Hamilton, Pope ordered his engineers to begin excavation of a canal that could enable Foote to bypass Island Number Ten. The canal connected the flooded fields above the Island Number Ten with a system of bayous that emptied into the Mississippi just upstream from New Madrid. By the first of April, the engineers (utilizing winches, brute strength, and an ingenious underwater saw) had opened a fifty-foot-wide passage from the Mississippi to the bayous that led to New Madrid. But the river now was low and the waterway was only four feet deep. The troop transports and supply barges managed to bypass the Confederate defenses but Foote's gunboats could not navigate in such shallow water. Facing stalemate again, Pope decided to make the crossing to Tennessee without the protection of the gunboats. This decision left Foote with little choice but to attempt to run past the enemy guns or bear the blame if Pope suffered heavy losses without the gunboats. Foote turned to the one commander who had thought it possible to run the batteries—Henry Walke of the *Carondelet*. It was Walke who had commanded the gunboats that supported Grant during the battle of Belmont. Foote now directed him to "avail yourself of the first foggy or rainy night" to run past Island Number Ten.[14]

The crew of the *Carondelet* was mostly from Philadelphia with a sizable group of Bostonians among them. A few men were seasoned blue-water sailors. As Walke later recalled, there were "just enough men-o'-war's men to leaven the lump with naval discipline." Walke himself had been born in Virginia but grew up in Ohio. He joined the navy at the age of eighteen and rose steadily in rank from midshipman to retire as a rear admiral in 1871. Walke served in the Mexican War and had fought bravely at Fort Donelson. But it was his heroic actions at Island Number Ten that attracted the admiration of an attentive North.[15]

On April 4 at 10:00 p.m. the *Carondelet* prepared to make the run to New Madrid. Walke protected his boat wherever he could with sacks of coal, stacks of cordwood, bales of hay, and a good deal of heavy chain used to strengthen the pilothouse armor protecting Walke's pilot, the experienced riverman William B. Hoel. As the *Carondelet* began to steam downstream, a fire broke out in one of its flue stacks. Walke closed the flue cap and extinguished the flame, but fire broke out again when the cap was opened. The flame made the *Carondelet* easy to spot. Confederate gunners soon opened fire and managed to hit the boat twice as it passed through the bend, but it sustained no significant damage, and as Walke came around the second bend near New Madrid, he fired his guns in a pattern that Pope had been alerted to recognize. By 1:00 a.m. the *Carondelet* was safely tied up at the New Madrid waterfront and the prospects for a successful troop crossing had brightened.

Pope quickly sent Foote a message reporting the safe arrival of the *Carondelet* and requesting that a second gunboat be sent downstream in a similar manner.

The "lives of thousands of men," exhorted Pope, and the success of the Federal campaign against Island Number Ten "hang upon your decision." Foote remained hesitant, but he agreed to send down a second boat. It made the run at 2:00 a.m. on April 7 in a heavy thunderstorm. Later that day, with the protection of the gunboats, Pope made his infantry crossing at Tiptonville. On April 8, as Pope's troops advanced against the rear of the rebel shore batteries, the defenses of Island Number Ten collapsed. Pope took five thousand prisoners as the demoralized Confederates scattered. As at Fort Henry, Eads's gunboats terrified the enemy. On March 17, a week after the gunboat attacks began, a surgeon with Tennessee troops on the island wrote to his wife reporting that "our officers tell the men openly that we are whipped and that we will be taken prisoners." In the days ahead, men whom the doctor knew to be healthy sought respite from the shelling in the hospital.[16]

The Federal victory in Arkansas at the Battle of Pea Ridge early in March, coupled with the victories at Shiloh and Island Number Ten a month later, seemed to validate Pope's assertion that the rebel flag no longer flew in Missouri. Federal successes in the West also caused Halleck's reputation to soar. To his credit, Halleck had been, as a biographer writes, "masterly in the way he organized and supported" Grant and Pope. But Halleck regarded Grant as disorderly and reckless, and a few days after the fall of Island Number Ten, Halleck took direct command of the massive concentration of Federal forces in southwest Tennessee. He left John M. Schofield, the commander of the Unionist Missouri militia, in charge of the state. Schofield recalled that Halleck left him "with the brief, but comprehensive, instructions to 'take care of Missouri.'" Initially, Schofield saw no difficulties in doing so. "Missouri was quiet," Schofield noted, "and there seemed no reason to apprehend any further serious difficulty in the state." By early June 1862, when Schofield succeeded Halleck as commander of the Department of the Missouri, it had become clear that Pope's declaration of victory in the state—and Schofield's perception of peace and prosperity—had both been premature.[17]

In the aftermath of the Confederate defeat at Pea Ridge, General Sterling Price sent a large number of his men back into Missouri to gather supplies and recruit fresh troops. Similarly, the new commander of the Confederate Trans-Mississippi Department, Thomas C. Hindman, authorized several raids into the Indian Territory and southwest Missouri to keep the enemy off balance and to gather much needed troops and supplies.

Perhaps the most daring of the Confederate raiders were led by Colonels Joseph C. Porter and John A. Poindexter who operated in north-central and northeastern Missouri—at times in collaboration with guerrilla bands, notably those led by "Captain" Alvin Cobb. Porter, who had joined Price's army from Marion County, returned to northeast Missouri. Poindexter, evidently undeterred by his defeat at Roan's Tan Yard in January, returned to north-central Missouri. Once their activities became evident, Schofield directed Colonel John McNeil and

Colonel Lewis Merrill to lead their mounted troops into the field to break up these Confederate bands and prevent the recruits from crossing the Missouri River and joining Price in Arkansas. "My troops were directed to move entirely without baggage," reported Schofield. The few "necessary articles of subsistence" they took with them would be carried on their horses. Schofield directed his troops "to take whatever else might be necessary," including fresh mounts, "from the rebels in the country." The goal was "to give the enemy no rest day or night until they should be totally broken up and destroyed."[18]

Porter began his operations by setting up a recruitment camp on the North Fabius River near Monticello in Lewis County. On July 13 he briefly occupied Memphis in Scotland County. McNeil and Merrill prevented Porter from remaining in any one place for long. Nevertheless, for the next month Porter succeeded in eluding the pursuing Federal troops. Moving south through Knox and Shelby Counties, Porter ambushed a battalion of Merrill's men (Merrill's Horse) on July 18 and fought another skirmish at Florida in Monroe County. Porter drove off a Federal attack at Santa Fe near the south fork of the Salt River in southern Monroe County and continued to move south through Audrain County. Colonel Odin Guitar, commanding Federal forces out of Jefferson City, stopped Porter's southern movement and forestalled any effort by the Confederates to cross the Missouri River. Porter moved north again through Paris and Newark and returned to western Lewis County.[19]

In his pursuit of Porter, McNeil led a combined force of cavalry and artillery numbering about one thousand men. Porter's brigade grew from a few hundred men to about twenty-five hundred. The guerrilla chieftain Alvin Cobb of Montgomery County briefly joined Porter's Missouri Brigade. Cobb was a striking figure. Six feet tall and powerfully built, his hair fell to his shoulders and his beard to his waist. He seldom spoke, and one of Porter's men described him as unpleasant, even sinister, in demeanor. He had lost his left hand and part of his left forearm. His stump was fitted with an iron hook with which he handled the reins of his horse. He carried a rifle and several revolvers. To one observer it appeared that Porter did not like to operate with him. Cobb typically led a detached "company" of about one hundred men.[20]

With Porter blocked to the south by Guitar, McNeil gave chase from the east. McNeil left Palmyra on July 29, passed through Clinton and Monroe Counties, and located Porter shortly after the Confederate commander left Paris. In the final pursuit from Newark to Kirksville, Porter slowed the Federals significantly by burning bridges and destroying fords. But at 10:00 a.m. on August 6, advance elements of McNeil's troops located him at Kirksville. Porter knew he was being closely pursued by McNeil, and he decided to stand and fight. He decided to concentrate his forces at Kirksville. The rebels numbered about two thousand in all but half were unarmed and only about five hundred were well armed. Porter warned the town's residents to leave and then barricaded his men in buildings around the town square and behind a rail fence along the railroad line on the west side of town.[21]

To ascertain the location of Porter's concealed sharpshooters, a squad of eight volunteers from Merrill's Horse rode into town. When they reached the square they drew the fire they desired. Only two men returned unscathed. Three were shot dead and another three were wounded. Five horses died in the initial reconnaissance. With the location of the enemy sharpshooters identified, McNeil deployed his artillery and fired into the buildings that concealed them and into the fields where Porter's men attempted to make their stand. McNeil's dismounted troops formed two battle lines, with the right wing on the north and east and the left wing on the south side of town. Over the next three hours, the Federal right wing drove Porter's men from the square while the left wing occupied the southern side of town and confronted Porter's main defensive line along the railroad line. Porter's line broke under the pressure, and his men fled into the wooded countryside west of town. Mounted Federals pursued them for a while, but Porter managed to make his way across the Chariton River. On August 8, remnants of Porter's forces skirmished with Federals near the Chariton River. On August 11, Porter disbanded his force, leaving each company to operate on its own.[22]

A number of the men who previously had joined Porter's brigade had been paroled by Federal forces. The day after the battle of Kirksville, fifteen captured Confederates were executed for violating their parole. More problematic was the execution the next day of the uniformed Confederate colonel Frisby McCullough. He had joined Porter to return to his home at Edina. Captured by Federal troops he was tried before a military commission and executed, presumably for fomenting guerrilla attacks.[23]

Meanwhile, in north-central Missouri, Poindexter labored to move his twelve hundred men east to join Porter. After driving Porter away from the Missouri River, Odin Guitar concentrated on Poindexter and caught him late in the day on August 10 as he attempted to cross the Chariton River. Poindexter's force greatly outnumbered Guitar's force of six hundred men and two pieces of artillery. But, as with Porter, a large portion of Poindexter's men were untrained and probably unarmed or poorly armed. In the fighting Schofield reported that "a very large number of the enemy were killed, wounded and drowned." Poindexter fled northward with what troops he could rally, in an attempt to join Porter, but General Benjamin Loan, operating out of northwest Missouri, stopped him. Pushed back by Loan, Poindexter was again attacked by Guitar. After a running fight of two days, Schofield reported that Poindexter's "entire force was killed, captured, or dispersed." Poindexter ("the banditti leader," as Schofield called him) wandered alone through the wooded countryside but after several days he was captured by Unionist militia.[24]

After disbanding his troops, Porter continued to operate as a partisan ranger in the region, and on September 12 he captured Palmyra. He freed the Confederate prisoners held there and also burned the records of the local provost marshal's office. His men abducted and murdered a local Unionist, Andrew Allsman. This precipitated the execution of ten Confederate prisoners by McNeil on October 18, an event remembered as the Palmyra Massacre.[25]

In northeastern and central Missouri, Federal efforts to break up Confederate recruitment activities largely succeeded. Guerrillas continued to operate in the countryside, but they did so only in small bands. In western Missouri Federal commanders were equally active in their efforts to defeat Confederate recruiters and their guerrilla allies, but at the battles of Independence and Lone Jack, which occurred within days of the Federal victory at Kirksville, it was the Confederates who emerged victorious. One of the Confederate recruiters in western Missouri was Sterling Price's cousin Colonel John T. Hughes, who, born in Kentucky, grew up in Fayette, in the heart of Missouri's slave-owning country. He had volunteered to fight in the Mexican War, and in 1861 he was quick to join Price's Missouri State Guard. Hughes had participated in the battle of Carthage, the Battle of Wilson's Creek, and the siege of Lexington. He had been slightly wounded at Lexington, but he recovered to participate in the Battle of Pea Ridge. In the summer of 1862, Hughes was one of the Confederate commanders selected by Price to return to Missouri to raise troops and challenge Federal control. Hughes established a recruitment camp at Lees Summit and began operating with one of the region's most feared guerrilla leaders, William Quantrill.[26]

Hughes was not as successful at recruiting as he had hoped to be. He had attracted only about three hundred men to Lees Summit, and he concluded that a victory over Federal forces combined with a movement north of the Missouri River would allow him to draw a far larger number of men into Confederate ranks. To facilitate this goal, Hughes looked north, to the relatively small Federal garrison at Independence on the south bank of the Missouri River. A victory over Federal forces there would benefit recruitment and open a passage across the Missouri. Quantrill brought his band of thirty men into the Lees Summit camp. Another Confederate recruiter, Upton Hays, also joined Hughes at Lees Summit with a small force. Hughes's combined force of recruits and guerrillas numbered about four hundred men.[27]

As Hughes planned his attack, he had reason to believe that the Federal commander at Independence, Colonel James T. Buel, was ill prepared for an attack. Buel knew of Hughes's presence at Lees Summit and probably contemplated attacking the camp, but Buel had stopped sending patrols into the countryside, fearing ambushes by Quantrill's guerrillas. Buel had no way of detecting Hughes's movements and thus gave his adversary the advantage of surprise. On August 10, one of Quantrill's men disguised himself as a local farmer and successfully reconnoitered Buel's forces in Independence. Buel commanded a detachment of about three hundred men. Most were camped in tents on open ground on the western side of town. Other elements of Buel's command were stationed in town. His provost marshal occupied the town jail. Buel himself established his headquarters in a bank building on the southwest corner of the town square. Hughes decided to launch a surprise attack just before dawn on August 11. Hughes convinced Quantrill to lead the attack. The guerrillas caught the Federal pickets by surprise on the edge of town and killed them before they could give warning of the attack. A Federal soldier near the square was the first to respond as Quantrill's men galloped into town: he fired his rifle and spread the alarm. The noise of battle awakened Buel who found his headquarters surrounded by guerrillas. Meanwhile, Hughes led the main Confederate force to the Federal camp where they wrought havoc on the soldiers still sleeping in their tents. The Federal troops who survived the surprise attack formed a defensive line behind a stone wall on the west side of town and drove off repeated Confederate attacks.

Hughes fell dead with a bullet in his forehead early in the fighting at the stone wall. Colonel Gideon W. Thompson assumed command and quickly sustained a wound that sent him to the rear. Upton Hays continued to lead the Confederates, although the Federals drove back as many as five assaults. Hays, too, sustained a slight wound in his foot.[28]

Meanwhile, Quantrill kept Buel and his bodyguard trapped in the bank building and isolated from his command. Quantrill's men took advantage of the opportunity to settle old scores with enemies in town: they executed men rousted from the jail and a hotel. The fighting continued for several hours with the Federal troops behind the stone wall holding their ground. But Quantrill grew weary of the stalemate at the bank and directed his men to set fire to a structure next door to it. As the flames spread, Quantrill ordered Buel to surrender or "roast." Realizing that he was trapped, Buel offered to surrender if he could do so to a Confederate officer and if he and his men would receive protection from the guerrillas. Colonel Thompson, returning to town to treat his wound, gave Buel the assurance he requested and the Federal commander surrendered. At the same time, Buel sent a message to the soldiers at the stone wall directing them to surrender as well. Thompson promptly paroled Buel and his surviving men. But Buel had lost about half of his command making the battle of Independence the worst Federal defeat since the capture of Lexington. However, the Confederates were unable to build on their victory. Hughes had launched his attack to gain access to a crossing of the Missouri River. The larger goal had been to enable recruits and guerrillas north of the river to move south to join Confederate forces. That ambition died with Hughes. After gathering what weapons and supplies they could take with them, Colonel Thompson and his men returned to their camp at Lees Summit.[29]

In the days after the Confederate victory at Independence, more rebel troops and recruits arrived in the area around Lees Summit. Confederate troops led by Colonel Jeremiah Vardaman ("Vard") Cockrell and recruits raised by Colonel John T. Coffee increased the number of rebel troops to about eight hundred. Vard

Cockrell was born near Warrensburg, Missouri, where he practiced law and became a Methodist minister. He joined the Missouri State Guard and rose to the rank of colonel. After the Battle of Pea Ridge, Cockrell was among the officers sent north to recruit troops in Missouri. Coffee had also joined the Missouri State Guard, but he operated independently of Sterling Price's army, remaining in Missouri to fight as a partisan ranger. In the wake of the Confederate victory at Independence, Cockrell and Coffee moved north to join Gideon Thompson. With a large number of fresh recruits, Coffee went into camp near Lone Jack, a few miles east of Lees Summit.[30]

In a fresh effort to disperse the rebels in western Missouri, Major Emory S. Foster led a combined force of eight hundred Federal troops from Warrensburg to Lexington and then west to confront the rebels gathered at Lees Summit and Lone Jack. Emory Foster and Vard Cockrell were both prominent citizens of Warrensburg who soon confronted each other in one of the most bitter battles of the war in Missouri. Foster was a new arrival in Warrensburg. His family had moved there from St. Louis in 1860, and Foster, a young man of twenty who still lived in his parents' home, set up shop as a photographer. With his brother, Marshall M. Foster, he also edited the *Warrensburg Missourian*, a Democratic paper with staunchly Unionist views. Marshall Foster was murdered by secessionists in February 1861. Emory Foster formed a Unionist home guard and sporadically fought raiding Confederates throughout the war.

On the morning of August 15, as Foster approached Lone Jack, he encountered Coffee with about sixteen hundred recruits. Foster attacked and succeeded in scattering the ill-trained and poorly armed enemy. Early the next morning, with Cockrell leading the attack, Foster faced a force of three thousand rebels, including troops commanded by Gideon Thompson and Upton Hays. At Hays's urgent request, elements of Quantrill's guerrilla band joined the fight. According to John Newman Edwards, who wrote one of the first histories of the war in the West and later shaped the legend of Jesse James, the battle of Lone Jack was fought with an unusual degree of vengeance on both sides. Cockrell and Foster almost certainly knew of each other, at least by reputation. The troops led by Hays were now fighting near their Jackson County homes. As Edwards put it, "sectional hate and civil feuds lent their desperation to the combatants." Hays's men, explained Edwards, "were in sight of their desolated homes, and the spoilers were in front of them." Similarly, the presence of Quantrill's guerrillas caused Foster's troops to conclude they were fighting for their lives.[31]

Much of the fighting focused on the Federal artillery, which rebels succeeded in capturing for a time. Bodies of men on both sides of the struggle littered the ground around the cannon. A hotel in town gave refuge to Federal sharpshooters, and rebels set it on fire. All the defenders, wrote Edwards, "perished in the flames." The fighting continued for five hours. Foster received a serious wound and was removed from the field to a nearby cabin. Foster's successor then ordered a retreat. As the Federal forces disengaged, they spiked their guns and made their way back to Lexington. The Federal troops retreated in order, and the rebels lost over 100 men in the fight. But the Federal forces had lost more than 150 men and they had left their wounded commander behind. According to Foster's own account, he was too badly hurt to retreat with his men. He lay helpless in a cabin and soon fell into the hands of Quantrill's men. Foster recalled that one of the guerrillas prepared to kill him and it was the future outlaw Cole Younger who intervened to save his life.[32]

Again the rebels were unable to build on their victory. They soon withdrew, retreating toward Arkansas, as Federal troops out of Kansas entered Missouri to clear the enemy from Jackson and adjacent counties. Leading the Federal force was General James G. Blunt, a native of Maine, an early settler in Kansas, and a Free State fighter who had ridden with Jim Lane. Blunt now led a well-armed Federal force with which Gideon Thompson and his commanders had no desire to engage. As in northeastern and north-central Missouri, guerrillas continued to operate in northwestern Missouri, but large Confederate forces were no longer present—and they would not be present again until Sterling Price's final raid in the fall of 1864.[33]

Schofield blamed Curtis for the guerrilla warfare that plagued Missouri during the period of Schofield's command (June–September 1862). After his victory at Pea Ridge, Curtis had tried to clear Arkansas of Confederates and had moved an army to Helena on the Mississippi River. This, in Schofield's view, left the southwest Missouri–Arkansas border unprotected. Schofield described guerrilla warfare in Missouri as "perhaps never before equaled in extent and intensity." Guerrilla raids, he continued "involved me in almost endless trouble and came near ruining my reputation as a successful commander." These Federal defeats were a major reason for Frank Blair's successful campaign to have Schofield replaced as Federal commander in Missouri.[34]

More Federal defeats lay ahead as Confederate forces in southwest Missouri continued to challenge Federal authority and both sides found Native American allies in the adjacent Indian Territory. On September 27, 1862, Colonel Douglas H. Cooper led Confederate troops, including Jo Shelby's cavalry and an Indian brigade, into Missouri to take control of Newtonia. Cooper was a veteran of the Mexican War who had fought with and been befriended by Jefferson Davis. When Davis became secretary of war in the 1850s, Cooper received an appointment as a Federal Indian agent. At the beginning of the Civil War, Cooper organized a brigade of pro-Confederate Indian troops known as the Chickasaw Mounted Rifles. At Newtonia, the town's grain mill gave Cooper's men welcome access to the fruits of the region's harvest. Cooper would soon be challenged by General Blunt who continued to move south after the Confederates retreated from Independence. On September 29, Blunt's scouts skirmished with Cooper's troops at Newtonia, and the next morning Blunt attacked in force. On the battlefield, tactical command rested with Shelby and with the German-born St. Louisan, Brigadier General Frederick Solomon. Both were veterans of the Battle of Wilson's Creek. Solomon had raised troops in Wisconsin and joined the Federal Indian Expedition in June 1862. He found allies among the Cherokee and now led them into battle against Cooper's Chickasaw Rifles. The fighting began at 7:00 a.m. and continued all day with the advantage falling first to the Federals and later, as Cooper received reinforcements, to the Confederates. By late afternoon, Blunt attempted to disengage, and as night fell he struggled unsuccessfully to maintain an orderly retreat. To cover his retreat, Blunt deployed his artillery on the road leading north to Sarcoxie. But the pursuing Confederates countered with artillery fire of their own. Using the muzzle flashes of the Federal guns to direct their fire, the rebel gunners delivered an effective barrage that instilled panic in the fleeing Federals, many of whom broke and ran. Cooper decisively defeated Blunt at the battle of Newtonia, but the Confederates and their Indian allies soon withdrew to Arkansas as Shelby's men fought a rearguard action to protect the retreat.[35]

As Confederate forces withdrew toward Arkansas, they enjoyed a final victory over a Federal garrison at Clark's Mill in south-central Missouri near the village of Vera Cruz, about thirty miles north of Gainesville and about forty miles north of the Arkansas border. At that location, Captain Hiram E. Barstow commanded a mixed force of about fifty men from his own Tenth Illinois Cavalry and another fifty men from the Missouri state militia. To the south, near Gainesville, two Confederate veterans of the Battles of Wilson's Creek and Pea Ridge—Colonels John Q. Burbridge and Colton Greene—recruited and armed more than fifteen hundred rebel troops. In the spring of 1862, both Confederate commanders had moved east of the Mississippi to fight with Sterling Price in Mississippi. But, by summer, Burbridge and Greene requested and received permission to return to Missouri to join in the widespread raiding and recruiting activities.[36]

Barstow had grown accustomed to reports of rebel activity in the vicinity of his small garrison. The reports had consistently proved to be false alarms, however, and Barstow had no reason to believe that the situation had changed when, at 2:00 a.m. on the morning of November 7, he received a report that several hundred Confederates had been in Gainesville the previous day "robbing Union families." He sent twenty men to Gainesville to investigate and himself led a party of eighteen men down the Vera Cruz road toward Rockbridge to intercept "bushwhackers" thought to be trying to slip past his post. About five miles north of Rockbridge, Barstow encountered a Confederate advance guard. He charged the enemy, drove them back, and then quickly fell back to his Clark's Mill camp. As he prepared to engage an enemy advancing from Rockbridge, Barstow learned that another sizable enemy force approached his post from the northeast. By mid-morning the Federal garrison was surrounded by more than fifteen hundred Confederates commanded by Burbridge and Greene. Fighting began at

11:00 a.m. and continued for five hours. Barstow was badly outnumbered and outgunned. Many of the Federal troops were armed only with Colt pistols, and Barstow defended his position with one two-pound field gun. Burbridge and Greene enjoyed a numerical advantage of more than ten to one, and they deployed four six-pound guns against the Federal post. Had he been aware of the enemy's strength, Barstow later reported, he would have abandoned his post after driving back the enemy's advance guard north of Rockbridge. By the time he realized the enemy's strength all escape routes had been cut off.

As daylight faded, Burbridge sent forward a messenger under a white flag demanding that Barstow surrender his command. Barstow complied, and he and his men were promptly paroled. Burbridge and Greene destroyed the garrison's blockhouse and several other outbuildings and then rapidly withdrew southward. Barstow made his way north to Marshfield—an outpost on the Federally controlled line of supply linking the railhead at Rolla with the Union military depot at Springfield—and filed his report.[37]

During his tenure as commander of the Department of the Missouri (June 5–September 24, 1862), Brigadier General John M. Schofield had been badly embarrassed by the guerrilla raids and Confederate recruitment activities that challenged Federal authority across the state. After being replaced by Major General Samuel R. Curtis (the victor of the Battle of Pea Ridge), Schofield took command of what became the Army of the Frontier. The Federal defeats at Newtonia on September 30 and Clark's Mill on November 7 occurred as Schofield gathered a powerful army of ten thousand troops to advance from Springfield into northern Arkansas to attack Confederate forces commanded there by Thomas C. Hindman. At the battle of Prairie Grove, Arkansas, in early December 1862, Hindman was badly defeated. By the end of December, Federals had forced Hindman's demoralized army south of the Arkansas River. In a bold attempt to revive Confederate fortunes in northern Arkansas, John Marmaduke (Hindman's cavalry commander) led a mounted force of nearly two thousand men into Missouri early in January.

When Marmaduke left Arkansas on December 31, 1862, his intention was to operate in the rear of the Army of the Frontier, particularly in the countryside between the Federal strongholds at Rolla and Springfield. From the railhead at Rolla, Federal wagon trains supplied the large military depot at Springfield, which in turn supported the Army of the Frontier in Arkansas. Marmaduke intended to threaten both places. At the very least he would disrupt Federal supplies; at best, he could force the Army of the Frontier to withdraw from Arkansas. A secondary purpose of the raid, evident from the outset, was the destruction of the system of Federal garrisons that provided the foundation for Unionist control of the countryside in southwest Missouri. As Marmaduke later reported, these outposts (like the one destroyed by Burbridge and Greene at Clark's Mill) were well-constructed defensive works from which one hundred well-armed and disciplined men could defend themselves against ten times as many attackers. These Federal outposts were intended to defend Unionists and suppress partisans and bushwhackers. They would be no match for Marmaduke's force, however, and the Confederate commander intended to lay waste to them and rekindle the spirit of rebellion in southwest Missouri.

On December 31, under orders from General Hindman, Marmaduke led his men to Yellville, Arkansas, about twenty miles south of the Missouri border. The Confederates then advanced into Missouri in three columns. Marmaduke led one column north through Forsyth to Ozark. The Federal garrison at Ozark withdrew as Marmaduke approached and carried the news of the rebel movement to Springfield. The rebels burned the fort at Ozark before continuing north toward Springfield. About twenty miles to the east, Colonel Emmett MacDonald's column destroyed a Federal fort at Lawrence Mill, about ten miles southwest of Ava. Fifteen miles further east, Colonel Joseph C. Porter advanced north to Hartville. It was Marmaduke's purpose at this point to "operate in the country between [Springfield] and Rolla." By dividing his force into three columns it was easier for his men to forage and it helped create the impression that Marmaduke commanded a force capable of controlling the entire region.[38]

Marmaduke's army suffered badly in the winter weather. His men entered Missouri poorly clothed and badly mounted. Many of the Confederates lost their horses to exhaustion and continued on foot, often shoeless, marching through mud and snow. They advanced, as Marmaduke reported, "without baggage wagons or cooking utensils." The Confederates were not slowed by supply trains, but their only supplies were what they carried with them on their horses or their backs. It was a point of pride for Marmaduke that his men advanced against the enemy "subsisting as best they could on the country through which they marched."[39]

Once he was in Missouri, Marmaduke's primary objective changed somewhat. On the evening of January 6, his scouts reported that Springfield "with its rich army stores, was weakly garrisoned, though strongly fortified." Marmaduke decided to move rapidly to attack Springfield hoping that with the element of surprise on his side he could capture the Federal outpost and resupply and remount his men. If he could take Springfield and hold it, the Army of the Frontier would be cut off from its line of supply and the Federal troops in Arkansas would be forced to retreat or face starvation. Marmaduke sent messengers to MacDonald and Porter with orders to join him at Springfield. The directive reached MacDonald successfully, but the courier dispatched to meet Porter did not locate him until January 10. By then it was too late for Porter's column to participate in the fighting at Springfield.[40]

Marmaduke's column arrived south of Springfield early on the morning of January 8. MacDonald joined him there at 10:00 a.m. Together they began shelling the earthwork fortifications and with their dismounted troops probed the

Federal defenses. Just before the Confederate attack began, the Federal commander at Springfield sent a telegram via Sedalia to his commander, Samuel R. Curtis in St. Louis, reporting that a large enemy force was seven miles south of town, advancing northward on the Ozark road. The commander at Springfield was Brigadier General Egbert Benson Brown, a native of New York State who had prospered as a grain merchant in Toledo, Ohio, before moving to St. Louis in 1852. In St. Louis he became an active figure in the railroad business. Brown first joined the Seventh Missouri Volunteers as a colonel. He later became brigadier general in the Missouri state militia. By November 1862, he was brigadier general of US Volunteers.[41]

As Marmaduke advanced against him, Brown prepared the defenses of Springfield. He called in militia forces from the surrounding area, and by noon he expected to have two thousand men under arms. Soldiers from the hospital who were able to bear arms formed what the men called the Quinine Brigade, a reference to the bitter medicinal tonic used to treat fevers. (They suffered two dead and fourteen wounded in the fighting.) To protect his supplies, Brown moved fifty thousand army rations from the supply depot in town to his fortifications. Supply trains from the west (presumably from Fort Scott) had arrived the previous night and supply trains from the east (the railhead at Rolla) had been sent back to Lebanon. Once the Confederates reached the outskirts of Springfield, Jo Shelby took tactical command of Marmaduke's column and began probing the Federal defenses on the southeast side of town from the Marshfield road to the main Ozark road. Brown had strengthened his defenses here by burning several houses to give his artillery a clear line of fire. In these uncoordinated Confederate attacks, the rebel troops were badly exposed. On the southwest side of town, MacDonald's brigade, supported by Shelby, found shelter in a ravine that allowed them to advance toward town. The ravine led to a hill upon which stood a two-story brick building surrounded by a stockade. Federal forces used the place as a prison and Brown had been slow to garrison it. MacDonald and Shelby took control of this strong point and soon threatened to break through the Federal defenses. At this point Brown led his bodyguard into the fight. He was badly wounded in the shoulder but his bold action held back the Confederate attack. Brown's adjutant later reported that the general had been "treacherously shot from a secesh residence." By 3:00 p.m. Brown reported that the enemy "are crowding the fighting," but his men behaved well and they held "the strong positions."[42]

The significance of the second battle of Springfield was immediately evident to General Curtis who telegraphed reports to Henry Halleck in Washington, DC. (In July 1862 Halleck had moved east to become general in chief of the Union army and to serve as the principal military administrator for President Lincoln and Secretary of War Stanton.) Rebels had come to the "outskirts of Springfield at 1 o'clock, and immediately began shelling the town with two cannon," Curtis reported. "Our troops responded from fort," continued Curtis. "Nothing decisive. Have directed General Brown to hold out as long as possible." In a second telegram to Halleck, Curtis reported that the fighting at Springfield had subsided at nightfall: "We hold all forts. Enemy occupy southwest corner of town. General Brown wounded in shoulder." Curtis identified the Confederate commander as Marmaduke and reported, "They fight for bread."[43]

Curtis expected Marmaduke to resume his attack the next morning, and he warned Brown to prepare for "a desperate effort" by the rebels. At 9:00 p.m on January 8, Curtis telegraphed a message of encouragement to Brown: "You and your troops are heroes. I hope God will spare you strength for to-morrow." Curtis assured Brown that two divisions of troops from the Army of the Frontier in Arkansas had been sent east from Fayetteville and that they would "soon be behind or near the foe. Don't weary in well doing."[44]

During the night of January 8, a detachment of Confederate troops tried but failed to locate Porter. On the morning of January 9, Marmaduke decided not to renew the attack. Shortly after dawn, he moved east toward Rolla. Along the way, small Federal garrisons fled, and Marmaduke's men captured supplies and destroyed forts where they found them. On January 10, Marmaduke finally formed a junction with Porter near Marshfield. Porter had destroyed Federal fortifications at Marshfield and further south at Hartville. On the night of January 10, Marmaduke moved toward Hartville knowing that a Federal force had arrived at that former garrison. This was a force of about seven hundred Union infantry and cavalry commanded by Colonel Samuel Merrill. Brigadier General Fitz Henry Warren had dispatched the force from Houston, Missouri, to reinforce Brown at Springfield. Finding Springfield secure but learning that rebels had attacked Hartville, Merrill moved east to that location and soon faced sustained attacks from Marmaduke, who feared that this Federal force might cut off his line of retreat back to Arkansas. Marmaduke attacked Merrill all day on January 11.

Marmaduke described the battle of Hartville as "desperate." He first engaged Merrill's force from the north and then moved his troops to the east side of town. Marmaduke intended his movements to drive the Federals out of Hartville toward the west or north and thereby open a line of retreat southward. Marmaduke lost over three hundred men in the fighting (compared with fewer than eighty casualties on the Federal side). Among the dead was Emmett MacDonald, the secessionist hero who refused to accept Federal parole after being captured at Camp Jackson. Also killed at Hartville was the former mayor of St. Louis, Lieutenant Colonel John M. Wimer. The bodies of both men were returned to St, Louis for burial. Fearing that MacDonald and Wimer would be viewed as martyrs in death and provide a catalyst for disloyal activities, the city's provost marshal raided the wake, confiscated the bodies, and buried them secretly. Also badly wounded at Hartville was Joseph C. Porter, and he later died from these wounds. The battle of Hartville was costly for Marmaduke, but he succeeded in pushing Merrill aside.

Merrill owed the survival of his force to the accuracy of his artillery. By 4:30 in the afternoon the Federal artillery had run out of ammunition, and Merrill withdrew north along the Lebanon road (he later turned east and returned to Houston). Marmaduke withdrew toward Arkansas and the intense fighting at Hartville left Federal forces in the region disinclined to pursue him.[45]

With Marmaduke now in retreat, Samuel Curtis lavished praise on General Brown. "Your gallant and successful defense of Springfield has added to the glory of the 8th January," he wrote, referring to the still popular celebration of Andrew Jackson's victory on that day at the Battle of New Orleans at the close of the War of 1812. On the same day, Curtis telegraphed the Unionist governor of Missouri, Hamilton Gamble: "All right in Springfield." Marmaduke had captured one field gun at Springfield but otherwise "got nothing but a good thrashing." Curtis dismissed as false any reports that Missouri militiamen had joined the enemy. These reports may have been prompted by the shooting of General Brown. Curtis insisted that the militiamen at Springfield "fought like heroes."[46]

From Hartville, Marmaduke marched over mountainous terrain, through rain and snow and icy mountain streams to Batesville, Arkansas, where he established a camp on the south side of the White River. The barren countryside through which he and his men traveled furnished "neither food for man nor horse." Marmaduke filed his initial report from Batesville on January 18, a week after the battle of Hartville. In his final report of February 1, he recorded that his entire force arrived at Batesville on January 25. Despite the hardships and the painful losses, Marmaduke deemed his raid a success. The Federal Army of the Frontier had "counter-marched rapidly to save Springfield," observed Marmaduke, although the movement of Federal troops east of Fayetteville had not enabled Hindman to return to northern Arkansas. Perhaps more important in Marmaduke's mind was the destruction of the Federal forts in the countryside between Springfield and Rolla. These forts, which had "overawed and kept in subjection the country," had been destroyed, "and the heart of the people revived again in the presence of Confederate troops."[47]

But Confederate troops had once more left Missouri. And fighting for the Confederacy outside of Missouri did not sit well with John Marmaduke and Jo Shelby; nor ultimately did it suit Sterling Price. In Missouri, the war had a personality and purpose that tended to dissolve with distance. When Marmaduke, Shelby, and Price were able to fight in Missouri, their cause became purposeful in ways that it could not in Arkansas and Mississippi. In retrospect, Price's victory at Lexington in September 1861 marked the zenith of secessionist power in Missouri. In the midst of the struggle, however, it was not at all clear to Missouri secessionists or to their foes that their hour had passed. Marmaduke, Shelby, and Price never acknowledged defeat and held fast to the conviction that their cause would triumph. It was in this spirit, after a winter of privation in Arkansas, that Marmaduke planned to return to Missouri again in April 1863.

The stated purpose of Marmaduke's second raid was to feed and supply his army. But he also wanted to continue to lay claim to Missouri. Marmaduke believed that Curtis's command in the state had been weakened, as Federal troops had been sent south to support Grant at Vicksburg. As always, Marmaduke believed that fresh recruits would rally to his banner. If he could raise tens of thousands of troops, he could threaten Jefferson City and even St. Louis. With lofty ambitions, Marmaduke assembled about five thousand men for his second raid. About twelve hundred of these men were without arms and about nine hundred were without mounts. They left northeast Arkansas on April 18 and marched north in two columns separated by about ten miles to maximize their access to the region's meager supplies of food and forage. Colonel Jo Shelby led one column through Van Buren; Colonel George W. Carter led the second column through Doniphan.

Once in Missouri, Marmaduke's plans changed quickly. He had originally intended to advance toward Rolla. But Federal forces had stripped the countryside of forage in order to discourage Confederate raids, and Marmaduke decided to operate "east of Ironton, capture the outpost (a regiment) at Patterson and strike [John] McNeil, who was at Bloomfield, with a force I estimated to be about 2000." At Patterson and Bloomfield, Marmaduke planned to capture the supplies his army badly needed. "If successful in capturing McNeil's forces," Marmaduke reported, "I anticipated that my whole command could be well armed and finely mounted for vigorous action." Marmaduke rode with Carter's column into Missouri. The two columns met at Patterson on the evening of April 20.[48]

At Patterson, Colonel Edwin Smart commanded a small Federal garrison. Early in the morning of April 20, advance elements of Carter's column captured the Federal pickets (a lieutenant and twenty-four men). Carter was then about twelve miles south of Patterson, and the Confederate raiders still enjoyed the advantage of surprise. They soon disclosed their presence, however, when overeager troops opened fire with their artillery before Marmaduke's infantry was in place to attack. As Marmaduke reported, the Federal garrison "took the alarm, and precipitously fled to Pilot Knob." Smart's men burned what supplies they could, but Marmaduke took possession of "a large supply of subsistence and some quartermaster's stores."[49]

Marmaduke now focused his attention on Bloomfield where Brigadier General John McNeil (the perpetrator of the Palmyra Massacre) commanded a Federal garrison. Marmaduke correctly estimated McNeil's command to be made up of about two thousand men. Again Marmaduke decided to divide his force. He rode with Carter's column and advanced southeast across the St. Francis River to attack Bloomfield. Marmaduke directed Shelby to move north to Fredericktown. Whether McNeil decided to stand and fight at Bloomfield or retreat, Marmaduke intended to trap him between Carter's and Shelby's columns. Unfortunately for Marmaduke's plans, heavy rains slowed his advance to Bloomfield. The St.

Francis River flooded and slowed the Confederate crossing. Worse, the passage through the Mingo Swamp beyond the St. Francis proved tortuous. Shelby faced no such difficulties and arrived at Fredericktown on April 22, a day before Carter's column overcame the obstacles of flood and swamp to reach Bloomfield on April 23.

Again Marmaduke lost the advantage of surprise. McNeil received reports of Marmaduke's advance toward Bloomfield, and he knew that Confederate raiders controlled the road north to Fredericktown. Contrary to Marmaduke's expectations and plans, McNeil retreated northeast to Cape Girardeau and took refuge in the formidable fortifications there. Earlier in the war in 1861, Grant had authorized the construction of four forts to protect the strategically important Mississippi River town located a few miles upstream from his headquarters at Cairo, Illinois. Marmaduke remained in Bloomfield while Carter gave chase to McNeil. On April 25, Marmaduke learned that Carter had pursued McNeil to within four miles of the Cape Girardeau fortifications. Realizing that Carter was now badly exposed, Marmaduke quickly made his way to Cape Girardeau and sent orders to Shelby at Fredericktown to make a night march of thirty miles to join him there.

On the night of April 25, McNeil sent civilians by steamboat to safety upstream. Also that night, two Federal gunboats and a troop transport of reinforcements arrived from Cairo. With the added protection of the gunboats, McNeil repositioned artillery from the town's two river forts to strengthen the two forts on the west side of town. One of these forts protected Cape Girardeau from attack along the Jackson road to the northwest. The other protected the town from attack on the roads leading to Gordonville and Bloomfield to the southwest and Commerce to the south. McNeil now commanded a consolidated force of about four thousand men. Marmaduke prepared to attack with fewer than five thousand effective troops.

Shelby's column arrived at Cape Girardeau on April 26. Traveling with Carter's column from the south, Marmaduke joined Shelby on the Jackson road west of town. While the Confederate commander studied the town's defenses, he directed Shelby to make a demonstration moving east along the Jackson road. According to Marmaduke's later report, Shelby engaged the enemy with more vigor than the commander had intended. "Shelby's demonstration amounted almost to an attack," Marmaduke reported. Marmaduke recalled that he felt compelled to bring up Carter's column to support Shelby. Both sides launched ineffective cavalry charges and exchanged artillery barrages. But Shelby's action, as Marmaduke reported it, committed rebel forces to a battle they could not win. The fighting began at 10:00 a.m. on April 26 and continued for the next four hours. McNeil's well-entrenched force proved impregnable, and by the time Marmaduke managed to withdraw at 2:00 p.m., he had suffered 325 casualties. McNeil reported only 17 dead and wounded. Marmaduke withdrew to Jackson where he camped for the night. He soon faced a new threat from the northwest.[50]

On the morning of April 26, General William Vandever left Fredericktown with a strong cavalry force. Vandever, a former congressman from Dubuque, Iowa, was a veteran of the Battle of Pea Ridge. He had been promoted to brigadier general in November 1862 and assigned to the Army of the Frontier. From his headquarters in St. Louis, Federal commander Samuel Curtis dispatched Vandever from Ironton to confront Shelby at Fredericktown. Learning that Shelby had left Fredericktown to join Marmaduke at Cape Girardeau, Vandever continued southeast to join McNeil at that location. During the night of April 26, Vandever's cavalry skirmished with elements of Marmaduke's force camped on the Jackson and Fredericktown road. By dawn on April 27, Marmaduke found himself confronting McNeil to the east and Vandever to the northwest. As his rear guard skirmished with Vandever, Marmaduke moved as quickly as he could south through White Water. He skirmished again with Vandever there and succeeded in destroying a bridge to slow the Federal pursuit. For the next several days, Vandever and McNeil maintained contact with Marmaduke as he retreated toward Bloomfield. At the Castor River on April 29 and again at Bloomfield on April 30, Marmaduke mounted rearguard actions that gave his engineers time to locate a crossing of the swollen St. Francis River at the Arkansas border. The crossing began on May 1 at Chalk Bluff. Again Marmaduke mounted a rearguard action as his wagons and artillery made the difficult crossing. Most of his men crossed into Arkansas that night. "By sun-up," Marmaduke reported, "my whole command was safely across. The pursuit had ceased."[51]

Marmaduke found some reason to regard his second raid as successful. He gained about 150 recruits (although he lost 120 "stragglers"). He also improved "the number and quality of horses." But the raid had failed in its major objectives. He had not succeeded in raising tens of thousands of recruits and he had not succeeded in punishing the hated John McNeil. Nor had Marmaduke provided his men with the splendid arms and horses he had hoped to acquire from McNeil. Except for the few supplies left behind by the Federals at Patterson, Marmaduke captured no military stores. The attack on the fortifications at Cape Girardeau had been wasteful, and Marmaduke returned to Arkansas with his army both diminished and exhausted. As one Confederate officer colorfully observed, Marmaduke's men emerged from the ordeal "more like an army of denizens of a semi-emphibio subterranean world than one of men and animals."[52]

Federal forces in Missouri repelled Marmaduke with relative ease. Nevertheless, Lincoln continued to struggle to find a military and political formula that would enable Federal forces to hold Missouri in the Union and keep the peace. Samuel Curtis, the victor at Pea Ridge, had commanded the Department of the Missouri since late September 1862. But his antislavery views put him at odds with Missouri's provisional governor, Hamilton Gamble. Shortly after Marmaduke's raid, Lincoln restored John M. Schofield to command, and Schofield returned to Missouri fully aware that guerrilla activities in the state had largely discredited his previous tenure as commander. In an attempt to maintain peace along the Missouri–Kansas border, Schofield appointed Brigadier General Thomas Ewing, Jr. (brother-in-law of William Tecumseh Sherman) to command the area. Ewing adopted an aggressive policy toward the families of guerrillas and ordered the arrest and imprisonment in Kansas City of known rebel women—the wives, daughters, sisters, and mothers of guerrillas in the field. On August 14, 1863, the building in which the women were confined collapsed in a wind storm. A sister of Bill Anderson was among those killed, as was a cousin of Cole Younger. Anderson and Younger were both members of Quantrill's guerrilla band. In retaliation, Quantrill led a murderous raid on Lawrence, Kansas, on August 19, 1863. A week later, on August 25, Ewing issued General Order, No. 11, directing the removal of civilians from several Missouri counties bordering Kansas. Partly as a result of Ewing's drastic response, Schofield managed to prevent Jim Lane from leading a Jayhawker invasion of Missouri. But conditions remained volatile in much of Missouri, and in September 1863, Jo Shelby gained the approval of Sterling Price to lead a raid into western Missouri. As with Marmaduke's raids, the military purpose was to gather supplies and raise recruits. But Shelby had other reasons to want to fight his way back into Missouri. When Shelby returned to Arkansas with Marmaduke's retreating troops, he learned that Federal authorities had banished his wife from Missouri (she and her children lived for the rest of the war with Shelby's stepfather in Lexington, Kentucky). There were scores to be settled, and even in retreat, Shelby made a point of passing through his antebellum home of Waverly.[53]

As Shelby entered Missouri at Pineville, John Coffee joined his ranks with four hundred men. Now about one thousand strong, the Confederates advanced toward Neosho starting early on the morning of October 4. Led by Coffee's men, they were approaching the town by midday. About two miles south of town they skirmished with Federal cavalry and drove them back. The Federal troops entered Neosho from one side of town as Coffee's men entered from the other. Soon several groups of Confederate cavalry converged on Neosho. Federal forces numbering about three hundred occupied the brick courthouse and held off the rebels for an hour and a half. Shelby brought an end to the standoff by deploying his artillery and firing into the building and delivering a message that he would raze the building unless the Federal garrison surrendered unconditionally. The Federal commander offered to surrender if all of his men—the regular Federal troops and the members of the enrolled Missouri militia—were treated as prisoners of war and allowed "to retain their clothing, money, &c." Shelby rejected the request and repeated his threat to destroy the courthouse. The Federal commander capitulated. Shelby gave written paroles to the Union officers but not to the militia men. Two members of the enrolled militia were killed by Coffee's men.[54]

Before leaving Neosho, Shelby supplied as many of his men as he could with fresh mounts, rifles, pistols and clothing. Some of the clothing consisted of

Federal uniforms. As the freshly equipped Confederates moved north, Shelby's biographer imagined "a curious sight: bluecoated cavalry trotting along beneath the Confederate flags with the red sumac in their hats which had become the insigne of Shelby's men." Confederate raiders in Federal uniforms could also be identified as guerrillas and summarily executed. Among the Federal troops pursuing Shelby was Major Emory S. Foster, the photographer from Warrensburg who had been badly wounded at Lone Jack and whose life had been spared by Cole Younger. Skirmishing with Shelby's rear guard as it approached Camp Cole, Foster reported that he had captured three of Shelby's men. "I did not shoot them," he explained to General Brown, "because the enemy have possession of several of our men."[55]

From Neosho, the rebels moved north. They passed through the desolate town of Sarcoxie, much of which had been burned by Federal forces. Shelby's men quickly took revenge by destroying the nearby town of Bowers' Mill, which Shelby described as "a notorious pest spot for the militia."[56] Shelby continued north, drove off the Federal garrison at Greenfield, and passed through Humanville on October 6. By the morning of October 7 the Confederates had reached Warsaw. They skirmished with Federal troops there but soon captured the town, and with it "vast quantities of all kinds of stores." Shelby crossed the Osage River and drove off small Federal garrisons at Cole Camp and Tipton as he advanced toward Boonville.[57]

By the time Shelby crossed the Osage, his force had grown to eighteen hundred men. Most were now well mounted, well fed and supplied, and well armed. As long as Shelby advanced against small Federal outposts his victories continued. Unless Federal forces could be concentrated in front of him, Shelby had little to fear from pursuing Federal troops. Shelby's skills in mounting rearguard actions were now well honed and with relatively small detachments of troops deployed in ambush he repeatedly stalled the pursuing Federal troops. The principal responsibility for stopping Shelby fell to Brigadier General E. B. Brown who had successfully defended Springfield during Marmaduke's first raid the previous January. Brown now commanded an area of 120 square miles in southwest Missouri with thirty-seven outposts distributed across the countryside for the purpose of suppressing guerrilla activity. As news of Shelby's raid reached him, Brown moved as rapidly as he could to concentrate troops at Sedalia, from which point his pursuit of Shelby began. On October 9, while Shelby skirmished with Major Emory Foster at Cole Camp, Brown (a few miles to the west) moved eleven companies of Missouri state militia and two field guns from Osceolo to Sedalia and directed the Federal troops following Shelby—from Tipton through Syracuse to Boonville—to disengage and move directly north to Marshall. These Federal troops had arrived at Marshall by 7:00 a.m. on October 13 and quickly took up a strong defensive position on high ground east of town. By 8:00 a.m., as the Federal troops hurriedly fed themselves and their horses, their pickets were driven in by Shelby's troops advancing toward Marshall from Boonville.[58]

At Boonville, as at Tipton, Shelby seized large amounts of boots, weapons, and horses before continuing his advance northwest on the Boonville–Marshall road with Brown's Federal troops still in pursuit. A few miles outside of Boonville, Shelby offered his enemy an excellent example of the rearguard action he had mastered. As his troops crossed the LaMine River on October 12, Shelby quickly set up an ambush on the "rugged and precipitous" river banks. He secluded a dismounted regiment on the wooded west side of the river and left two companies of soldiers on the east side to skirmish with the pursuing Federals and lead them into the trap. As Brown's troops approached the river, the rebel skirmishers engaged them in a firefight and then fled across the river in "apparent confusion." The Federal troops took the bait and charged the fleeing enemy only to face a sheet of deadly fire on the other side. Shelby thought his men had killed or wounded fifty of the enemy in this action. In any case he had stalled the Federal pursuit. On the evening of October 12, Shelby camped about six miles southeast of Marshall. Scouts visited Arrow Rock on the Missouri River to the east and reported no enemy activity there. On the morning of October 13, confident that his flanks were secure, Shelby prepared to attack Marshall. He was unaware that General Brown had disengaged the Federal pursuit and had succeeded in locating a strong military presence there. Brown had correctly anticipated that Shelby intended to pass through Marshall on his way to his antebellum hometown of Waverly. For the first time in the raid, Shelby faced a strong force in his front, as another strong force led out of Sedalia by Brown closed in on him from his rear.[59]

In the three hours of fighting that took place at Marshall the Federal forces held their ground and turned back several rebel charges. Unable to dislodge the defenders and hearing Brown's artillery open fire to his rear, Shelby realized that he was very nearly trapped. Brown's Federals cut Shelby's force in two. Shelby, with about six hundred men, dashed to safety to the north while the rest of his command (about three hundred) fled east for about eight miles and then turned south. Shelby kept his men on the move throughout the night of October 13. They passed through Waverly before dawn on October 14. Shelby's captured supplies now became a burden, and he sank his wagons in the Missouri River before heading south. He fought repeated rearguard actions on October 14, 15, and 16 as he passed through Warrensburg and crossed the Osage River. The Federal pursuit continued on October 17, 18, and 19 as Shelby passed through Carthage. The dismal retreat contrasted sharply with the early days of the raid. Shelby had been welcomed by southern-sympathizing civilians, particularly at Boonville, and he found "the people of Missouri, as a mass, true to the South and her institutions." In his triumphal advance into Missouri, Shelby had attracted fresh recruits. But after his defeat at Marshall he lost many of his men, and he concluded that Missourians needed "the strong presence of a Confederate army to make them volunteer." As he passed once more through southwest Missouri to the Arkansas border, he found most of the countryside laid waste by years of war. He reported that most of the "southern, southwestern and some of the middle countries of Missouri are completely desolated." In many places he traveled forty miles without encountering a residence. On the road to Arkansas he found "delicate females fleeing southward" driving their teams "barefooted, ragged, and suffering for even bread." Shelby reunited his command in Arkansas and made his way safely across the Arkansas River. His raid had briefly thrown Federal forces in disarray, but General Brown had decisively defeated Shelby at Marshall. Back in Arkansas, Shelby's diminished force had little to show for its valor and sacrifice.[60]

ROBERT VAN HORN

EMMET MACDONALD

James A. Mulligan

William P. Carlin

David Rice Atchison

DAVID HUNTER

Benjamin M. Prentiss

Caleb Dorsey

SAMUEL R. CURTIS

ANDREW H. FOOTE

JOHN POPE

SCHUYLER HAMILTON

Henry Walke

THOMAS C. HINDMAN

JOHN MCNEIL

Lewis Merrill

Odin Guitar

Emory S. Foster

James G. Blunt

Thomas Ewing, Jr.

John M. Wimer

William Rosecrans

E. Kirby Smith

Sidney Jackman

A.J. Smith

Thomas Fletcher

ALFRED PLEASONTON

JOSEPH A. MOWER

Grenville Dodge

Chapter Six

"He Saw the Rebellion Vanishing before Him"

In the year that separated Shelby's raid (October 1863) from Price's expedition (October 1864), Federal forces adopted a determined effort to coordinate the activities of armies in the East and West and to carve the Confederacy into militarily disjointed sections. Ulysses Grant's victory at Vicksburg in July 1863 was an essential first step in this direction, extending Federal control throughout the lower Mississippi valley. Grant's subsequent victories over Braxton Bragg at Chattanooga in November 1863 opened an invasion route to Atlanta. In March 1864, Grant took command in the East and assumed overall responsibility for Federal military efforts. Confederates had never coordinated their military activities in the East and West; in this new military climate it became nearly impossible to do so. Nevertheless, powerful Confederate forces continued to operate in the trans-Mississippi theater. They posed less of a threat to Federal operations east of the Mississippi but they continued to threaten Federal control in the West. General Nathanial Banks launched the Red River campaign (March–May 1864) in an unsuccessful effort to break Confederate resistance west of the Mississippi. Banks's efforts brought Price back to the trans-Mississippi region to strengthen Kirby Smith's command. The collapse of the Red River campaign left a substantial rebel presence threatening Missouri from the south. This was the situation encountered by Missouri's new Federal commander, William Rosecrans, who arrived in St. Louis late in January 1864. Rosecrans had been badly beaten by Bragg at Chickamauga and nearly defeated at Chattanooga. When Grant took over at Chattanooga, Rosecrans came to Missouri where Lincoln expected that the general's administrative abilities would be put to good use.

Rosecrans found that his new command was the scene of constant skirmishing. With large numbers of rebel troops in northern Arkansas, southern Missouri and the Missouri River corridor remained vulnerable. Rebel raids continued and Federal cavalry scoured the countryside in repeated attempts to root out the menace. The Federal commander at Springfield reported that groups of the enemy "are constantly moving north in bodies of from 50 to 125." Late in May, as Banks's Red River threat evaporated, about one hundred rebels attacked the Federal garrison at Lamar. The rebels were driven off without loss on the Federal side but they continued to roam the countryside. The force that had attacked Lamar had skirted the Federal garrison at Neosho and passed though Granby two days earlier. Federal cavalry chased the rebels as they moved further north but without effect. The Federal commander lamented that with the limited resources available to him it was impossible "to intercept them or bring them to an engagement."[1]

In May 1864, William Tecumseh Sherman launched his Atlanta campaign and captured the city early in September. As Sherman advanced into Georgia, Kirby Smith entertained with increasing sympathy Sterling Price's proposal to return in strength to Missouri. The collapse of the Red River campaign meant that Smith faced no immediate danger in Arkansas. The concentration of Federal forces at Atlanta and the ease with which small bands of Confederates operated in southern Missouri suggested to Smith that Rosecrans's forces were stretched thin and that St. Louis might be vulnerable to a bold attack. An invasion of Missouri might compel Federal forces to withdraw from central Georgia. Price still believed that thousands of Missourians would join his army of liberation.

Union general Samuel R. Curtis, now at Fort Leavenworth, believed that Price's successes in Arkansas "inspired him with new energies." Curtis had been victorious over Price at Pea Ridge, and he considered himself "familiar with his purpose, often declared to his followers of making another effort to establish himself on the Missouri River." At the very least a Confederate invasion of Missouri would embarrass the Lincoln administration and disrupt Missouri Unionists as they prepared for the fall elections. Curtis had returned to Fort Leavenworth after fighting Indians on the upper Arkansas River in Colorado. On September 17 he learned that Price had crossed the Arkansas River and had begun to assemble an army. Curtis had no doubt that an invasion of Missouri was imminent. Unfortunately most of his troops were too far west to be of use in new fighting in Missouri. But, on the positive side, Curtis found Fort Leavenworth well supplied with mountain howitzers. These lightweight guns would greatly strengthen the cavalry forces that he hurriedly began to organize. Curtis also advised the governor of Kansas, Thomas Carney, that it would be necessary to call out the militia. Curtis gathered together a regular US army force of about four thousand men and denominated it the Army of the Border.[2]

When Kirby Smith contemplated sending Price into Missouri he may have been motivated by personal as well as military considerations. Like Ben McCulloch before him, Smith regarded Price and his men with disdain. When Price first returned to the trans-Mississippi theater, Smith criticized him for failing to maintain discipline in his ranks. Too often, the Missourians acted like plunderers, not soldiers. "In taking command of the District of Arkansas," Smith advised Price, "I hope you will make it your aim to reduce and discipline the cavalry." Smith ordered that "no new mounted regiments should be received." Any new conscripts to Price's army should be assigned to infantry regiments. Moreover,

Smith directed that "all inefficient and ill-mounted cavalry commands should be dismounted," and "every cavalry company to which depredation or outrages can be traced is to be immediately dismounted." Smith urged Price to "reduce one-half your cavalry to infantry, and introduce order and discipline in the remaining portion." If Price did so, concluded Smith, "I honestly believe you will do more to relieve our people and benefit our cause than by gaining a victory."[3]

On August 4, 1864, through his chief of staff, Smith formally issued the orders that authorized Price to make plans to invade Missouri. "General: You will make immediate arrangements for a movement into Missouri, with the entire cavalry force of your district." Price should "make Saint Louis the objective point of your movement" with the understanding that the recruitment of large numbers of troops remained an overriding goal. Smith authorized Price to organize his army into three divisions, noting that these were "skeleton organizations" to be filled by new recruits as a "large addition to your force is expected." Old concerns about the lack of discipline in Price's army remained. "You will scrupulously avoid all wanton acts of destruction and devastation," Smith instructed. "Restrain your men," Smith advised, "and impress upon them that their aim should be to secure success in a just and holy cause and not to gratify personal feeling and revenge."[4]

On September 13, 1864, Price arrived in Pocahontas, Arkansas, near the south-central Missouri border. Two of Price's division commanders—Jo Shelby and John Marmaduke—were experienced Missouri raiders. The third division's commander was Brigadier General James Fleming Fagan, a Kentucky native whose family had settled in Arkansas. A veteran of the Mexican War, Fagan commanded the Arkansas troops who joined Price's Missourians. At Pocahontas, Price assembled an army of about twelve thousand men. But the skeleton divisions included many recent conscripts and captured deserters. As many as four thousand of Price's men were unarmed. Price expected the army to grow in size once he entered Missouri and he intended to supply it with arms and stores captured from Federal forces. To assure a degree of military stability in his potentially unwieldy force, Price organized each division around an effective fighting brigade. Shelby's division included his Iron Brigade, now commanded by Colonel David Shanks as Shelby assumed the responsibilities of division commander. At the beginning of the war, Shanks had raised a regiment of cavalry near his home in Jackson County and fought throughout the war with Shelby's brigade. In sharp contrast to the Iron Brigade, the other brigade in Shelby's division was composed largely of recent recruits and only five hundred of the fifteen hundred men were armed. Commanding this skeleton brigade was the veteran border ruffian and partisan ranger Colonel Sidney Jackman, born in Kentucky in 1826, who had moved as a boy to Howard County, Missouri. He later bought a farm in western Missouri and fought in the Border War against Free State settlers in Kansas. For most of the war, Jackman remained in western Missouri fighting as a partisan. In May 1864 he and his men crossed into Arkansas and joined Price's army. The fighting core of Fagan's division was the brigade commanded by Brigadier General William L. Cabell, a Virginia native and an 1850 graduate of West Point. After joining the Confederate army, Cabell was assigned to the trans-Mississippi Department. Marmaduke's division relied on veteran troops commanded by the sixty-two-year-old Fayette lawyer Brigadier General John B. Clark. Throughout the raid, these veterans bore the brunt of the fighting.[5]

At his headquarters in the Planters House Hotel in St. Louis, Rosecrans learned of Price's concentration of troops near the Missouri border. The Federal commander responded cautiously, leaving the initiative entirely in Price's hands. Perhaps Rosecrans was intimidated by Price's success in driving back Frederick Steele's Federal Army of Arkansas. In any case, Rosecrans chose to wait and let Price make the first move. There was some logic to Rosecrans's timid response. Guerrilla attacks were frequent in Missouri and any concentration of Federal troops to confront Price necessitated the abandonment of many of the small outposts that Rosecrans and his predecessors had created in their continuing attempt to pacify the countryside. A concentration of Federal forces would be a boon to the guerrillas. Moreover, if Rosecrans led a Federal army south to confront Price in Arkansas, he risked being outflanked, an outcome that could leave St. Louis dangerously exposed. But Rosecrans displayed timidity throughout Price's Missouri expedition. In his final report of July 1865 to Secretary of War Edwin M. Stanton, Ulysses Grant criticized Rosecrans's caution. Elsewhere Federal commanders made good use of their advantages in manpower and supplies, Grant noted. Rosecrans did not. "The impunity with which Price was enabled to roam over the State of Missouri for a long time, and the incalculable mischief done by him, shows to how little purpose a superior force may be used." Grant concluded that Rosecrans should have concentrated his forces and "beaten and driven Price" before the Confederates could do much damage in Missouri. Grant thought Rosecrans should have acted early in September when it was clear to Grant and Stanton that Shelby had joined Price in northern Arkansas. To meet the developing threat, Rosecrans received reinforcements: a division of veteran troops commanded by Major General Andrew Jackson Smith, a West Point–trained veteran of the Mexican War who had served in the Vicksburg and Red River campaigns. The War Department diverted Smith's command to St. Louis from Cairo where he had been preparing to move east to support Sherman at Atlanta. While Rosecrans waited for Price to attack, Smith deployed his troops in the defenses of St. Louis.[6]

Price entered Missouri on September 19 and advanced in three columns separated by between ten and thirty miles. He directed that the columns form a junction at Fredericktown. Price rode with Fagan who advanced along a central course through Greenville. Marmaduke's division advanced on Fagan's right, passing through Poplar Bluff. Shelby's division advanced on Fagan's left through Doniphan and Patterson. Shelby arrived in Fredericktown on September 24 and was soon joined there by Fagan and Marmaduke. As Price assembled his army, the news of the Confederate invasion reached Rosecrans. On the night September 24, the Federal commander directed Brigadier General Thomas Ewing to reinforce Pilot Knob, the southern terminus of the Iron Mountain Railroad. At the same time Rosecrans deployed two brigades under General A. J. Smith at DeSoto, also on the Iron Mountain Railroad. Rosecrans prepared to defend St. Louis; Price was free to strike where he chose.[7]

At Fort Davidson, north of Pilot Knob, Ewing commanded a force of fifteen hundred men including two hundred veteran troops from Smith's command. These Iowa troops were veterans of Shiloh and the Vicksburg and Red River campaigns. They significantly bolstered the Federal garrison. The Federal force defended a hexagonal earthwork that commanded an unobstructed field of fire for several hundred yards in all direction. But Fort Davidson was far from impregnable. Pilot Knob Mountain and Shepherd Mountain rose above the fort to the south and rendered the place vulnerable to artillery bombardment. Ewing acknowledged that Fort Davidson was "indefensible against any large army having serviceable artillery." But his engineers had not been able to locate a better location for a defensive position to protect the Iron Mountain Railroad. The original earthwork had been erected in 1862 when Grant commanded Federal forces in the region. Earlier in the summer of 1864, Ewing did what he could to strengthen the position. He had obstructions placed on the roads leading up the relatively gentle southern and western slopes of Shepherd Mountain, and he cleared the steeper northern slope of timber. The northern slope of Shepherd Mountain was within musket range of the fort, and Ewing wanted to create a clear line of fire to discourage an attack from that location. He also deepened the ditch (to somewhat over six feet) in front of the fort's nine-foot parapet. He did what he could to shore up the eroded parapet and he added rifle pits on either side of the fort to extend its defenses.[8]

Ewing had not been educated to be a soldier but he proved himself to be a very competent commander. He was the son of the prominent Ohio Whig politician Thomas Ewing, Sr. The younger Ewing had graduated from Brown University and served as Zachary Taylor's private secretary while his father served as secretary of the interior. At that time the entire Ewing family resided in Washington, DC, and it was there that Ewing's sister married William Tecumseh Sherman. Later in the 1850s, Ewing practiced law in Cincinnati and then moved to Kansas to promote railroad construction. When the Civil War began, he raised the Eleventh Kansas Infantry Regiment to which he was elected colonel. His successes in the field led to his promotion to brigadier general in March 1863. It was Ewing who had issued General Order No. 11 in retaliation for Quantrill's raid on Lawrence, Kansas. When Price learned that Ewing was at Pilot Knob he made it his first priority to strike against that Federal garrison.[9]

As planned, Price's three columns formed a junction at Fredericktown. Fagan and Price joined Shelby there on September 24; Marmaduke arrived on September 25. The division commanders conferred with Price that night. Shelby wanted

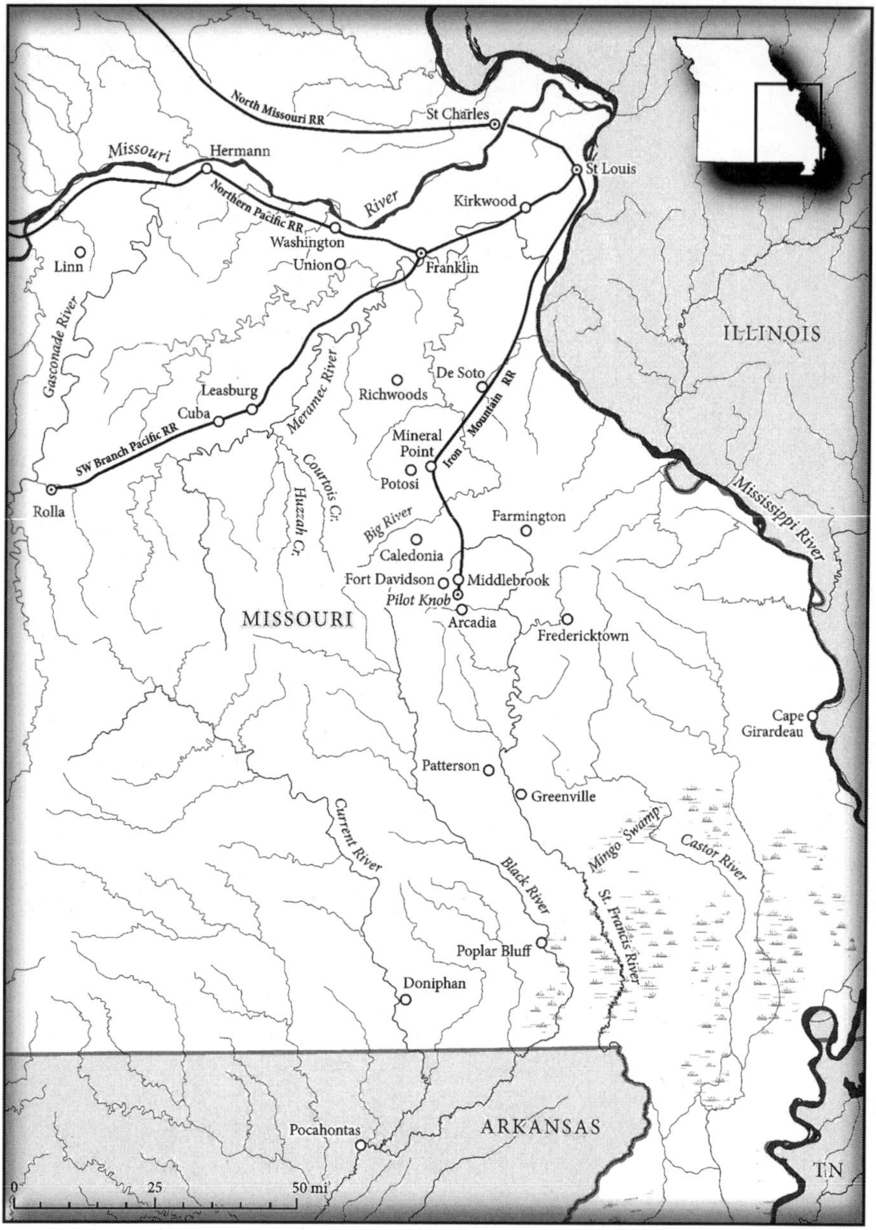

to bypass Pilot Knob and strike directly at St. Louis. Marmaduke and Fagan favored attacking Pilot Knob to gain needed arms and supplies. They also thought it could be dangerous to leave a significant Federal force in their rear. Price did not immediately issue orders regarding an attack on Fort Davidson, but early the next morning (September 26), he sent Shelby north of Pilot Knob to destroy rail bridges and sections of the Iron Mountain Railroad. At the same time, Price sent Marmaduke's and Fagan's divisions west to Arcadia.[10]

Fagan's division led the march to Arcadia. At Fort Davidson, Ewing learned that a Confederate army was concentrating at Fredericktown. On the morning of September 26 he sent two companies south to scout the road to Ironton (a distance of about two miles south of Pilot Knob) and the road from Ironton east to Fredericktown. Early in the afternoon Ewing's scouts skirmished with Fagan's advance troops east of Ironton in the narrow gorge of Shut-in Gap. The Federals fell back to Ironton where they joined a third company of Federal troops to form a defensive line. Ewing reinforced this position with detachments of infantry, artillery, and cavalry. The Union troops succeeded in driving the Confederates back to Shut-in Gap, but as the main body of Fagan's and Marmaduke's divisions moved up, the Federal force gradually fell back to Ironton. Nightfall and rain brought a halt to the fighting.[11]

Rosecrans had directed Ewing to hold Fort Davidson against detachments of rebel troops but to evacuate the position if faced with Price's entire command. Rosecrans's overriding concern was to keep as many of Ewing's and Smith's troops as possible between Price and St. Louis. By midnight Ewing felt certain that most of Price's army had arrived in the Arcadia valley. But he resolved to make a stand at Fort Davidson believing that he could slow and perhaps blunt Price's invasion before retreating toward the defenses of St. Louis. As Ewing prepared for the expected Confederate attack he sent north by rail all of the quartermaster and commissary stores not immediately needed by his men as well as all railroad rolling stock and quartermaster wagons. He also put his engineers to work constructing six "barbettes," platforms that allowed his gunners to fire down from the fort's parapets. General Smith had deployed his troops at DeSoto and Mineral Point, and Ewing reported to him regularly by telegraph until the line was cut at about 11:00 a.m. on September 27.[12]

Earlier on the morning of September 27, Fagan and Marmaduke began a coordinated advance and steadily drove the Federal troops through the Arcadia valley toward the defenses of Fort Davidson. Where the Ironton road crossed Knob Creek, Pilot Knob Mountain rose to the north and Shepherd Mountain rose to the south to form a narrow valley known as Ironton Gap. Here Ewing formed a new defensive line, locating infantry on the eastern slope of Shepherd Mountain and cavalry on the western slope of Pilot Knob. For a time Federal forces held their ground at Ironton Gap. Price sent a mounted force around Shepherd Mountain to probe the defenses of Fort Davidson from the west. As these Confederates rounded Shepherd Mountain and approached the fort, they found themselves badly exposed in open terrain where they were easily driven away by two companies of skirmishers supported by the fort's artillery. Ewing reported that Price's men twice displayed a flag of truce; but Ewing had no intention of discussing the terms of his surrender and he directed his men to ignore the flags.

Price pressed his attack on the Federal line at Ironton Gap. Marmaduke advanced on the rebel left over the eastern slope of Shepherd Mountain. Fagan advanced on the right over the western slope of Pilot Knob. Ewing watched as his men retreated and as "the enemy followed them along the hill-sides in strong force." But as Price's men approached the fort, they were driven back by artillery and the Federals briefly retook the gap. By this time, however, Price had located two artillery pieces on Shepherd Mountain, and Ewing quickly brought all of his forces and their artillery into the relative security of the fort.[13]

Marmaduke located his division of about three thousand men along the northern slope of Shepherd Mountain where they were supported by the field guns. Fagan deployed his four thousand troops along the northern slope of Pilot Knob. Price had decided to storm the fort with his infantry rather than take the time necessary to deploy more artillery on Shepherd Mountain and conduct a bombardment that would eventually force Ewing's surrender. Price, Fagan, and Marmaduke apparently agreed that they could make short work of Fort Davidson and move on before more Federal forces could be concentrated against them.

Price believed that he had Ewing trapped. To the north Shelby's division cut the Iron Mountain Railroad and prevented reinforcement from reaching Ewing. Price also believed that Shelby blocked a retreat by Ewing along the railroad and the parallel Middlebrook road. During the assault on Fort Davidson, Price also detached a brigade from Fagan's division and moved it north of the fort to block any Federal retreat along the Potosi road.[14]

The Confederate assault on Fort Davidson began at 2:00 p.m. as their artillery opened fire from Shepherd Mountain. These guns were soon silenced, however, by effective artillery fire from the fort. Federal artillery fire also tore into the ranks of Marmaduke's and Fagan's troops who now faced a daunting task of crossing nine hundred yards of open ground. Price had directed Marmaduke and Fagan to take care to press forward in a coordinated attack to maximize the Confederate's numerical advantage. But when Fagan's division advanced, it was not immediately joined by Marmaduke's troops. Fagan's division swept onto the open ground on the southeast side of the fort, presenting themselves, as Ewing reported, "In handsome style, yelling and on the double-quick." Federal troops opened fire on the rebels with musket fire from the fort and from the northern line of rifle pits. The seven guns in the fort fired canister into the Confederate ranks. Ewing described the bloody assault: "They rushed on most gallantly but were broken, confused, and swept down by our rapid and well-directed fire until the advance reached the ditch, when the attacking forces fled in dismay, leaving apparently almost half their comrades dead or wounded on the plain."[15]

The concentration of Federal fire caused Fagan's right flank (filled with inexperienced troops) to break away and leave Cabell's seasoned troops alone to press on to the ditch. There, even the best of Fagan's men faltered and then fled in disorder. Marmaduke's division suffered a similar fate. Marmaduke's untested men refused to leave the relative protection of a dry creek bed that traversed the plain about halfway between the base of Shepherd Mountain and the fort. Only Clark's veterans advanced to the fort's ditch where they, too, wavered and then fled back to the creek bed.[16]

With nightfall the fighting ended, and Ewing learned from prisoners that Price had entered Missouri with about twelve thousand men and ten field guns. He also learned that Shelby's division had moved north from Fredericktown to Farmington. As Ewing took stock of his situation, he realized he could not hold the hillsides to his south and thereby prevent Price from locating more artillery there. Also, Ewing had lost about a quarter of his force since the fighting began at Shut-in Gap. The Federal commander decided to evacuate the fort that night and attempt to form a junction with General Smith to the north in the vicinity of Mineral Point. For his part, Price had seen more than a thousand of his best troops killed in the assault on Ford Davidson. He called off the attack but prepared to resume his assault the next morning. That night Price tried to get word to Shelby to rejoin the main force at Pilot Knob. Shelby never got these instructions. Expecting Shelby's return, Price instructed his troops to prepare scaling ladders for a fresh assault on Fort Davidson.

That evening Ewing planned his evacuation. He knew the dangers facing him once he moved his command outside the protection of the fort. Making matters worse for Ewing, Price's men had set fire to an ironworks at the north base of Pilot Knob. Iron workers had gathered what Ewing described as an "immense pile of charcoal" to fire the iron furnace. Flames from the burning ironworks ignited the charcoal, and in Ewing's description, it now "glowed and flamed all night, making the valley as light as noonday." The only escape route available to Ewing was the Potosi road, if he could make his way past the brigade of Fagan's troops camped nearby.[17]

Ewing began preparing his men for retreat at midnight, and the evacuation started at 3:00 a.m. Ewing assigned his second in command, Colonel Thomas Fletcher (soon to be Missouri's governor-elect) the task of manufacturing a slow fuse to blow up the fort's large magazine an hour after the evacuation was complete. Fletcher then led the infantry out the fort's sally port, around the ditch, and into the shadow of the north rifle pits. The Federals used tents on the drawbridge to muffle the sound of horse hoofs and artillery caissons. They followed a "byway to the Potosi road" and successfully eluded Fagan's Confederates camped nearby. Ewing's deceptions worked surprisingly well. Price initially thought that the predawn explosion of the fort's magazine was caused by an accident. Several more hours passed before Price discovered Ewing's departure. Belatedly Marmaduke led the Confederate cavalry in pursuit.[18]

At Caledonia, Ewing routed a detachment of about twenty-five Confederates and learned that Shelby had taken Potosi and that General Smith had retreated from Mineral Point. Indeed, Smith had also retreated from DeSoto and positioned himself at Kirkwood, north of the Meramec River. This was consistent with Rosecrans's directions to hold "the most advanced position compatible with the certainty of keeping between the enemy and St. Louis." Ewing realized that it was no longer possible for him to form a junction with Smith. Ewing left the Potosi road and continued his retreat to the northwest, heading toward Rolla. The enemy troops that Ewing drove off at Caledonia were advance elements of Shelby's division, which was now making its way south from Potosi to rejoin Price at Pilot Knob. Unaware that Ewing had diverted his retreat to the northwest, Shelby paused to prepare a defensive line two miles north of Caledonia intending to block what he supposed was Ewing's retreat to Potosi. Price's tardy response to Ewing's evacuation and Shelby's deployment north of Caledonia gave Ewing essential time to move unmolested about thirty miles northwest of Pilot Knob.[19]

At sundown on September 27, Ewing paused to rest his troops until midnight and then resumed his march. Realizing that taking the main road leading west to Rolla could potentially expose his command to being surrounded by enemy cavalry, Ewing turned north and followed a "sharp spur of the Ozark range" defined on the east and west by the steep valleys of Courtois and Huzza Creeks. Along this route Ewing's flanks were protected by "the gorge of the Huzza [and] walled in with untraversable cliffs." This route led to Leasburg and to the southern branch of the Pacific Railroad. As Ewing's retreat continued on September 28, Marmaduke's cavalry began to skirmish with the Federal rear guard. The mountainous terrain made it nearly impossible for Marmaduke's cavalry to flank the Federal force and halt its retreat. About four miles from the rail line, however, the Leasburg road left the rugged but protective terrain behind and passed over a stretch of rolling wooded hills. Here Marmaduke made a concerted effort to flank Ewing's force before it could reach the railroad line and the defensive breastworks located there.[20]

This proved a critical moment for the survival of Ewing's command. The civilian refugees who retreated with the Federal troops from Pilot Knob—"men, women, and children, white and black"—panicked as the Confederates pressed their attack. The "affrighted non-combatants" nearly "sacrificed" his command, Ewing reported. But the Federal troops managed repeatedly to unlimber their artillery and "stagger the pursuers with a few rounds, and move on." That night behind the breastworks that protected the rail line Ewing's men could see the nearest railroad stations to the northeast and southwest in flames. They spent the night fortifying their position at Leasburg. The next morning the Confederates returned and sporadic fighting continued through the night and into the next morning. At about 2:00 p.m. on September 30 the Confederates broke off their attack and within an hour Ewing had learned the reason. At 4:00 p.m. a Federal cavalry force of five hundred men arrived from Rolla. Now with strong cavalry support, Ewing completed his retreat to Rolla. On October 6, with "pride and pleasure," Rosecrans praised "the gallant conduct" of Ewing and his men.[21]

Price remained in Pilot Knob until September 29. He then directed Shelby to feint toward St. Louis, as he moved the main body of his troops north through Potosi and arrived at Richwoods on September 30. Fagan sent three hundred men to burn the rail depot at DeSoto while Cabell's brigade tore up a section of the Pacific Railroad east of Franklin. Meanwhile, Marmaduke sent a detachment to burn the railroad depot at Cuba. As they passed through the countryside, the Confederates tore up several miles of the southern branch of the Pacific Railroad. Advancing from Union, Marmaduke took Washington on October 2 and Hermann on October 3. On October 4, Marmaduke detached four hundred men to destroy the Pacific Railroad Bridge over the Gasconade River and a portion of Shelby's division took Linn. Price's army then forced crossings of the Osage about seven miles southeast of Jefferson City. Five miles east of the state capital, Price drove the Federal defenders into their entrenchments and then went into camp two miles south of Jefferson City. Price had skirted the defenses of St. Louis. He also avoided the fortifications at Jefferson City. Instead, he moved on to Boonville and sent M. Jeff Thompson with about one thousand men to take Sedalia.[22]

In central Missouri, Price expected to benefit substantially from the support of friendly civilian populations in the state's large slaveholding counties. He also expected to gain support from guerrillas. Earlier in September, Price had managed to get a message delivered to the guerrilla chief George Todd, informing that veteran of the first battle of Independence that Confederates would soon invade Missouri. Price asked Todd and other guerrilla leaders to assist by attacking Union outposts and disrupting Federal communications and supply lines. On September 24, while Price gathered his forces at Fredericktown, guerrillas led by William ("Bloody Bill") Anderson rendezvoused with several guerrilla bands south of Fayette in Howard County. Todd was there, as was William Quantrill and John Thrailkill. It was unusual for guerrillas to gather in such large numbers. They typically operated in bands of fifty or fewer and remained elusive by breaking into even smaller groups when attacked. Near Fayette, however, the guerrilla leaders brought together as many as two hundred men, and most were eager to attack the Federal garrison there. Quantrill demurred. He deemed the Federal position to be too strong and rode off while the remaining guerrillas prepared to attack.[23]

Anderson's men planned to lead the Fayette raid. Wearing Federal uniforms, they were accustomed to having the advantage of surprise as they moved close to an unsuspecting enemy before unleashing an attack. At Fayette, however, the presence of a black man in a Federal uniform infuriated Anderson's men. They shot the black soldier and prematurely alerted the defenders to their presence. The guerrillas were badly exposed in the street as the Federal soldiers fired into their ranks from the protection of brick and stone buildings. Badly shot up, the guerrillas rode out of Fayette without the loot they had hoped to gather. But the massing of guerrillas in Howard and Boone Counties led to the massacre of unarmed Federal troops at Centralia on September 27 and the destruction of Major Ave Johnson's pursuing militia command later that day. The guerrillas were brutal, but they could also be militarily effective. Price hoped that the guerrilla attacks would keep Federal forces off balance and ill prepared to consolidate to resist his invasion. When Price marched into Boonville on October 10, the leading guerrilla chiefs came to meet with him.[24]

At Boonville, Price gave the guerrillas legitimacy as Confederate partisan rangers. He directed Anderson to move north of the Missouri River and destroy the North Missouri Railroad from central Missouri toward St. Charles, "as far east as practicable." Price also directed Quantrill to destroy the Hannibal–St. Joseph line. Todd's men served as scouts as Price continued to drive westward. But the guerrillas did not serve Price well. Anderson burned depots as far east as Montgomery County but soon turned west again to loot in the rear of Price's army, taking advantage of the retreat of Federal forces toward Independence and Kansas City. Quantrill's band had grown too small to do much damage, and the eagerness of Todd's men to murder Federal prisoners exacerbated the lack of military discipline that had plagued Price's command from the beginning of the Missouri expedition. In his final report, Price acknowledged detaching Anderson and Quantrill for partisan raids, but he criticized them for utterly failing to accomplish their tasks.[25]

On October 13, Price left Boonville and established a camp a few miles west at Chouteau Springs. From there he dispatched General John B. Clark's brigade to capture the Federal garrison at Glasgow several miles upstream from Boonville. It was probably not a coincidence that Clark's wife was in Glasgow, living in the household of the wealthy planter Benjamin Lewis. The Clarks may have believed that their home in Fayette was vulnerable to guerrilla attack despite their southern sympathies. Fayette had a small Federal garrison that had managed to drive off a guerrilla attack, but Glasgow, about ten miles to the northwest, was more easily defended by Federal forces because of its location on the Missouri River. Price had his eye on Glasgow because he had been told that the Federal government had established a large depot of military supplies there. His army had attracted hundreds of new recruits as it entered central Missouri, and Price was eager to arm them. Price strengthened Clark's brigade with an additional five hundred men and directed Jo Shelby to support the attack on Glasgow with a regiment of infantry and two artillery pieces. The plan was for Shelby to take control of the south bank of the Missouri River opposite Glasgow and to open fire at dawn on October 15 with his artillery and sharpshooters.

An important target for Shelby was the steamer *West Wind*, tied up at the levee and thought to be outfitted as a gunboat. The *West Wind* had been dispatched from Fort Leavenworth by General Samuel Curtis on October 5 to support the supply ship *Benton*, which Curtis dispatched to Lexington to move military stores to safer locations as Price's army advanced toward Jefferson City. The *West*

Wind carried six companies of the Forty-Third Missouri Infantry commanded by Colonel Chester Harding, Jr., a native of Massachusetts and the son of a prominent portrait painter. Harding had graduated from Harvard before moving to St. Louis as a young man where he studied law under the direction of his brother-in-law Judge John M. Krum of the St. Louis Circuit Court. By 1852, Harding was a partner in the prominent St. Louis firm of Krum and Harding. When the Civil War began, Harding first served as an adjutant with Nathaniel Lyon and later raised a regiment and fought with General John Pope at the Battle of Corinth. Now aboard the *West Wind*, Harding's task was to protect the *Benton*, clear the banks of the Missouri of guerrillas, and eventually, make his way to Jefferson City to reinforce the state capital for the expected Confederate attack.[26]

The river was low as the *West Wind* and *Benton* made their way downstream from Fort Leavenworth. The deeper-drafted *West Wind* frequently ran aground. For this reason the riverboats could not travel in the dark, and they needed an infantry force for protection against guerrillas. On the first night out of Leavenworth, Harding's force tied up at Camden. On October 6, Harding landed four companies of troops at Wellington and marched them to Lexington to clear the countryside of guerrillas and to facilitate the landing of the *Benton*. At Lexington, Federal forces freighted the *Benton* with quartermaster and commissary stores not immediately needed by the garrison there. Both the *Benton* and the *West Wind* continued downstream, gathering and distributing supplies and driving off guerrillas. On October 11, near Brunswick, Harding landed troops at the mouth of the Grand River and proceeded cautiously upstream where his Federal troops skirmished with guerrillas and drove them off. On October 12, Harding's force started for Glasgow. The *West Wind* ran aground about a mile above Cambridge and was not able to work its way free until the afternoon of October 13. With his force stalled, Harding received a dispatch from Glasgow indicating that the telegraph line had been cut. The commander of the Federal garrison expected to be attacked by guerrillas and he requested support. Harding arrived at Glasgow on the evening of October 13.[27]

At Glasgow Harding assumed command of a force of 481 officers and men and an additional 150 militiamen and armed citizens. With an effective force of 550 men without artillery, Harding met with his officers "and leading citizens" to plan the town's defenses. From the officers of the troops already garrisoning Glasgow, Harding learned that they had been ordered by General Rosecrans to defend the place if attacked. From the officers and citizens Harding also learned that "no fears of an attack from Price's regular forces had been entertained." What concerned the Federal officers and the leading citizens of Glasgow was "the concentration of conscripts and bushwhackers" in the vicinity. Harding now knew that Jefferson City was no longer in danger and that Price's main force was downstream at Boonville and Arrow Rock. He decided against any further movement toward the state capital and agreed to support the Federal forces in Glasgow, at least until the telegraph could be repaired and the immediate danger of guerrilla attack dissipated. Harding sent the *Benton* back upstream to Fort Leavenworth, and it successfully made the trip without infantry support. Deemed an encumbrance because it drew too much water, the *West Wind* remained moored at the Glasgow levee.

Benjamin Lewis was undoubtedly one of the leading citizens who met with Harding and convinced him to add the strength of his command to the town's defenses. Lewis had been one of the largest slaveholders in the state. He had owned 150 slaves when the war began, and although he was now in the process of becoming an employer of free labor, he remained one of the state's wealthiest tobacco planters and cigar manufacturers. The Lewis home north of Glasgow was one of the grandest mansions in the state. Lewis had family ties through marriage to Confederate generals Clark and Shelby, and Harding undoubtedly knew that Clark's wife resided at the Lewis home. The leading citizens who met with Harding must have impressed upon him the reality that despite Lewis's kinship ties with leading southerners, he and his social circle in Glasgow were staunch Unionists and that their wealth together with their loyalties made them visible and vulnerable targets for guerrilla attacks. Harding located two companies of troops near the Lewis home. That force soon held off a regiment of Clark's Confederate troops as they advanced toward Glasgow along the Keytesville road.

Harding prepared to defend Glasgow from guerrilla attack and considered "the garrison of the place, re-enforced by my command . . . ample to defend it." He knew that Price's main force had reached the Missouri River at Boonville, but he also believed (wrongly) that Price had been "routed" at Jefferson City and that the Confederate army was closely hemmed in by pursuing Federal troops. Confident that he could defend the loyal citizens of Glasgow from marauding guerrillas, Harding sent mounted patrols two miles out of town to scout on the Keytesville and Huntsville roads to the north and on the Fayette and Boonville Plank roads to the south. Harding also removed the plank flooring of the bridges crossing Greggs Creek south of town and Bear Creek north of town and stationed strong infantry forces at both places to control these approaches to Glasgow. Perceiving the greatest threat of attack to be from Fayette and Boonville, Harding also positioned infantry at regular intervals along a ridge running eastward from the Missouri River to the Fayette road.[28]

On October 14 Shelby and Clark moved toward Glasgow with regular Confederate troops. Shelby did not need to cross the Missouri to reach his assigned position, and as planned, he opened fire on the *West Wind* and on the town's defenders at 5:00 a.m. on October 15. The Missouri River bends sharply above Glasgow and flows directly south past the town. Shelby's artillery and sharpshooters fired on the town from the west while Clark planned to encircle the town on three sides with his flanks anchored at the river. Difficulties in crossing the river at Arrow Rock had delayed Clark. His troops were still three miles south of Glasgow when they heard Shelby's artillery open fire. Clark approached Glasgow at 7:00 a.m. and found the Federals arrayed in a defensive line along Greggs Creek. Clark soon learned that the Federals were stretched thin. Confederates outnumbered the Union troops by at least two to one and the defenders of Glasgow were quickly forced to fall back to town where their defensive line was extremely compact and buildings, fences, and recently constructed rifle pits provided protection. In addition, the high ground at the center of town offered some defensive advantage.[29]

Clark's brigade faced determined resistance but steadily forced the enemy into their fortifications on Hereford Hill. As Harding's adjutant later reported, the Federal right flank and its center were very closely engaged by the Confederates. The combatants were "separated by only the width of village lots, our boys sheltered by the front fence and the enemy firing from behind those in the rear." Shelby's sharpshooters made it exceedingly dangerous for Federal troops to cross streets that led to the river. Shelby's artillery also disabled the *West Wind* and inflicted considerable damage on nearby buildings. As Clark's brigade came into the field in force, the Federal defenders managed to turn back several assaults. They were particularly successful on the north side of town near the Lewis house. By noon, however, after eight hours of fighting, it was clear to Harding that a Confederate victory was inevitable. At 1:00 p.m. Clark positioned his artillery for a final assault, and Harding asked if his adversary would accept an honorable surrender. Clark agreed that Harding's men would be treated as prisoners of war, that they could keep their personal property, and that officers could keep their side arms. The personal property of the town's residents would also be respected. At 1:30 p.m. Harding surrendered his command. With no capacity to house prisoners, Clark paroled Harding and his men. Price had dispatched a steamboat to Glasgow to bring Shelby's men across the river for the final assault. When the boat arrived, it carried Harding and his men across the Missouri and they made their way with a Confederate escort to Boonville.[30]

Clark did not find the huge cache of military stores he had expected. The *Benton* had made its way back to Leavenworth with most of what Clark had fought to acquire. The Confederates did gather up some supplies, however, particularly a large number of winter coats. They were blue coats, however, and it must have caused Clark some concern when he allowed them to be distributed among his men. Soon many of the Confederate regulars, as well as the guerrillas, were dressed in Union blue. The ominous shadow of guerrilla war fell over the battle of Glasgow in other ways as well. Unionists and Federal forces in Glasgow had protected Clark's wife at the Lewis house, and Clark took care to protect the paroled Federal prisoners as they were escorted to Boonville. With obvious relief, Harding's adjutant made special notice of "the uniform, kind, and gentlemanly treatment we received at the hands of the Confederate officers." Among the officers recognized in this regard were Clark and Shelby, of course, but also William

Quantrill. Clark probably enjoyed a visit with his wife in Glasgow. He then made his way back across the Missouri River on October 17 and rejoined Price's army on October 18.[31]

The withdrawal of Confederate troops from Glagow left the town defenseless to guerrilla attack. Clark and Shelby had made good on their pledge to protect civilians and their property. Now they were gone. Notwithstanding his "gentlemanly" demeanor at Harding's surrender, Quantrill returned to Glasgow on the evening of October 17 and robbed the bank of twenty-one thousand dollars. He and his men then rode off without inflicting further damage. But the arrival of Bloody Bill Anderson on October 21 brought a reign of terror to town, particularly to the Lewis household. After raiding the North Missouri Railroad as directed by Price, Anderson turned west to plunder in the wake of Price's army. Suddenly he turned east and made his way to Glasgow where he descended on the Lewis home. Suffering threats and blows, Lewis tried to placate the guerrilla leader with a cash payment of one thousand dollars. That sum was not nearly enough to satisfy Anderson. Over the protestations of Mrs. Clark (who in vain presented the guerrilla chieftain with a letter from her husband thanking Lewis for his hospitality), Anderson subjected Lewis to brutal beatings in his home and in the streets. The torture did not cease until Lewis's relatives and friends collected another five thousand dollars for Anderson. Lewis never fully recovered from his ordeal and died in his early forties in February 1866.[32]

Price's army united again on October 17 at Marshall, and the next day they advanced to Shelby's hometown of Waverly. Discipline had been fragile since the beginning of the expedition. When the Confederate army passed through central Missouri where many of the men had homes, desertion and disorder become commonplace. In large numbers, and without seeking official leave, many men went home. Amid the disarray Fagan complained that no effort was made to supply his Arkansas troops with rations. In a remarkable communication to Price, Fagan admonished his commander concerning the duties of "the proper officers of the staff of the army." It was the responsibility of Price and his staff to locate and distribute rations. His men, Fagan wrote, "deem it strange that in such a plentiful country as the one in which we are now operating breadstuffs cannot be supplied at least while we are moving so leisurely."[33]

As Price's Confederates passed through central Missouri, Rosecrans belatedly devised plans to trap him. Rosecrans followed Price westward with forty-five hundred cavalry under General Alfred Pleasonton (a veteran of the eastern campaigns who recently had been transferred to central Missouri) and nine thousand infantry under General A.J. Smith who had been reinforced by General Joseph A. Mower from Arkansas. To the west, Price faced Curtis who commanded the Department of Kansas. On Price's march from Jefferson City to Boonville, Pleasonton's mounted troops engaged Price from the rear, slowing him as more Union troops joined the chase. But, with telegraph wires cut, Rosecrans found it difficult to communicate effectively with Curtis or to coordinate with him. Curtis prepared three lines of defense to prepare his command for Price's advancing army. Curtis deployed the black troops under his command to labor on the fortifications. They were joined, Curtis reported, by civilians of all walks of life: "lawyers, doctors, divines, and merchants entered the service." Curtis's first line of defense was on the west bank of the Big Blue River, a few miles west of Independence. Curtis constructed a second line of defense south and east of Kansas City, Missouri. If these defensive lines were breached, Wyandotte, Kansas, on the north bank of the Kansas River "would be a dernier resort." Curtis positioned Major General James G. Blunt with the US Volunteers at Hickman Mills, Missouri, on the Federal right wing south of Westport. He positioned General George Deitzler with the Kansas militia at Shawneetown, Kansas, on his left wing. Curtis directed Blunt to demonstrate in the direction of Warrensburg while Deitzler demonstrated in the direction of Lexington. Soon, Curtis hoped, he would locate Price's army and determine its size and movements.[34]

Blunt was eager for a fight. He had been in command of Federal troops that had fallen victim to Quantrill's murderous attack at Baxter Springs, Kansas, in October 1863 (Curtis's son had died in the attack). Blunt had arrived at Fort Leavenworth from Arkansas on October 9. By October 15 he had moved into camp at Hickman Mills. Because Deitzler was reluctant to move his Kansas militiamen very far away from the Missouri border, the task of searching for Price fell to Blunt and his two thousand regulars. Blunt first advanced southeastward, arriving at Pleasant Hill shortly after midnight on the morning on October 17. He then proceeded eastward on the Warrensburg road. About ten miles east of Pleasant Hill, Blunt encountered a squad of Missouri militiamen and Union civilians fleeing westward. They reported that Shelby had taken Sedalia and they feared he would move next on Warrensburg. Blunt sent scouts forward to reconnoiter at Warrensburg. He soon learned that after taking Sedalia Shelby had rejoined Price and the Confederate army was now near Waverly. Blunt then occupied Lexington and prepared to meet the enemy south of that place, keeping the Independence Rroad to his rear as an avenue of retreat.[35]

For the first time in his Missouri expedition, Price faced a significant military force to his front. On October 19, Shelby's column led the Confederate advance from Waverly to Lexington. Skirmishing continued for nearly two hours as Price slowly brought his army forward. Finally, when Price deployed his long-range artillery, Blunt realized his short-range mountain howitzers "could not reply with effect." With an overwhelming advantage in numbers, Price tried to envelope both flanks of the Federal force, but Blunt successfully retreated toward Independence. During the retreat, Blunt's mountain howitzers effectively supported a succession of rearguard actions. At 9:00 a.m. on October 20, Blunt reached the crossing of the Little Blue River, about nine miles east of Independence. On the west bank of the river he set up a new defensive line and sent a dispatch to

Independence requesting rations and reinforcements. Curtis, however, did not plan to make a major fight at the Little Blue. He wanted to slow Price's advance to give his engineers and laborers as much time as possible to strengthen the defenses on the west bank of the Big Blue. Instead of sending reinforcements, Curtis ordered Blunt to leave a small force on the Little Blue and to fall back with the bulk of his command to Independence.[36]

Somewhat reluctantly Blunt obeyed. He left Colonel Thomas Moonlight on the Little Blue with orders to burn the bridge and hold the ford as long as possible. A native of Scotland, Moonlight had emigrated to the United States as a young man and served in the army. When the Civil War began, he joined the Eleventh Kansas Cavalry as colonel; his task now was to slow Price's advance while Curtis dug in beyond the Big Blue and Pleasonton pressed against Price's rear.

On the morning of October 21, Curtis met with Deitzler at Independence and directed the Kansas militia commander to occupy the defenses at the Big Blue, bring up all his available forces, and prepare for battle there. Curtis noted that the sound of fighting coming from the Little Blue imbued Deitzler "with fresh zeal and energy." Curtis's defensive line west of the Big Blue stretched about fifteen miles from the Missouri River to the north to Hickman Mills to the south. There Curtis had assembled a defensive force of about fifteen thousand men, including "a considerable colored force." With his main defensive line in place, Curtis moved forward with Blunt to support Moonlight. They rejoined the Scotsman at 10:00 a.m. on October 21. By this time Moonlight had been forced to fall back about two miles from the Little Blue. Curtis and Blunt found him holding a new defensive line where his men were protected by stone walls, fences, and houses. With Blunt's return, the Federals managed to push the Confederates back for a time, but again Price's superiority in numbers gradually took effect. Blunt slowly withdrew as the enemy again threatened to outflank him. Moonlight mounted a series of rearguard actions to support the retreat, and Blunt's men skirmished with rebels though the streets of Independence. At nightfall, the fighting ceased. By midnight, Blunt had relocated his entire force in the prepared defenses on the west bank of the Big Blue. Earlier that afternoon Rosecrans managed to telegraph Curtis informing him that Pleasonton's cavalry had reached Lexington that morning and the Federal infantry would arrive there that evening. Curtis continued to strengthen his defenses at the Big Blue. At 5:00 p.m. he telegraphed Rosecrans that he was confident that he could stop Price. And if Rosecrans could move to Hickman Mills, Curtis was confident that "we will bag Price."[37]

Blunt successfully slowed Price at Lexington and at the Little Blue. This gave Pleasonton time to press Price from the east. And the presence of Pleasonton alarmed Price, whose movement across Missouri had been unhurried. Once he turned west from Ironton, the Federal garrisons in front of him had posed no significant threat. Passing through central Missouri, Price's men steadily gathered up commissary supplies, weapons, ammunition, and booty. By the time they reached Lexington, the Confederate army carried with it six hundred heavily laden wagons and three thousand head of cattle. Now, however, Price felt the need to move quickly. With Curtis moving toward him out of Kansas and Pleasonton attacking his rear Price realized he could be trapped, with his route of retreat into Arkansas cut off. From Price's perspective, it was essential for him to cross the Big Blue and defeat Curtis before Pleasonton converged on him from the east. With Curtis defeated, Price could continue his retreat controlling Pleasonton's pursuit with rearguard ambushes and attacks. To accomplish this, Price sent Shelby with part of Fagan's division forward to attack Curtis. The rest of Fagan's command guarded the immense Confederate wagon train. Marmaduke mounted rearguard actions to slow Pleasonton while Price struggled to move his army and supplies across the Big Blue.

Fighting on the Big Blue began at 9:00 a.m. on October 22, 1864. On the west bank of the river, Federal forces were well entrenched in formidable defenses extending from the Missouri River to Hickman's Mills. At the two principal crossings of the Big Blue, Moonlight held Simmon's Ford to the north while Blunt defended Byram's Ford further south. Blunt now relied on an old rival, Colonel Charles R. Jennison, to place obstructions in the river and defend the crossing. Both Blunt and the New York–born Jennison had fought with Kansas Jayhawkers during the Border War, but Jennison deeply resented Blunt's rising reputation as a military commander. Jennison resigned his commission as colonel of the Seventh Regiment of Kansas Volunteers in May 1862, shortly after Blunt won promotion from colonel to brigadier general. Thereafter, Jennison's tendency toward banditry grew, and he fought as a partisan with little respect for military discipline. After the Lawrence massacre, however, Governor Carney prevailed on Jennison to raise and lead a new regiment of Kansas militia. Now Jennison followed orders from General Blunt to confront elements of Jo Shelby's division as the Confederates desperately sought to cross the Big Blue.[38]

By 10:00 a.m. Shelby had divided his division to probe the Federal defenses. An hour later, he decided to attack in force at Byram's Ford. Shelby launched a series of attacks against Jennison's brigade and for several hours the Kansans drove them back. By 2:00 p.m., while Jennison's Kansans and Shelby's Missourians continued to fight at Byram's Ford, Shelby led a strong mounted force upstream where they managed to cross the Big Blue and turn Jennison's left flank. Jennison withdrew from Byram's Ford toward the northwest. When Curtis learned that Shelby had broken through his lines above Byram's Ford, he hastened to reform his defensive line south and east of Westport. Fighting continued until nightfall. In the gathering darkness, Curtis saw the enemy campfires spread "over a vast field south and southwest of Westport." Jennison added, "As the night wore on, we seemed encircled by the camp-fires of the rebels, which gleamed menacingly from the woods."[39]

During the night of October 22, the Confederates consolidated their position at Byram's Ford, and Price successfully moved his army across the Big Blue and prepared to advance toward Little Santa Fe and begin his retreat into Arkansas.

Price now controlled all of the Blue River south of Byram's Ford and had captured about one hundred Kansas militiamen who had been cut off by the crossing. But Curtis continued to menace him from the north and Pleasanton pressed in from the east. Price concluded that he could not begin his retreat until he had driven Curtis from the field while he continued to hold off Pleasanton. Byram's Ford now became a vital defensive position for the Confederates. Price positioned Marmaduke's division there to stop Pleasanton while he turned Shelby's division northward in an attempt to drive back Curtis.

During the night, Curtis reorganized his right wing south of Westport. To his rear lay the security of the defenses of Kansas City. There Curtis believed that "the citizens and soldiers had so improved the natural strength" of the place "as to make this position almost impregnable." That evening Curtis learned that Pleasonton had arrived at Independence and had begun to strike at Price's rear as he crossed the Big Blue. Leaving his heavy artillery, as well as the unmounted militia and Home Guard in the Kansas City entrenchments, Curtis went into camp north of Brush Creek, a tributary of the Big Blue flowing east to west south of Westport. Curtis saw the spirits of his troops rise as they regrouped. They were now "well furnished with food, forage, and ammunition," reported Curtis. They also had time to rest before Curtis took the offensive shortly before dawn on October 23.[40]

In the predawn morning darkness, Curtis sent Blunt forward to probe the Confederate lines south of Brush Creek. Blunt crossed the creek but was quickly pushed back by a strong enemy force. The Battle of Westport began at dawn as Jennison, Blunt, and Deitzler attacked Shelby's division at Brush Creek, attempting to drive the rebels from the wooded banks of the creek onto the open prairie to the south. The first Federal advance faltered, and Shelby's men drove the Kansans back across Brush Creek and beyond. It was now 7:30 a.m. Curtis joined Blunt at Westport, and the two men perched themselves on the roof of a hotel to watch as the two armies skirmished and exchanged artillery fire. At 10:00 a.m. the Confederates drove back a second Federal advance. Hoping to move his troops forward, Curtis went to the front and at 11:00 a.m. assumed personal command. After his troops stopped a Confederate advance, Curtis prepared for a third Federal attack. As he surveyed the terrain at Brush Creek, Curtis met a civilian, an old man "with trembling, sinking steps," who led him to a ravine through which Curtis's men moved their field guns to the south side of the creek. With artillery support, Curtis ordered Jennison to attack the center of the Confederate line with all of the mounted men available—Jennison's Kansans, Colonel James H. Ford's Second Colorado Cavalry, four companies of Wisconsin cavalry, and General Blunt's mounted bodyguard. Jennison led the charge, and soon Curtis's entire line advanced onto the prairie south of the creek. As they did so, they heard artillery fire to their left signaling that Pleasonton had engaged Marmaduke at Byram's Ford. Soon a large column of cavalry advanced toward them from the east, about a mile further south. It soon became clear that these were Pleasonton's men. Deitzler described the emotions of the moment: "We are inspired with new and intense interest; we look and listen; we are not long in doubt; we hear the artillery. . . ; they have at last reached us and given the enemy's right a taste of their powder; we now have them; the retreat became a perfect rout; we cannot keep pace with them." At the moment of Union victory, Curtis's thoughts turned to the old man who had guided him across Brush Creek. "Like many other brave Missourians of that day," reported Curtis, the old man "saw the rebellion vanishing before him and his home and country free."[41]

Jennison's charge cleared rebels from the high ground and stone fences south of Brush Creek. Federal troops quickly poured out of the wooded creek bed and occupied the former Confederate positions. Earlier that morning Pleasanton launched his attack on Marmaduke's division at Byram's Ford. After three hours of fighting, Marmaduke fell back and Pleasanton crossed the Big Blue. By 2:00 p.m. Pleasonton had formed a junction with Curtis's left flank and Price was threatened with destruction. Fortunately for Price, General John McNeil had failed to fully carry out Pleasonton's orders to advance from Independence to Little Santa Fe. Pleasonton had sent McNeil in that direction at midnight on October 22, but McNeil and his men had been fighting Price's rear guard all day. The commander decided to rest his horses and men near Byram's Ford before dawn on October 23. He then made his way to Hickman Mills, but he failed to concentrate his forces effectively to block Price's retreat.[42]

Price had been routed at Westport, but he had gained his line of retreat. At 2:30 p.m. Curtis and Pleasonton paused in their pursuit at Indian Creek to meet with Governor Carney and their commanders. Curtis now commanded an army that advanced southward on a front reaching from Hickman Mills to the state line. At Carney's request Curtis discharged the Kansas militia, confident that with Pleasonton's reinforcements he could successfully pursue the weakened Confederates. Curtis and Pleasonton pressed on to Little Santa Fe where they halted for the night. Later that evening, Rosecrans telegraphed the Federal commanders urging them forward and informing them that he would send supplies to them via Pleasant Hill. While at Little Santa Fe, Curtis organized his army of pursuit into two divisions. Blunt commanded the first division, composed of Kansas troops. Pleasonton took command of the second division, composed mostly of troops from Missouri, Iowa, and Indiana. The Federal pursuit of Price continued on the morning of October 24, down the Line Road toward Fort Scott, Kansas.[43]

The Federal pursuit continued all day. By 8:00 p.m. the night had become "very dark and rainy" and Curtis halted. His troops had outrun their supply train but found an abundance of cattle abandoned by the fleeing rebels. While his army ate and rested, Curtis sent scouts forward to keep track of Price's movements. At about 1:00 a.m. on October 25, Curtis learned that his scouts had located a large Confederate camp at the Marais des Cygnes River. Curtis sent a reconnoitering

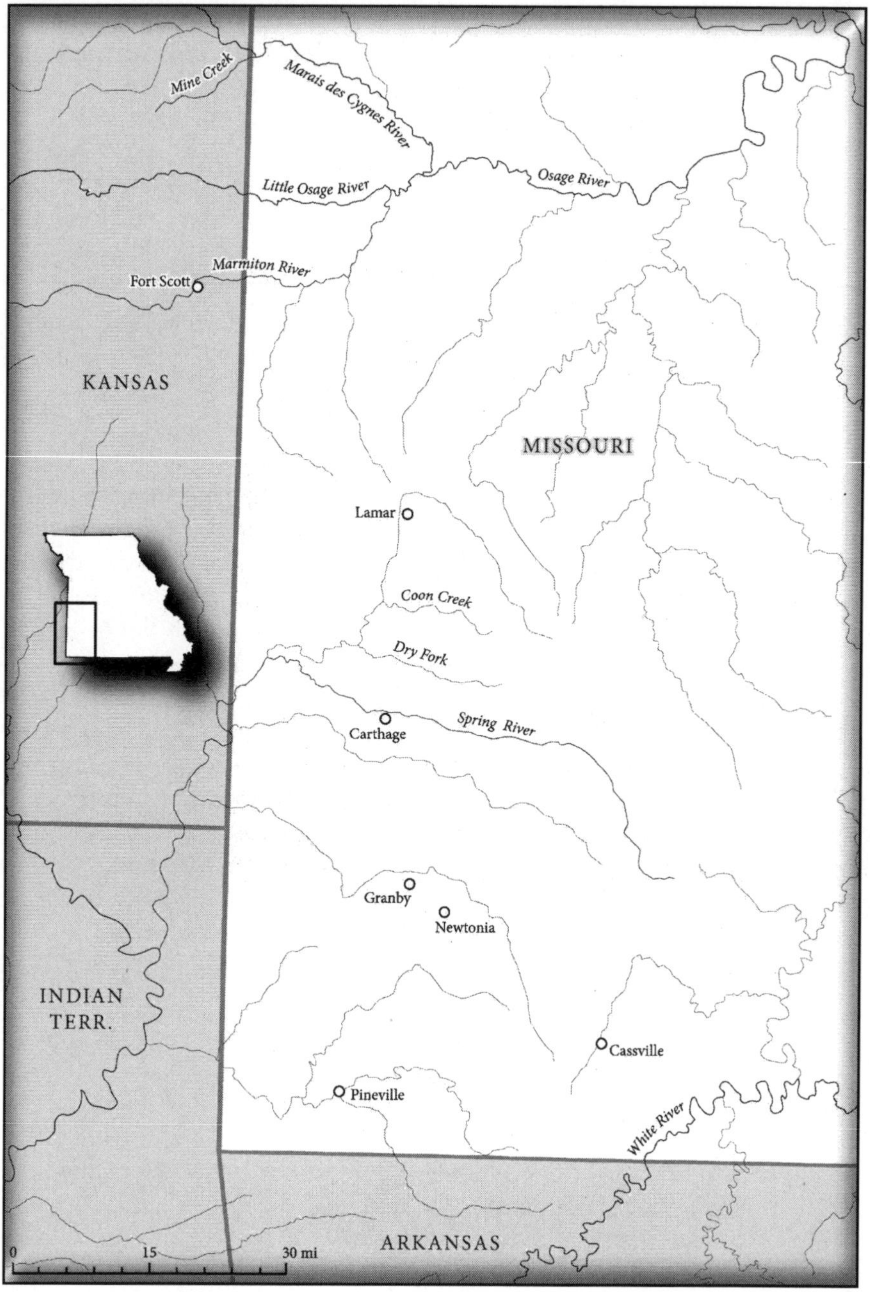
Mine Creek
Marais des Cygnes River
Little Osage River
Osage River
Marmiton River
Fort Scott
KANSAS
MISSOURI
Lamar
Coon Creek
Dry Fork
Carthage
Spring River
Granby
Newtonia
INDIAN TERR.
Cassville
Pineville
White River
ARKANSAS
0
15
30 mi

party forward and launched a predawn attack that drove the startled enemy from their camp and quickly broke up their effort to slow the Federal pursuit at the river's ford. Harassed, but with no foe in front of him, Price continued to make good his escape, but the Federal attacks were nevertheless taking their toll. At the Marais des Cygnes, Price's men abandoned many personal items and supplies as they hastily fled. A few miles further south, Price prepared to pass his wagon train over Mine Creek and the Little Osage. Here again he felt compelled to stand and fight. Between the two streams rose an open prairie. Price mounted a rearguard action that held the Federal troops at bay for two hours while his wagons and troops crossed the Little Osage. Again the Federal attack weakened the retreating Confederates. Curtis watched the fighting on the prairie with a commander's pride and a veteran soldier's sense of awe. "Both armies were in full view," recounted Curtis, "and the rapid onward movement of the whole force presented the most extensive, beautiful, and animated view of hostile armies I have ever witnessed."[44]

In the fighting that day, Federal troops captured two Confederate generals: Brigadier General William L. Cabell, and one of Price's division commanders, Major General John S. Marmaduke. Colonel Charles W. Blair of the Fourteenth Kansas Cavalry witnessed Marmaduke's capture by Corporal James Dunlavy, Company D of the Third Iowa Cavalry. Blair saw Dunlavy galloping toward Price firing his carbine. In the confusion of battle, Marmaduke seemed to mistake Dunlavy for one of his own men. Desperately trying to rally his men to stop a Federal cavalry charge, Marmaduke rode toward Dunlavy, apparently to reprimand him for firing on friendly troops. Dunlavy reined his horse to a stop and calmly waited until Marmaduke came within twenty or thirty yards of him. Although badly wounded in his right forearm, Dunlavy retained enough strength and composure to level his carbine at the general and order him to dismount. Marmaduke did so and quickly appealed to Blair, as a fellow officer, for protection. Blair found Marmaduke a new mount and then escorted the defeated Confederate general with Corporal Dunlavy to General Curtis.[45]

The fighting at Marais des Cygnes and Mine Creek produced another welcome outcome for Federal forces. After crossing the Little Osage, Price left the Fort Scott road and "bearing a little east of south his movement soon rendered it certain" that he had abandoned the idea of attacking Fort Scott. Price made a stand again at the Marmiton River and again took a beating at the hands of the pursuing Federals. After that fight Pleasonton took his cavalry to Fort Scott for what he believed was a well-deserved rest. Curtis had wanted to camp in the field and send back to Fort Scott for supplies, but Blunt had already joined Pleasonton. Curtis soon acquiesced, and he and his men too enjoyed a good meal and a comfortable night's sleep at Fort Scott. On the morning of October 26, Price took advantage of the Federal withdrawal and continued his retreat, turning eastward to cross back into Missouri in Barton County about twenty-five miles from Fort

Scott. Price now headed toward Lamar. The Federal respite at Fort Scott had allowed Price to put some significant distance between his army and his enemy.

Curtis now continued his pursuit of Price into Missouri, without Pleasonton who remained with his troops at Fort Scott. At 3:00 a.m. on October 28, Curtis rested "at the ruins of Carthage." Later that day, at Diamond Grove Prairie north of Granby, Price paroled his Federal prisoners, easing Curtis's concern about their treatment. Curtis now passed through Granby and approached Newtonia. Blunt led the Federal forces through Newtonia and located Price's camp on the Pineville road south of town. Again Curtis attacked, broke up the rebel camp, and drove Price south toward Cassville.[46]

Curtis went into camp the evening of October 28 confident that he could capture Price in the Ozark or Boston Mountains before the remnants of the Confederate army could reach the Arkansas River. But on the morning of October 29 he received a dispatch (dated October 27) from Pleasonton at Fort Scott saying that new orders had been received from General Rosecrans at Warrensburg. Rosecrans directed Curtis to stop his pursuit of Price and disband his command. Curtis was to return to Fort Leavenworth and his brigade commanders, Generals John B. Sanborn and John McNeil, were to return to Springfield and Rolla respectively. Curtis was loath to obey. He was convinced that Pleasonton, who claimed that ill health required him to remain at Fort Scott, had successfully lobbied Rosecrans to resume a defensive posture in Missouri. Although Curtis was more than sixty miles away from the nearest telegraph office, he managed to get a message to Halleck in Washington, DC, challenging Rosecrans's order. At midnight on October 29, Curtis received a telegraphic reply from Halleck stating that General Grant (now lieutenant general and commander in chief of all Federal forces) wanted Price pursued to the Arkansas River. Armed with these directions from Rosecrans's superior, Curtis called back his withdrawn brigades and directed them to join him at Cassville. There Curtis reassembled a force of about one thousand mounted troops and continued his pursuit of Price. In northwest Arkansas, Price and Curtis revisited the familiar terrain of Pea Ridge. Price attacked a Federal garrison at Fayetteville but withdrew as Curtis approached. Price succeeded in crossing the Arkansas River and evaded capture, but his Confederate army had been destroyed as a fighting force. Curtis stopped at the Arkansas River and returned to Fort Scott in easy marches scouring the nearly barren countryside for forage and food.[47]

Rosecrans remained in command in Missouri until early December when the War Department transferred him to Cincinnati. The Massachusetts-born Iowan Grenville Dodge became the new commander of the Department of Missouri until July 1865. Dodge presided over a military district that was now free of organized Confederate military units, a point made official by Governor Thomas Fletcher on March 7, 1865. But guerrillas, typically in small bands of ten or less, continued to raid. Now, following Price's retreat and with the surrender of Kirby

Smith’s Arkansas command, all legitimate pretexts for partisan warfare had vanished. Federal forces had always dealt harshly with guerrillas. It was now openly Federal policy to kill them on sight. General E. B. Brown reported on January 16 that troops under his command had repeatedly skirmished with small bands of guerrillas in Texas County. Over several days, the Federal soldiers killed nine guerrillas and wounded one (who managed to escape). The Federal soldiers “must be good marksmen,” quipped General Brown, “as it is seldom so large a proportion of [their] hits prove fatal.” The guerrilla chieftain Jim Jackson continued to operate north of the Missouri River. A former Texas Ranger who had fought with John Hunt Morgan in Kentucky, Jackson supported Price’s Missouri expedition by launching a twelve-hour raid into southeast Iowa on October 12. Federal patrols tracked him down near Glasgow in mid-January 1865. They killed a companion and forced Jackson to flee on foot leaving behind his boots and hat. On the dead guerrilla, the Federal soldiers found a belt with six pistols. Jackson continued to elude Federal forces until eventually he was captured and hanged in June 1865. William Quantrill left Missouri for Kentucky where he too died in June 1865. Other guerrillas continued to fight, and the exploits of Jesse James (not yet fifteen when the first shots of the war in Missouri were fired at Boonville in June 1861) enlivened a popular culture that cherished the memory of the Lost Cause. The military campaigns of the Civil War had ended; the national task of assigning meaning to the Civil War had just begun.[48]

CONCLUSION

Frank Blair, arguably the most aggressive Unionist in Missouri during the secession crisis, returned to the state in June 1865 after three years of military service in the field. Blair had led the fight against Governor Claiborne Jackson's policy of armed neutrality in the spring of 1861, and he had briefly seen military action in Missouri at the battle of Boonville. Elected to Congress in 1860, Blair left Missouri after the Federal victory at Boonville and hastened to Washington, DC, to attend the special session of Congress called by President Lincoln. Initially delighted by Lincoln's appointment of John C. Fremont as Federal commander in Missouri, Blair soon became a fierce foe of the imperious general and successfully maneuvered to secure Fremont's removal from Missouri in October 1861. When Congress went into recess in July 1862, Blair accepted a military command and served in the field for the next three years, rising to the rank of major general. He led his Missouri, Illinois, and Ohio troops at Vicksburg, Chattanooga, Atlanta, and in the march across Georgia. He was a prominent commander in a Federal army that marched across the South from the Mississippi River to the Atlantic coast. The war ended for Blair in North Carolina, and he bid farewell to his troops at Louisville on July 11, 1865, as they mustered out of Federal military service.[1]

Blair returned to Missouri eager to regain his antebellum prominence in public life. His lengthy absence from the state required a new burst of political energy, the more so because he returned a determined foe of the Radical Republicans. Radicals in Missouri had drafted a new state constitution, which imposed an ironclad loyalty oath on voters and on all professional men practicing with a license from the state. The intent was clear: to establish and maintain the ascendance of Unionists in public life. In Blair's view the vanquished rebels in Missouri were unjustly disenfranchised. And under Radical control, the Republican Party had become a cabal, plundering public coffers and intent upon suppressing the democratic will of the people. Blair quickly returned to his conservative Democratic Party roots and became a leading figure in Missouri and across the nation, advancing the postwar Democratic opposition to Republican political hegemony. Blair returned to Missouri on June 20. Two days later, three hundred guests gathered at the Lindell Hotel in St. Louis to attend a banquet in his honor and to hear him speak in support of President Andrew Johnson's lenient Reconstruction policies. No one had done more than Blair to defeat the southern rebellion. No one would do more than Blair to limit the political and social consequences of emancipation and the military defeat of the Confederacy.[2]

With the military defeat of the rebellion, Blair favored a swift restoration of the antebellum rights of the states. He had made his conservative views clear early in the war. As a congressman he had supported compensated emancipation in the District of Columbia and for Missouri, and he later accepted the necessity of the Thirteenth Amendment. But he continued to argue in favor of colonizing African Americans outside of the United States, and he bitterly opposed the Fourteenth and Fifteenth Amendments. Now back in Missouri, Blair eagerly forged political alliances with former rebels.[3]

Eventually, returning Confederates like John Marmaduke benefited from Blair's efforts. Captured by Federal forces during the Confederate retreat after the Battle of Westport in October 1864, Marmaduke remained a prisoner of war at Johnson's Island in Ohio until the end of war. Once freed, he returned to Missouri, settled in St. Louis, and became active in Democratic politics. Conservatives in Missouri succeeded (through court orders and legislation) in defeating the Radical loyalty oath and thereby restored the antebellum political rights of former rebels. Blair died in 1875, but had he lived, he would undoubtedly have supported Marmaduke in his victorious 1884 campaign for governor.

Ironically, Marmaduke's capture may have eased his return to civilian life. For Jo Shelby and Sterling Price, the war ground on after their defeat at Westport. They continued their retreat from Westport through Arkansas to Texas. Defiant to the end, both men were loath to surrender. Shelby managed to hold together a disciplined brigade. Once in Texas, he believed that Confederates could assemble a well-equipped, battle-tested army of sixty thousand men to continue the fight. It was not to be. Learning of Lee's surrender in Virginia, General Kirby Smith surrendered his trans-Mississippi Confederate command. Unwilling to follow Smith, Price and Shelby fled to Mexico where the French had recently installed the Emperor Ferdinand Maximilian and hundreds of defeated Confederates hoped to find refuge from the victorious Union army. Their exile and Maximilian's regime were short-lived. But Shelby's and Price's actions expressed the deep-seated alienation felt by many Missouri Confederates who had fought long and hard under unfavorable circumstances to resist Federal control of their state.[4]

By contrast, Union commanders in Missouri welcomed victory with the equanimity of seasoned and successful soldiers. After disengaging with Price's retreating army at the Kansas–Missouri border, Alfred Pleasonton returned to his command in central Missouri. In March 1865 he received the brevet rank of brigadier general in recognition of his services in Missouri. Samuel Curtis returned to Kansas after pursuing Price to the Arkansas River. He briefly led his Federal forces into southern Minnesota to suppress an Indian uprising. When the war ended, the sixty-year-old general returned to civilian life in Iowa. He died in

Council Bluffs in 1866. Andrew Jackson Smith enjoyed a number of military successes in 1864. He defeated Nathan Bedford Forrest at Tupelo, Mississippi, in July 1864, although Forrest's troopers remained a menace until the end of the war. After his victory at Tupelo, Smith moved to Missouri to help meet the challenge of Price's invasion. Once Price was driven from the state, Smith moved east to join General George H. Thomas's army at Nashville. Smith was promoted to the brevet rank of major general for his role in the overwhelming defeat of John Bell Hood at the Battle of Nashville in December 1864. After the war, Smith served for a few years in the West and then resigned from the army to become postmaster of St. Louis, Missouri, where he died in 1897.[5]

Thomas Ewing also won promotion to major general in March 1865. Ewing had fought well at Fort Davidson and skillfully eluded pursuing Confederates as he made his way to the Federal stronghold at Rolla. Ewing accepted his promotion and expressed his gratitude in person to President Lincoln, but he was eager to return to private life, and he promptly resigned to do so. By contrast, Ewing's commander, William Rosecrans, had not distinguished himself during Price's invasion. Indeed, in his final report to the War Department, Grant singled Rosecrans out for criticism. After the Confederate defeat at Westport, Rosecrans remained in command in Missouri until relieved by Grenville Dodge in December 1864. Rosecrans resigned from the army in 1867 but managed to face rebuke from Grant once more. President Andrew Johnson appointed Rosecrans US minister to Mexico in 1868. The next year, when Grant became president, he promptly removed Rosecrans from office. Rosecrans then settled in California, pursued a variety of economic ventures there, and became prominent in Democratic Party politics. Rosecrans served two terms as a US congressman from California (1881–1884). He died in California in 1898.[6]

Grant, who died in 1885, spent the last months of his life writing his *Personal Memoirs*, which were published in two volumes the year of his death. Grant concluded his *Memoirs* with the observation that "The cause of the great War of the Rebellion against the United States will have to be attributed to slavery." But Grant understood as well as anyone that the war, particularly the war in Missouri, was not just about slavery. In July 1861, when Grant first moved his Illinois regiment across the Mississippi River from Quincy, Illinois, to Palmyra and then marched about twenty-five miles through the Missouri countryside in an attempt to engage Thomas Harris's Missouri State Guard recruits near the town of Florida, the Federal troops found the region deserted. Despite the fact that Federal forces openly cooperated with proslavery Unionists in Missouri, Grant sensed the deep apprehensions felt by most Missouri civilians toward what he called the National troops. "We did not see a person, old or young, male or female except two horsemen who were on a road that crossed ours," Grant recalled. The horsemen "decamped as fast as their horses could carry them" at the sight of the Union troops. The laws of war, as Grant and most Civil War commanders understood them, provided some protection to civilians. Grant saw to it that his men did not enter any of the abandoned houses along their line of march. Later, while in Jefferson City, Grant witnessed the desperate condition of Union refugees. "For the Union man in Missouri who staid at home during the rebellion," Grant observed, "if he was not immediately under the protection of National troops, was at perpetual war with his neighbors."[7]

In Grant's view, the National troops restored the rule of law where they took control in Missouri and eventually across the South. But in his first military movement of the war, Grant sensed a profound interaction between his army and the civil society it encountered in Missouri. The war was not just about slavery. Viewed from Grant's perspective, Federal troops protected the rule of law—and with it the law of slavery—in Missouri until the state constitutional convention abolished the institution on January 11, 1865.[8] But slavery touched every aspect of the war nevertheless. The Missouri civilians who fled before Grant's National troops knew that their antebellum way of life was threatened by Federal military control of the state. The Civil War was not just about slavery, but slavery could not be divorced from the war and the victories and defeats of Union and Confederate armies in the field mattered a great deal to everyone.

Notes

Introduction

1. James M. McPherson and James K. Hogue, *Ordeal by Fire: The Civil War and Reconstruction* (Boston: McGraw Hill, 2009), 173.

2. For the Union perspective, see Wiley Britton, *The Civil War on the Border*, 2 vols. (New York: G. P. Putnam, 1891); for the Confederate perspective, see Col. John C. Moore, "Missouri," in Gen. Clement A. Evan, ed., *Confederate Military History: A Library of Confederate States History, Written by Distinguished Men of the South* (Atlanta: Confederate Publishing Company, 1899), vol. 9. Britton was a Kansas cavalry officer; Moore served with John Marmaduke and Jo Shelby.

3. On the emergence of the Lost Cause ideology across the South and its impact on national memories of the Civil War, see David W. Blight, *Race and Reunion: The Civil War in American Memory* (Cambridge: Harvard University Press, 2001). On Edwards's role in popularizing Jesse James, see T. J. Stiles, *Jesse James: Last Rebel of the Civil War* (New York: A. A. Knopf, 2002), 288–91. Edwards's contribution to the military history of the war in Missouri is John Newman Edwards, *Shelby and His Men: Or, the War in the West* (Cincinnati: Miami Printing and Publishing Co., 1867; reprint, Waverly, MO: General Joseph Shelby Memorial Fund, 1993). For an analysis of social banditry and an interpretation of Jesse James as a defender of traditional social relations, see Eric Hobsbawm, *Bandits* (New York: Dell, 1969).

4. Michael Fellman, *Inside War: The Guerrilla Conflict in Missouri during the Civil War* (New York: Oxford University Press, 1989); Louis S. Gerteis, "A Border War," *Reviews in American History* (December 1989): 559–65; Mark W. Geiger, *Financial Fraud and Guerrilla Violence in Missouri's Civil War, 1861–1865* (New Haven: Yale University Press, 2010).

5. William E. Parrish, *Turbulent Partnership: Missouri and the Union, 1861–1865* (Columbia: University of Missouri Press, 1963); Albert E. Castel, *General Sterling Price and the Civil War in the West* (Baton Rouge: Louisiana State University Press, 1968); Robert E. Shalhope, *Sterling Price: Portrait of a Southerner* (Columbia: University of Missouri Press, 1971); Howard N. Monnett, *Action before Westport, 1864* (Kansas City: Westport Historical Society, 1964); Edwin C. Bearss, *The Battle of Wilson's Creek* (Bozeman, Montana: Artcraft Printing, 1975); James Denny and John Bradbury, *The Civil War's First Blood: Missouri, 1854–1861* (Boonville, MO: Missouri Life, 2007); William Garrett Piston and Richard W. Hatcher III, *Wilson's Creek: The Second Battle of the Civil War and the Men Who Fought It* (Chapel Hill: University of North Carolina Press, 2000).

6. On the insecurity generated by guerrilla actions, see Daniel E. Sutherland, *A Savage Conflict: The Decisive Role of Guerrillas in the American Civil War* (Chapel Hill: University of North Carolina Press, 2009), 246–66. On the laws of war in conventional military campaigns, see Mark E. Neely, Jr., *The Civil War and the Limits of Destruction* (Cambridge: Harvard University Press, 2007), 41–71.

7. John G. Nicolay and John Hay, eds., *Abraham Lincoln Complete Works: Comprising His Speeches, Letters, State Papers, and Miscellaneous Writings* (New York: Century, 1894), 2:59.

8. See the Civil War Sites Advisory Commission Report on the Nation's Civil War Battlefields (1993), online.

Chapter 1

1. On Missouri's small-scale slaveholding culture, see Diane Mutti Burke, *On Slavery's Border: Missouri's Small-Slaveholding Households, 1815–1865* (Athens: University of Georgia Press, 2010), 17–51.

2. On the 1860 presidential election, see David M. Potter, *The Impending Crisis, 1848–1861*, completed and edited by Don E. Fehrenbacher (New York: Harper and Row, 1976), 430–47. Douglas and Bell ran nearly even in the state. Douglas won a narrow plurality of 58,800 votes to Bell's 58,400 votes.

3. Basil Duke, *Reminiscences of General Basil W. Duke, C.S.A.* (Garden City, NY: Doubleday, Page, 1911), 32. Duke's reminiscences were originally published serially, beginning in 1905.

4. Thomas L. Snead, *The Fight for Missouri from the Election of Lincoln to the Death of Lyon* (New York: C. Scribner's Sons, 1886), 17–18.

5. Ibid., 22–23.

6. Ibid., 137.

7. Affidavit of Charles T. Tracy, May 6, 1863, Reel F1218, Missouri's Union Provost Marshal Papers, 1861–1866, Missouri State Archives, Jefferson City. On McLaren's continued business activities in St. Louis, see Walter B. Stevens, *St. Louis: The Fourth City, 1764–1911* (St. Louis: S. J. Clarke, 1911), 1:213.

8. Robert V. Kennedy, *Kennedy's Saint Louis City Directory for the Year 1857* (St. Louis: R. V. Kennedy, 1857; also 1858), 44; Report of Maj. Gen. Sterling Price, September 26, 1862, in *The War of the Rebellion: A Compilation of the Official Records of the Union and Confederate Armies* (Washington, DC: Government Printing Office, 1881), series I, volume xvii, pt. 1, 120 (hereafter cited as *OR*).

9. Gary Robert Matthews, *Basil Wilson Duke, C.S.A.: The Right Man in the Right Place* (Lexington: University of Kentucky Press, 2005), 18–19, 248–61; Duke, *Reminiscences*, 37–38; John H. Eicher and David J. Eicher, *Civil War High Commands* (Stanford, CA: Stanford University Press, 2001), 217. Greene and Duke survived the war. Unable to reestablish his business interests in St. Louis, Greene moved to Memphis where he rebuilt his wealth and died in 1900. Duke fought with John Hunt Morgan and succeeded him in command when he died. Duke returned to Kentucky where he devoted himself to writing military history and contributing to the ideology of the Lost Cause.

10. Greene and Shaler distinguished themselves at the Battle of Pea Ridge. Shaler too survived the war. Active in railroad construction in Mexico, he became superintendent of the Panama Railroad when the United States took control of the canal zone. He died in his summer home in Ocean City, New Jersey, in 1910. See Shaler's obituary in the *New York Times*, September 8, 1910. See also Report of Brig. Gen. D. M. Frost, March 19, 1862, *OR*, I, viii, 324; Eicher and Eicher, *High Commands*, 217.

11. Duke, *Reminiscences*, 38. On McCoy as a guerrilla, see Edwards, *Shelby and His Men*, 493–95. A close friend of Shelby, Edwards served as his adjutant during the war. After the war, as a journalist Edwards romanticized and eulogized the exploits of what he described as Missouri's five leading guerrillas turned bandits: the James brothers, the Younger brothers, and Arthur C. McCoy. See Stiles, *Jesse James*, 242, 274–75.

12. Robert E. Miller, "Daniel Marsh Frost, C.S.A.," *Missouri Historical Review* 85 (July 1991): 381–401. Frost's business interests included the fur trade. His activities in this area involved him prominently in the formation of the Dakota Territory. See Clement A. Lounsberry, *Early*

History of North Dakota: Essential Outlines of American History (Washington, DC: Liberty Press, 1919), 263.

13. William E. Parrish, *Frank Blair: Lincoln's Conservative* (Columbia: University of Missouri Press, 1998), 93. See also Louis S. Gerteis, *Civil War St. Louis* (Lawrence: University Press of Kansas, 2001), 85, 89; Snead, *The Fight for Missouri*, 133–35, 147.

14. Snead, *The Fight for Missouri*, 101; George Rollie Adams, *General William S. Harney: Prince of Dragoons* (Lincoln: University of Nebraska Press, 2001), 216–29. Rather than accept reassignment, Bell retired to his farm in St. Charles. See William C. Winter, *Civil War in St. Louis: A Guided Tour* (St. Louis: Missouri Historical Society Press, 1994), 39. A biographical sketch of Daniel Frost appears in William Hyde and Howard L. Conard, eds., *Encyclopedia of the History of St. Louis: A Compendium of History and Biography for Ready Reference* (St. Louis: Southern History Company, 1899), 2:822.

15. Gerteis, *Civil War St. Louis*, 95–96; Parrish, *Frank Blair*, 2, 48, 79–111.

16. Gerteis, *Civil War St. Louis*, 71, 74, 90. A biographical sketch of John How appears in Hyde and Conard, *Encyclopedia*, 2:1065. How lost most of his fortune in wartime speculation. After the war, mining interests led him into the West and he moved to San Francisco where he died in 1885.

17. Gerteis, *Civil War St. Louis*, 59, 89, 357; Parrish, *Frank Blair*, 87; *New York Times*, January 23, 1884; Lincoln to Charles D. Drake and Others, October 5, 1863, in Nicolay and Hay, *Lincoln, Complete Works*, 2:420. The racial views of Blair and Glover are expressed in Francis P. Blair, Jr., *The Destiny of the Races of This Continent. An Address Delivered Before the Mercantile Library Association of Boston, Massachusetts. On the 26th of January, 1859* (Washington, DC: Buell & Blanchard, 1859); Samuel T. Glover, *Speech of Samuel T. Glover at the Ratification Meeting in St. Louis, Held at the Court House, July 22, 1863* (St. Louis: Daily Union Steam Printing House, 1863), 17; Samuel T. Glover, *A Review of State & National Questions* (St. Louis: George Knapp and Co., 1866), 1–7.

18. J. G. Rosengarten, *The German Soldier in the Wars of the United States* (Philadelphia: J. B. Lippincott Company, 1890), 242.

19. Sweeny participated in the capture of Camp Jackson and was severely wounded at Wilson's Creek. He recovered and served with Ulysses S. Grant at Fort Donelson and Corinth, and with William T. Sherman in the Atlanta campaign. He retired from the army in 1870 and died at his home on Long Island, New York, in 1892. *New York Times*, April 12, 1892.

20. Totten was brevetted lieutenant colonel for bravery at the Battle of Wilson's Creek. For a time he held the rank of brigadier general as commander of federally funded militia in central Missouri. He was brevetted colonel in the regular army in March 1865 for his role in the siege of Mobile. He retired from the army in 1870 and died in Sedalia, Missouri, in 1871. Report of Brig. Gen. James Totten, March 29, 1862, *OR*, I, viii, 349–50; Piston and Hatcher, *Wilson's Creek*, 13; *New York Times*, October 4, 1871.

21. Lyon filed charges against his commander at Fort Riley, an action that led to the dismissal of the senior officer from the army. See Christopher Phillips, *Damned Yankee: The Life of General Nathanial Lyon* (Columbia: University of Missouri Press, 1990), 56–59, 75, 90, 101, 112, 127.

22. [Albert Tracy], "The Utah War Journal of Captain Albert Tracy, 1858–1860," *Utah Historical Quarterly* 13 (1945): ix–x; Ray W. Irwin, ed., "Missouri in Crisis: The Journal of Captain Albert Tracy, 1861," *Missouri Historical Review* 51 (October 1956): 11–13.

23. Saxton served as Lyon's quartermaster until July 1861, when he began serving in the same capacity with General George McClellan in western Virginia. He later became active in raising black troops. Tracy also served in western Virginia and then in the Atlanta campaign. Bonneville retired from the army in 1861 at the age of sixty-five but continued for a time to serve as a recruiting officer and commandant at Benton Barracks. Churchill was arrested for disloyalty

later in 1861 and banished from St. Louis in 1863. He returned to his native Kentucky. Gerteis, *Civil War St. Louis*, 90–91. Saxton's work among the "Contraband" in South Carolina is treated in detail in Willie Lee Rose, *Rehearsal for Reconstruction: The Port Royal Experiment* (Indianapolis: Bobbs-Merrill, 1964), 153–55. See also Richard Zuczek, ed., *Encyclopedia of the Reconstruction Era* (Westport, CT: Greenwood Press, 2006), 545; Junius P. Rodriguez, ed., *The Louisiana Purchase: A Historical and Geographical Encyclopedia* (Santa Barbara: ABC-CLIO, 2002), 45; Report of Brig. Gen. Benjamin F. Kelly to Colonel Albert Tracy, Assistant Adjutant-General, April 12, 1862, *OR*, I, xii, pt. 1, 423; Mark W. Johnson, *That Body of Brave Men: U.S. Regular Infantry and the Civil War in the West* (Cambridge: Da Capo Press, 2003), 667–68.

24. Gerteis, *Civil War St. Louis*, 91–92.

25. Ibid., 93; John M. Schofield, *Forty-Six Years in the Army* (New York: Century, 1897), 47–49; Donald B. Connelly, *John M. Schofield and the Politics of Generalship* (Chapel Hill: University of North Carolina Press, 2006), 23–26.

26. Gerteis, *Civil War St. Louis*, 93.

27. Ibid., 94.

28. John F. Poole, "I'm Going to Fight Mit Sigel" (New York: H. De Marsan, n.d.). A copy of Poole's published lyrics is available online in the Duke University Libraries Digital Collection.

29. A. Richard Edwards et al., *Edwards's Great West and Her Commercial Metropolis* (St. Louis: Office of Edwards's Monthly, 1860), 556–59; Stevens, *St. Louis*, 1:165; Henry Boernstein, *Memoirs of a Nobody: The Missouri Years of an Austrian Radical, 1849–1866*, trans. and ed. Steven Rowan (St. Louis: Missouri Historical Society Press, 1997), 317–37, 350; *New York Times*, July 14, 1862. Boernstein served as consul until 1866 and then remained in Germany and Austria for the rest of his life. He died in 1892.

30. St. Louis city directories show that Schuettner (sometimes spelled Schittner) served as superintendent of the city engineer's office in 1864 and as street commissioner in 1867. He died in 1868. See Boernstein, *Memoirs*, 282n; Robert J. Rombauer, *The Union Cause in St. Louis in 1861: An Historical Sketch* (St. Louis: Nixon-Jones, 1909), xiii, 198, 394; Chester Harding, Jr., to Nathaniel Lyon, July 21, 1861, *OR*, I, iii, 401.

31. Rosengarten, *The German Soldier*, 257; [Ulysses S. Grant], *Personal Memoirs of U. S. Grant* (New York: Charles L. Webster & Company, 1885), 1:212–13.

32. D. M. Frost to Capt. N. Lyon, May 11, 1861, *OR*, I, iii, 7.

33. *New York Times*, November 6, 1867. The *Times* reported that Duke, P. G. T. Beauregard, and M. Jeff Thompson were in St. Louis and were serenaded by their supporters. Duke made his comments on that occasion. See also Marshall D. Hier, "Basil W. Duke: Legend Made Vivid," *St. Louis Bar Journal* 43 (Fall 1996): 45–47; "Brig. Gen. Basil Wilson Duke," *Confederate Veteran* 24, no. 1 (January 1916): 485; Duke, *Reminiscences*, 44–56.

34. Phillip Thomas Tucker, *The Forgotten Stonewall of the West: Major General John Stevens Bowen* (Macon, GA: Mercer University Press, 1997), 23–81. Bowen later participated in the Vicksburg campaign. A few days after the city's surrender, as he made his way east to Atlanta he died of dysentery. Gerteis, *Civil War St. Louis*, 102, 180.

35. Stevens, *St. Louis*, 1: 838–41; Winter, *Civil War in St. Louis*, 42, 140. A biographical sketch of John Knapp appears in Hyde and Conard, *Encyclopedia*, 2:1185.

36. Prichard was wounded at the Battle of Nashville. Soon after leaving the Federal army in 1865, he received an appointment as lieutenant colonel in the new Missouri Militia. He returned to DeKalb County after the war but in 1879 moved to Kansas. In 1892 he was elected as a Populist to the house of the state legislature. In 1896 he won election to the state senate as a Populist. He died in Kansas in 1901. See the *Handbook of the Kansas Legislature, 1897* (Topeka: Crane and Company, 1897); Fred R. Kline, ed., *George Caleb Bingham Catalogue Raisonné Supplement*, online; Ira Berlin et al., *Freedom: A Documentary History of Emancipation, 1861–1867* (Cambridge: Cambridge University Press, 1985), series 1, 1:467–68.

37. He died at the Battle of Murfreesboro in December 1862. See Report of Lieut. Col. Bernard Laiboldt, January 7, 1863, *OR*, I, xx, pt. 1, 367; Rombauer, *The Union Cause*, 367; Michael E. Banasik, ed., *Missouri in 1861: The Civil War Letters of Franc B. Wilkie, Newspaper Correspondent* (Iowa City: Camp Pope Bookshop, 2001), 97; Piston and Hatcher, *Wilson's Creek*, 228.

38. Cavender recovered from a severe wound sustained at Wilson's Creek and rose to brevet brigadier general in March 1865 after winning a commendation for his "gallant and meritorious service" with General Grant at Fort Donelson and the Battle of Shiloh. After the war, Cavender resided in prestigious Benton Place in St. Louis and remained active in Republican politics. He died in St. Louis in 1886. Rombauer, *The Union Cause*, 358; Winter, *Civil War in St. Louis*, 120; Snead, *The Fight for Missouri*, 152–54; Report of Lieut Col. George L. Andrews, August 28, 1861, *OR*, I, iii, 77; *New York Times*, July 19, 1876; Walter B. Stevens, *Centennial History of Missouri* (Chicago: S. J. Clarke, 1921), 2:807; J. Thomas Scharf, *History of St. Louis City and County, From the Earliest Periods to the Present Day: Including Biographical Sketches of Representartive Men* (Philadelphia: L. H. Everts, 1883), 2:1844.

39. Snead, *The Fight for Missouri*, 164; Gerteis, *Civil War St. Louis*, 95.

40. Snead, *The Fight for Missouri*, 162–64.

41. Winter, *Civil War in St. Louis*, 114. Following the capture of Camp Jackson, Brown's regiment reinforced Sigel after the Battle of Carthage. Thereafter Brown's troops patrolled the Ironton area before mustering out at the end of their three months of service. Brown himself had no interest in further military service and happily returned to the political sphere. See Norma L. Peterson, *Freedom and Franchise: The Political Career of B. Gratz Brown* (Columbia: University of Missouri Press, 1965), 103; *Anzeiger des Westens*, March 19, 1862, in Steven Rowan, ed. and tr., *Germans for a Free Missouri: Translations from the St. Louis Radical Press, 1857–1862* (Columbia: University of Missouri Press, 1983), 312.

42. When Almstedt's regiment mustered out in August 1861, he accepted a commission as colonel of the Second Missouri Light Artillery. He resigned that commission in August 1863 and served from 1864 to 1868 in the army's paymaster's department. He was briefly reassigned to artillery duty during Sterling Price's invasion of Missouri in 1864. Almstedt died in Fenton, Missouri, in 1884. See Kenneth Kronnenberg et al., *Lives and Letters of an Immigrant Family: The Van Dreveldts' Experiences along the Missouri, 1844–1866* (Lincoln: University of Nebraska Press, 1998), 146; Winter, *Civil War in St. Louis*, 131–32; Stevens, *Centennial History*, 393; Scharf, *St. Louis City and County*, 1182; Richard Josiah Hinton, *Rebel Invasion of Missouri and Kansas and the Campaign of the Army of the Border, Against General Sterling Price, in October and November, 1864* (Chicago: Church and Goodman, 1865), 40.

43. After the war, Kallmann participated in the construction of the Eads Bridge and then continued his engineering career in Detroit where he died in 1904. Stifel and his men engaged in the fight at Boonville and later sparred with Jo Shelby near Lexington. At the end of his three months of service, Stifel returned to his brewing business. See Gerteis, *Civil War St. Louis*, 96; Report of Brig. Gen. U.S. Grant, August 11, 1861, *OR*, I, iii, 130; Paul Leake, *History of Detroit: Chronicle of Its Progress, Its Industries, Its Institutions and the People of the Fair City of the Straits* (Chicago: The Lewis Publishing Company, 1812), 3:905–8; Winter, *Civil War in St. Louis*, 124. A biographical sketch of Charles Stifel appears in Hyde and Conard, *Encyclopedia*, 4:2141.

44. Piston and Hatcher, *Wilson's Creek*, 34–35.

45. Unless otherwise noted, the following discussion of the capture of Camp Jackson relies on Gerteis, *Civil War St. Louis*, 107–13.

46. *OR*, I, iii, 6–7.

47. Frost joined the Confederate army after the fighting at Wilson's Creek (August 1861) and Lexington (September 1861). Although Frost finally cast his lot with the Confederacy, his commitment to the cause continued to seem less than wholehearted. He rejected as too small a field command of a Missouri brigade prior to the Battle of Pea Ridge (March 1862). He served instead

as a staff officer, first with Braxton Bragg and then with Thomas C. Hindman. Frost saw action in December 1862 at the Battle of Prairie Grove. But in the spring of 1863, after his wife had been banished from St. Louis, Frost left the army without leave to move his family first to Matamoras, Mexico, and then to Canada. During his absence with his family, the Confederacy dropped him from the rolls of the army. He later sought but did not receive a new command. Pardoned by President Andrew Johnson in October 1865, Frost returned to his Hazelwood estate where he died in 1900. See Miller, "Daniel Marsh Frost," 381–401; Winter, *Civil War in St. Louis*, 140; Gerteis, *Civil War St. Louis*, 180–81, 358n30.

48. Adams, *William S. Harney*, 227–37. See also WM. S. Harney, Brigadier-General, U.S. Army, General Orders, No. 10, May 11, 1861; Harney to Liet. Col. E. D. Townsend, Asst. Adjt. Gen., Hdqrs. of the Army, Washington, D.C., May 13, 1861; Harney, "Proclamation," May 12, 1861; Harney "To the People of the State of Missouri," May 14, 1861, *OR*, I, iii, 369–72.

49. Sterling Price and Wm. S. Harney to the People of the State of Missouri, May 21, 1861, *OR*, I, iii, 374–75.

50. Gerteis, *Civil War St. Louis*, 118.

51. Snead, *The Fight for Missouri*, 181–84; Piston and Hatcher, *Wilson's Creek*, 37; Donald J. Stanton, Goodwin F. Berquist, and Paul C. Bowers, eds., *The Civil War Reminiscences of General M. Jeff Thompson* (Dayton: Morningside House, 1988), 69. Watkins chose to take no part in the gathering conflict, although he retained the informal title of General for the rest of his life. See also William Van Ness Bay, *Reminiscences of the Bench and Bar of Missouri* (St. Louis: F. H. Thomas and Company, 1878), 37–40.

52. Stanton et al., *Thompson*, 55, 60, 62–63; Doris Land Mueller, *M. Jeff Thompson: Missouri's Swamp Fox of the Confederacy* (Columbia: University of Missouri Press, 2007), 28–32. In October 1861, Federal forces defeated Thompson at the Battle of Fredericktown and he retreated south into Arkansas. After the war, he settled in New Orleans and worked as an engineer. He returned to St. Joseph shortly before his death in 1876.

53. On Randolph, see *American Ancestry: Giving the Name and Descent, In the Male Line, of Americans Whose Ancestors Settled in the United States Previous to the Declaration of Independence, A.D. 1776* (n.p.: Joel Munsell's Sons, 1893), 8:221; Annette Gordon-Reed, *Sally Hemmings: An American Controversy* (Charlottesville: University of Virginia Press, 1997), 198. On Harris, see Banasik, *Missouri in 1861*, 349; [Grant], *Memoirs*, 1:250; Thomas L. Snead, Acting Adjutant General, to Brigadier-General Harris, Second Military District, August 26, 1861, *OR*, I, iii, 684.

After formally seceding from the Union, the pro-Jackson state legislature elected Harris a delegate to the Provisional Confederate Congress. Early in December 1861, Martin E. Green replaced Harris as brigadier general of the Second Division of Missouri State Guard. Also a native of Virginia, Green was the brother of Missouri's ardently proslavery senator James S. Green. He was judge of the Lewis County Court when the war began. He commanded a regiment of mounted troops before succeeding Harris. After his promotion to brigadier general, Green fought at Pea Ridge. He was killed by a Federal sharpshooter during the siege of Vicksburg. See Ezra J. Warner, *Generals in Gray: Lives of the Confederate Commanders* (Baton Rouge: Louisiana State University Press, 1992), 116–17; Benson J. Lossing, *Pictorial History of the Civil War in the United States of America* (Hartford: T. Belknap, Publishers, 1868), 2:463; Report of Brig. Gen. Thomas A. Harris, September 23, 1861, *OR*, I, iii, 190–92; H. Little, Adjutant General, General Orders, No. 111, December 2, 1861, *OR*, I, liii, 758; Walter Williams, ed., *A History of Northeast Missouri* (Chicago: Lewis, 1913), 1:56–57.

54. Report of Brig. Gen. John B. Clark, July 19, 1861, and Clark to General A. S. Johnston, September 23, 1861, *OR*, I, iii, 30–32, 706–7; *Biographical Directory of United States Congresses*, online. Clark presumably attended the fifth and final session of the Provisional Congress, which met in Richmond in November 1861. He was subsequently elected senator from Missouri to the

first Confederate Congress and a representative from Missouri in the second Confederate Congress. After the war he resumed his law practice in Fayette and died there in 1885.

55. Bay, *Bench and Bar*, 137–38.

56. A fellow conservative Unionist, Missouri's provisional governor Willard P. Hall secured work for Doniphan as a Federal pension claims agent. Hall's Radical Republican successor, Thomas C. Fletcher, arranged for Doniphan's replacement in January 1865. Doniphan warmly supported Andrew Johnson and chaired the Missouri delegation to the Democratic National Convention that met in St. Louis in 1876. Several years earlier, in August 1868, Doniphan moved from St. Louis to Richmond, Missouri (near Lexington). He continued to practice law but did not prosper. He died in a boardinghouse in Richmond in 1887 at the age of seventy-nine. Richard D. Launius, *Alexander William Doniphan: Portrait of a Missouri Moderate* (Columbia: University of Missouri Press, 1997), 234, 253–54, 261–63, 266–67, 269.

57. Steen later commanded a regiment under Mosby Parsons at the Battle of Prairie Grove where he was killed in December 1862. Some sources mistakenly report that Steen attended West Point. See Piston and Hatcher, *Wilson's Creek*, 114–15, 252.

58. Piston and Hatcher, *Wilson's Creek*, 88. After fighting with Claiborne Jackson in Missouri, Parsons fought the rest of the war in Arkansas. Rather than surrender to Federal troops, he escaped to Mexico where he was killed by bandits in August 1865. See Warner, *Generals in Gray*, 228–29.

59. After fighting with Sterling Price in Missouri, McBride was detached to recruit Confederate troops at Little Rock. He died of illness in March 1864. See Bruce S. Allardice, *More Generals in Gray* (Baton Rouge: Louisiana State University Press, 1995), 155–56.

60. Wounded at Pea Ridge, Rains was removed from command for "incompetence and insobriety." He moved to Texas to regain his health. Although Rains returned to Missouri during Price's 1864 raid to recruit Confederate soldiers, he returned to Texas and made his home there until his death in 1880. See ibid., 190–91.

61. Winter, *Civil War in St. Louis*, 115–16; Lawrence O. Christensen et al., eds., *Dictionary of Missouri Biography* (Columbia: University of Missouri Press, 1999), 188–89.

62. Marmaduke rose to the rank of brigadier general in the Confederate army. See Christensen et al., *Dictionary of Missouri Biography*, 519–21.

63. Gerteis, *Civil War St. Louis*, 118, 122–24.

64. Claiborne F. Jackson, "To The People of Missouri," June 12, 1861, *OR*, I, liii, 696.

65. Henry Little, Assistant Adjutant General, General Orders, No. 11, June 12, 1861, *OR*, I, iii, 592.

Chapter 2

1. Piston and Hatcher, *Wilson's Creek*, 99–110; Snead, *The Fight for Missouri*, 229–30.

2. Christensen et al., *Dictionary of Missouri Biography*, 625–27.

3. N. Lyon, Brig. Gen., to Maj. Gen. George B. McClellan, June 22, 1861, *OR*, I, iii, 12; Snead, *The Fight for Missouri*, 210–11.

4. Early in July, Boernstein moved into the governor's mansion with his wife. On July 26, with his period of enlistment over, he relinquished command of Jefferson City to Colonel James Mulligan who arrived with a regiment of Iowa troops. Boernstein, *Memoirs*, 330, 335.

5. Thomas W. Cutrer, *Ben McCulloch and the Frontier Military Tradition* (Chapel Hill: University of North Carolina Press, 1993), 10–21, 48, 89–103, 124, 131–39, 163, 190–95.

6. Phillips, *Damned Yankee*, 219. For an overview of the battle of Boonville, see Paul Rorvig, "The Significant Skirmish: The Battle of Boonville, June 17, 1861," *Missouri Historical Review* 86 (January 1992): 127–48.

7. This account of the Battle of Boonville relies on N. Lyon, Brigadier-General of Volunteers, to Gen. George B. McClellan, Commanding Division of Volunteers, June 30, 1861, *OR*, I, iii, 12–14.

8. Rorvig, "The Significant Skirmish," 141.

9. Thomas Wallace Knox, *Camp-fire and Cotton-field, Southern Adventure in Time of War: Life with the Union Armies, and Residence on a Louisiana Plantation* (New York: Blelock, 1865), 41; Lyon to McClellan, *OR*, I, iii, 12–14.

10. Robert Neumann, "The Richest Man in Greene County," *Greene County Historical Society Bulletin* 58, no. 2 (May–August 1997); Snead, *The Fight for Missouri*, 215–16.

11. Twice badly wounded, Guibor fought throughout the war, from Wilson's Creek to his surrender in 1865 in North Carolina. See Winter, *Civil War in St. Louis*, 137–38. After the war, Guibor returned to St. Louis where he served as vice president (1886) and president (1887) of the Ex-Confederate Historical and Benevolent Association. He died in St. Louis in 1899. See Hyde and Conard, *Encyclopedia*, 2:404; also Snead, *The Fight for Missouri*, 218.

12. Blair resigned his command of the First Missouri Volunteers after the fight at Boonville. Elected to the US Congress in 1860, he returned to St. Louis and then traveled to Washington, DC, to attend the special session of Congress called by President Lincoln. In November 1862, Blair returned to the field as a brigadier general, joining Maj. Gen. John A. McCernand at Helena, Arkansas. During the Vicksburg campaign and throughout the rest of the war, Blair fought with William Tecumseh Sherman. See Parrish, *Frank Blair*, 156–57.

13. Daniel O'Flaherty, *Jo Shelby: Undefeated Rebel* (Chapel Hill: University of North Carolina Press, 1954), 7, 14–16, 28, 36, 46, 51, 58–59, 66.

14. Snead, *The Fight for Missouri*, 219. Weightman was killed at the Battle of Wilson's Creek. See Report of Maj. Gen. Sterling Price, August 12, 1861, *OR*, I, iii, 101; Piston and Hatcher, *Wilson's Creek*, 155. There is some uncertainty regarding the date and place of Weightman's birth. *The Biographical Directory of the United States Congress* (online), using information probably supplied by Weightman, reported that he was born in Washington, DC, in 1816. However, *Appleton's Cyclopedia of American Biography* (online) reported that he was born in Maryland in 1818.

15. Badly wounded in the foot toward the end of the Battle of Wilson's Creek, Cawthorn died eight days after undergoing an amputation. Members of the Sons of Confederate Veterans, Col. John T. Coffee Camp No. 1934, found a gravestone at the site of Cawthorn's farm. It bore the initials "J.H.C." and indicated that Cawthorn was born on May 3, 1809, and died on August 18, 1861. See *Nevada, Missouri, Daily Mail & Herald-Tribune*, April 27, 2006, and Hyde and Conard, *Encyclopedia*, 1:550.

Bledsoe's battery fought in western campaigns throughout the war. He died at his home in Pleasant Hill, Missouri, in February 1899. See *New York Times*, February 8, 1899, and William Elsey Connelley, *War with Mexico, 1846–1847: Doniphan's Expedition and the Conquest of New Mexico and California* (Kansas City: Bryant and Douglas, 1907), 537.

16. Wounded in the hand at Wilson's Creek, Kelly went on to serve with the Confederate army throughout the war. After the war he returned to St. Louis. In poor health, he died in 1870. See Michael E. Banasik, ed., *Serving with Honor: The Diary of Captain Eathan Allen Pinnell of the Eighth Missouri Infantry (Confederate)* (Iowa City: Camp Pope Bookshop, 1999), 378–79, 168n; Piston and Hatcher, *Wilson's Creek*, 38, 84, 87–88. Brown died in September 1861 while leading an attack on Unionist Home Guards defending Boonville. See Banasik, *Missouri in 1861*, 198n.

17. Joseph A. Mudd, "What I Saw at Wilson's Creek," *Missouri Historical Review* 7 (January 1913): 89–105. Wounded in the head by a Minie ball at Wilson's Creek, Burbridge recovered and became colonel of a Confederate regiment in January 1862. He fought at Pea Ridge and joined Marmaduke's Missouri expedition in 1863. Captured near Little Rock in August 1863, Burbridge spent some time in the Gratiot Street Prison before being transferred to Johnson Island in Baltimore Harbor. He was exchanged in February 1864 and returned to Arkansas and joined Price's Missouri raid in 1864. Burbridge survived the war and settled in Jacksonville, Florida, where he

made his living as a real estate dealer. His heirs began legal proceedings regarding his estate in October 1898 following his death. See Banasik, *Serving with Honor*, 378–80; Charles H. Smith, *Jacksonville and Florida Facts* (Jacksonville: H. and W. B. Drew, 1906), 13; *The Southern Reporter* 26 (St. Paul: West, 1900): 1017.

18. Piston and Hatcher, *Wilson's Creek*, 85. Clark recovered from a wound he received at Wilson's Creek and went on to represent Missouri in the Confederate Congress. Major fought at Vicksburg, rose to the rank of brigadier general, and played a leading role in blunting Nathaniel P. Banks's Red River campaign in 1864. After the war, Major settled in Louisiana for a time and then moved to Texas. He died in Austin in 1877 at the age of forty-one. See Texas State Historical Society, *The Handbook of Texas* (online).

19. Rives was killed at Pea Ridge. After Pea Ridge, Hughes returned to Missouri to recruit troops and died leading an attack on the Federal garrison at Independence in August 1862. See Report of Maj. Gen. Sterling Price, March 22, 1862, *OR*, I, viii, 306; Allardice, *More Generals in Gray*, 132–33; Snead, *The Fight for Missouri*, 219.

20. Snead, *The Fight for Missouri*, 230–37.

21. Lyon to McClellan, June 22, 1861, *OR*, I, iii, 12. For the composition of Sturgis's battalion, I have relied on Schofield, *Forty-Six Years in the Army*, 37. Schofield joined Lyon at Boonville on June 26 and began his duties as adjutant general. For the total strength of Sturgis's force I have relied on Piston and Hatcher, *Wilson's Creek*, 69. After the Battle of Wilson's Creek the War Department transferred Sturgis to the East and he rose to the brevet rank of brigadier general. In June 1864 he suffered a humiliating defeat by Nathan Bedford Forrest at Brice's Crossroads in Mississippi. Sturgis never rose to military prominence thereafter, although he remained in the army until he retired in 1886. See Eicher and Eicher, *High Commands*, 518.

22. Snead, *The Fight for Missouri*, 222; F. Sigel, Colonel, Commanding Second Brigade, Missouri Volunteers, to Brigadier-General Sweeny, Commanding Southwest Expedition, July 11, 1861, *OR*, I, iii, 16–19; Piston and Hatcher, *Wilson's Creek*, 69–80.

23. Sigel to Sweeny, *OR*, I, iii, 16–19; Snead, *The Fight for Missouri*, 223.

24. Snead, *The Fight for Missouri*, 224.

25. Piston and Hatcher, *Wilson's Creek*, 103.

26. O'Flaherty, *Shelby*, 68–69.

27. Snead, *The Fight for Missouri*, 225.

28. Stephen Douglas Engle, *Yankee Dutchman: The Life of Franz Sigel* (Fayetteville: University of Arkansas Press, 1993; Baton Rouge: Louisiana State University Press, 1999), 1–27, 33, 42–43, 86.

29. James S. Rains, Brig. Gen., Comdg. Second Division, Missouri State Guard, to Brig Gen. W. Hough, Adjutant-General, Missouri State Guard, July 20, 1861, *OR*, I, iii, 20–22.

30. Snead, *The Fight for Missouri*, 227.

31. M. M. Parsons, Brigadier-General, to Gov. C. F. Jackson, Commander-in-Chief Missouri State Guard, July 10, 1861, *OR*, I, iii, 34–37.

32. Captain Joseph Conrad to Co. F. Sigel, July 11, 1861, *OR*, I, iii, 38.

33. N. Lyon, Brigadier-General, Commanding Army of the West, to J. M. Schofield, Assistant Adjutant-General, July 25, 1861, *OR*, I, iii, 19; Snead, *The Fight for Missouri*, 227–28.

34. T. W. Sweeny, Captain, Second Infantry, to Hon. Simon Cameron, Secretary of War, July 12, 1861, *OR*. I, iii, 15–16.

35. O'Flaherty, *Shelby*, 72–73, 75.

36. Promoted to brigadier general in January 1862, McIntosh commanded a brigade at the Battle of Pea Ridge, where he was killed. See Eicher and Eicher, *High Commands*, 379.

37. At Pea Ridge, Hebert led an infantry brigade and was captured. After his exchange in 1862, he was appointed brigadier general and led an infantry brigade. Captured at Vicksburg and again exchanged, Hebert served as an engineer in North Carolina and as an artillery commander at

Fort Fisher. After the war he made his living as editor of the *Iberville South*. He died in 1901. See ibid., 292.

38. At Pea Ridge, Greer sustained a minor wound and briefly commanded McCulloch's division following McCulloch's death. In October 1862, Greer was appointed brigadier general and became chief of conscription for the Trans-Mississippi Department. He died in 1877. See ibid., 266–67.

39. Churchill was promoted to brigadier general and fought at Pea Ridge. He then served as commander at Arkansas Post on the Arkansas River. In January 1863, Arkansas Post came under attack by a Federal force commanded by John A. McClernand and supported by gunboats commanded by Admiral David Porter. After more than a day of resisting the heavy bombardment from the gunboats and a Federal force ten times larger than his, Churchill surrendered. Most of his men were exchanged but Federal authorities held Churchill for three months as a prisoner of war at Camp Chase near Columbus, Ohio.

After his release, Churchill commanded an Arkansas infantry division during the 1864 Red River campaign. He then inflicted heavy losses in Arkansas on Union troops commanded by Frederick Steele. Churchill was promoted to major general in March 1865. After the war he returned to his plantation near Little Rock and led the fight against Reconstruction. He served three terms as Democratic state treasurer (beginning in 1874) and in 1880 won election as the Democratic governor of Arkansas. He died in 1905. See ibid., 172–73; Warner, *Generals in Gray*, 49–50.

40. After Wilson's Creek, McRae's battalion became a full regiment, the Twenty-First Arkansas Infantry. McRae commanded this regiment at the Battle of Pea Ridge. Later in 1862, McRae raised a second regiment and was promoted to brigadier general in November 1862. After the war he was active in the Ku Klux Klan in Arkansas and for several years evaded arrest for accessory to murder. When Democrats returned to power in Arkansas in 1872, McRae came out of hiding, and eventually a jury acquitted him and a codefendant. He died in 1899. See Eicher and Eicher, *High Commands*, 384; Warner, *Generals in Gray*, 206–7; Piston and Hatcher, *Wilson's Creek*, 335.

41. After the Battle of Wilson's Creek, Pearce disbanded his brigade. For the rest of the war he served as a major in the Confederate Commissary Department in Arkansas. After the war Pearce secured a pardon from President Johnson, and by 1867 he had returned to Osage Mills where he rebuilt his home, a mill, and a store. He later moved to Texas and died in Dallas in 1894. See Allardice, *More Generals in Gray*, 179–80.

42. Paul Beckwith, *Creoles of St. Louis* (St. Louis: Nixon-Jones Printing Co., 1893), 97–98; William Hugh Robarts, *Mexican War Veterans: A Complete Roster of the Regular and Volunteer Troops in the War Between the United States and Mexico From 1846 To 1848* (Washington, DC: A.S. Witherbee and Co., 1887), 61–2l; Evan, *Confederate Military History*, 10:284–85. After the Civil War, Walker resumed law practice in Fayetteville in 1865. Active in the Democratic Party, he won election to the US Senate in 1878. He declined to seek reelection in 1884 and returned to his law practice. He died in Fayetteville in 1906. Walker is mistakenly identified as "Jonathan D. Walker" in Piston and Hatcher, *Wilson's Creek*, 275, 336. See also Evan, *Confederate Military History*, 10:286; *Biographical Directory of the United States Congress* (online).

43. Dockery later commanded the Nineteenth Arkansas Infantry Regiment at Corinth and participated in the defenses of Vicksburg. Paroled after the fall of Vicksburg, Dockery became brigadier general in August 1863 and fought in Arkansas for the duration of the war. After the war, he became active in promoting railroads and dabbled in Democratic politics. He later moved to New York City where he died in 1898. See Eicher and Eicher, *High Commands*, 211; Piston and Hatcher, *Wilson's Creek*, 98, 336; William Edward Woodruff, *With the Light Guns in '61–'65* (Little Rock: Central Printing, 1903), 21.

The description of Carroll as an elderly planter is in Evan, *Confederate Military History*, 10:286. After Wilson's Creek, and with the end of his initial enlistment, DeRosey Carroll evidently returned to his plantation. In January 1863 he was murdered on his plantation by the Unionist guerilla Captain Martin D. Hunt. See David Pickering and Judy Falls, *Brush Men and Vigilantes: Civil War Dissent in Texas* (College Station: Texas A&M University Press, 2004), 76–77.

44. By late September 1861 the original company of volunteers had disbanded. Most of them, including Woodruff, joined the Confederate army. In November 1861, Woodruff received orders to recruit a new light battery to be called Weaver Artillery. Promoted to major in 1863, Woodruff commanded the Weaver Artillery for the rest of the war. Early in the 1880s, Woodruff attended a reunion in Springfield of the northern and southern participants in the Battle of Wilson's Creek, See Woodruff, *With the Light Guns*, 9, 34, 50–51, 57, 64.

45. After defeating pro-Confederate troops commanded by Jeff Thompson at Fredericktown in October 1861, J. B. Plummer won promotion to brigadier general. See Eicher and Eicher, *High Commands*, 431–32. After the Battle of Wilson's Creek, Osterhaus fought at Pea Ridge and was promoted to brigadier general. He remained in the field throughout the war, serving in the Vicksburg campaign, the Chattanooga campaign, and in the march through Georgia. At the close of the war, he was military commander of Mississippi. He later served the United States as consul general at Lyons during the Franco-Prussian War. He lived the rest of his life in Germany. In January 1917, a few months before the United States declared war against Germany, Osterhaus died in Berlin at the age of ninety-four. See *New York Times*, January 6, 1917; Piston and Hatcher, *Wilson's Creek*, 182–83; Rowan, *Germans for a Free Missouri*, 230n.

46. After Wilson's Creek, Wood remained in southwest Missouri commanding mounted forces attached to Missouri troops headquartered in Rolla. His troopers ranged into northwestern Arkansas and largely succeeded in clearing southwest Missouri of Confederates. He resigned in 1863 and returned to Kansas where he became brigadier general of the Kansas State Militia. He was murdered in 1891 in a dispute over the location of a county seat. William E. Connelley, *History of Kansas State and People* (Chicago: American Historical Society, 1928), 1165, 1169, 1171; Potter, *The Impending Crisis*, 207; Piston and Hatcher, *Wilson's Creek*, 68, 181; S. N. Wood to Col. G. M. Dodge, November 18, 1861, *OR*, I, iii, 366.

47. Albert G. Brackett, *History of the United States Cavalry, From the Formation of the Federal Government to the 1st of June, 1863* (New York: Harper and Brothers, 1865), 321; *Official Army Register, for August, 1862* (Washington, DC: Government Printing Office, 1862), 18; Piston and Hatcher, *Wilson's Creek*, 184. Overall, US cavalry units were short of officers because of the large number of resignations by men joining the Confederacy. The Second Cavalry became the Second Dragoons when the US Cavalry was reorganized in August 1861. In November 1861 Stanley was promoted to brigadier general and took part in the Island Number Ten campaign. He then served in the Army of the Tennessee under Grant and in the Army of the Cumberland under Rosecrans. Stanley was with Sherman in the Atlanta campaign and thereafter defended Nashville against Hood. After the Civil War, Stanley participated in the Indian wars. He retired in 1892 and died in Washington, DC, in 1902. See Whitelaw Reid, *Ohio in the War: Her Statesmen, Generals and Soldiers* (Cincinnati: Moore, Wilstach & Baldwin, 1868), 1:796–98.

Sturgis commended Canfield for his "conspicuous" gallantry "from the beginning to the close" of the Battle of Wilson's Creek. See Report of S. D. Sturgis, Major, First Cavalry, Commanding, August 21, 1861, *OR*, I, iii, 70. After the Battle of Wilson's Creek, Canfield evidently rejoined Company C of the Second Cavalry, which made its way east to join the rest of the regiment. Promoted to captain, Canfield died at Beverley's Ford, Virginia, on June 9, 1863, in the largest cavalry battle of the Civil War (Brandy Station). See Jesse Bowman Young, *The Battle of Gettysburg: A Comprehensive Narrative* (New York: Harper and Brothers, 1913), 415.

48. Albert was wounded and captured at Wilson's Creek. He was later exchanged and served with Fremont in the Department of the West and, subsequently, in the Mountain Department. See *Kennedy's St. Louis Directory, 1860*; Rombauer, *The Union Cause*, 103–4; Andrew Rolle, *John Charles Fremont: Character as Destiny* (Norman: University of Oklahoma Press, 1991), 196; Eugene Pivany, *Hungarians in the American Civil War* (Cleveland: n.p., 1913), 16; Piston and Hatcher, *Wilson's Creek*, 189.

49. Wounded three times at the Battle of Pea Ridge, Carr won the Medal of Honor for his bravery there. He served as the district commander in St. Louis until March 1863 when he joined the Vicksburg campaign. In 1865, he returned to Missouri to marry Mary Magwire of St. Louis. He was well-known as an Indian fighter in the decades after the Civil War. His command faced a dangerous attack by Apaches in August 1881 and the *New York Times* mistakenly reported his death. Carr retired in 1893 and died in 1910. See *New York Times*, September 4, 1881; Eicher and Eicher, *High Commands*, 164–65; James T. King, *War Eagle: A Life of Eugene A. Carr* (Lincoln: University of Nebraska Press, 1963), 29–45, 58.

50. J. C. Fremont, Major-General, Commanding, to Col. E. D. Townsend, Asst. Adjt. Gen., August 13, 1961, *OR*, I, iii. 56. Farrand later commanded cavalry at the Forts Henry and Donelson campaign and, later in 1862, became aide-de-camp to General William S. Rosecrans. He left the army in 1871 and settled in Colorado, where he died in 1900. See Piston and Hatcher, *Wilson's Creek*, 190; *New York Times*, July 10, 1858.

51. Andrews served throughout the war and remained in the army until his retirement in 1892. See Banasik, *Missouri in 1861*, 136 n249; Piston and Hatcher, *Wilson's Creek*, 120–21.

52. Steele later participated in the Vicksburg campaign and rose to the rank of major general. He then took command of Federal forces in Arkansas where President Lincoln appointed him military governor. Steele soon drew criticism from Arkansas Unionists for his leniency toward Confederates. Relieved of duty in Arkansas in November 1864, he commanded Federal forces in the lengthy assault on Mobile, Alabama. He died on leave of absence in California in 1868. See Eicher and Eicher, *High Commands*, 507–8; Patricia J. Palmer, *Frederick Steele: Forgotten General* (Stanford: Stanford University Libraries, 1971), 6–14.

53. After Wilson's Creek, DuBois briefly served on General Halleck's staff and then fought with Sherman at Corinth and Vicksburg. By the end of the war, DuBois had received the brevet rank of lieutenant colonel. He retired from the army in 1876 with a "disability contracted in the line of duty" and died at his home in Hudson, New York, in 1879 at the age of forty-six. See *New York Times*, August 1, 1879; Piston and Hatcher, *Wilson's Creek*, 166.

54. Wounded at Wilson's Creek, Deitzler recovered to accept a commission as brigadier general in the Army of the Tennessee. Deitzler participated in the Battle of Corinth and during the Vicksburg campaign directed the construction of the Lake Providence Canal. Ill health caused him to return to Kansas where he became major general, commanding all of the Kansas State Militia. He played an important role in defeating Sterling Price at the Battle of Westport. He engaged in business activities after the war and died in a carriage accident in Tucson, Arizona, in 1884. See Oswald Garrison Villard, *John Brown* (Boston: Houghton Mifflin, 1911), 142; *New York Times*, April 12, 1884; *National Cyclopedia of American Biography* (online).

After the Battle of Wilson's Creek, Merritt briefly served on McClellan's staff and was then posted at Fort Leavenworth. He resigned from the army late in 1862 and returned to Iowa where he died in 1891. See L. F. Andrews, *Pioneers of Polk County, Iowa, and Reminiscences of Early Days* (Des Moines: Baker-Trisler, 1903), 1:205–7; Benjamin F. Gue, *History of Iowa from the Earliest Times to the Beginning of the Twentieth Century* (New York: Century History Company, 1903), 4:188; Piston and Hatcher, *Wilson's Creek*, 205, 323.

55. Beardsley and the Thirteenth Illinois later fought with the Army of the Tennessee. Piston and Hatcher, *Wilson's Creek*, 79–80. See also *First Reunion of the Survivors of the Army of the Ten-*

nessee and Its Four Corps (Washington, DC: Wilson, Humphreys & Co., [1892]), 156; Landmark Designation (1987) for the James M. Beardsley House, Rock Island, Illinois (online).

Chapter 3

1. Snead, *The Fight for Missouri*, 240–43. For a recent account of the first year of the war in Missouri, see Denny and Bradbury, *First Blood*.

2. Nathaniel Cheairs Hughes, Jr., and Roy P. Stonesifer, Jr., *The Life and Wars of Gideon J. Pillow* (Chapel Hill: University of North Carolina Press, 1993), 172–77.

3. L. Polk, Major-General, Commanding Second Division, to Hon. L. P. Walker, Secretary of War, July 23, 1861, *OR*, I, iii, 612–14; Snead, *The Fight for Missouri*, 243–44; Hughes and Stonesifer, *Pillow*, 177.

4. Gid. J. Pillow, Brigadier-General, Commanding, to Major-General Polk, July 28, 1861, *OR*, I, iii, 619; Hughes and Stonesifer, *Pillow*, 177–79 (179).

5. Hughes and Stonesifer, *Pillow*, 181–83.

6. W. J. Hardee, Brigadier-General, to Major General Polk, July 29, 1861, *OR*, I, iii, 619–20; Snead, *The Fight for Missouri*, 245; Duke, *Reminiscences*, 80; [Grant], *Memoirs*, 1:256–67.

7. Piston, *Wilson's Creek*, 128–63.

8. J. M. Schofield, Acting Adjutant–General, Orders, No. [unnumbered], July 26, 1861, *OR*, I, iii, 407. To their credit, most commanders in the Union and Confederate armies identified their own sense of military honor with maintaining discipline among their troops and shielding civilians from the ravages of war. Accounts of looting and other crimes abounded, of course, but throughout the war, commanders on both sides of the conflict shared Lyon's implicit opinion that the rule of law shaped civilized warfare. See Gerald F. Linderman, *Embattled Courage: The Experience of Combat in the American Civil War* (New York: Free Press, 1987), 34–60; Neely, *Limits of Destruction*, 41–71.

9. Snead, *The Fight for Missouri*, 245–47. For the strength of McCulloch and Price's army, I have relied on Piston and Hatcher, *Wilson's Creek*, 335–37.

10. Snead, *The Fight for Missouri*, 253. Lyon's army consisted of 5,431 men in the field plus about 1,200 reserves left in Springfield. See Piston and Hatcher, *Wilson's Creek*, 338.

11. Knox, *Camp-fire and Cotton-field*, 54–55.

12. Piston and Hatcher, *Wilson's Creek*, 139.

13. Snead, *The Fight for Missouri*, 254 (quote); Cutrer, *McCulloch*, 223; Woodruff, *With the Light Guns*, 36–37.

14. Cutrer, *McCulloch*, 226–27.

15. Snead, *The Fight for Missouri*, 261.

16. Ben. McCulloch, Brigadier-General, Commanding, to Brig. Gen. S. Cooper, Adjutant-General C.S. Army, August 12, 1861, and to Hon. J. P. Benjamin, Secretary of War, December 22, 1861, *OR*, I, iii, 104–7, 743–49; Snead, *The Fight for Missouri*, 256–58, 263.

17. Snead, *The Fight for Missouri*, 266–67; Lyon is quoted in Knox, *Camp-fire and Cotton-field*, 55. Some historians have offered the psychological speculation that Lyon was nearing a mental breakdown as these decisions were being made. The evidence suggests only that Lyon displayed a degree of apprehension as he prepared to attack. See Piston and Hatcher, *Wilson's Creek*, 170; Phillips, *Damned Yankee*, 246, 248.

18. Snead, *The Fight for Missouri*, 258–61.

19. Ibid., 268.

20. Piston and Hatcher, *Wilson's Creek*, 179–290.

21. Snead, *The Fight for Missouri*, 271, 272.

22. Piston and Hatcher, *Wilson's Creek*, 203.

23. Snead, *The Fight for Missouri*, 270.

24. Knox, *Camp-fire and Cotton-field*, 59.

25. Captain J. B. Plummer to Second Lieut. James Powell, August 16, 1861, *OR*, I, iii, 72–73; Piston and Hatcher, *Wilson's Creek*, 206–20.

26. Jas. Totten, Capt. Second Artillery, to Capt. Gordon Granger, Acting Adjutant-General, Army of the West, August 19, 1861, *OR*, I, iii, 73; Woodruff, *With the Light Guns*, 44–45.

27. Plummer to Powell, August 16, 1861, *OR*, I, iii, 72–73.

28. Castel, *Price*, 45; Piston and Hatcher, *Wilson's Creek*, 221–31.

29. F. Sigel, Commanding Second Brigade, Missouri Volunteers, to General [Fremont], August 18, 1861, *OR*, I iii, 87–88.

30. J. M. Schofield, Brigadier General, U.S. Volunteers, to Major General Halleck, Commanding Department of the Missouri, February 13, 1862, *OR*, I, iii, 94–95.

31. John V. DuBois, Second Lieutenant, Mounted Rifles, to Capt. Gordon Granger, August 17, 1861, *OR*, I, iii, 80; Castel, *Price*, 43.

32. Piston and Hatcher, *Wilson's Creek*, 235–45.

33. Snead, *The Fight for Missouri*, 275–76.

34. At the Battle of Wilson's Creek, Price and McCulloch sustained total casualties (killed, wounded, and missing) of 1,222 men. The Missouri State Guard's losses, 724 men, accounted for 60 percent of the total losses. Although Gratiot joined the fight on Bloody Hill, most of Bart Pearce's Arkansas troops remained east of Wilson's Creek prepared to defend themselves from a Federal assault that never came. See Woodruff, *With the Light Guns*, 47–48; Piston and Hatcher, *Wilson's Creek*, 337.

35. Report of Capt. James Totten, Second US Artillery, August 19, 1861, *OR*, I, iii, 74; Snead, *The Fight for Missouri*, 282; Piston and Hatcher, *Wilson's Creek*, 270–73.

36. See Schofield, *Forty-Six Years in the Army*, 44.

37. Snead, *The Fight for Missouri*, 283; Piston and Hatcher, *Wilson's Creek*, 262–86.

38. Knox, *Camp-fire and Cotton-field*, 75, 106.

39. Fred'k Steele, Captain, Second Infantry, to Capt. G. Granger, August 17, 1861, *OR*, I, iii, 79. Decades later, five men who fought at Wilson's Creek received congressional Medals of Honor. Two of them received the medal for their heroism during the retreat. In the retreat, some of Totten's men abandoned a cannon when the lead horses pulling the caisson fell dead from Confederate fire. Although wounded in the shoulder, Corporal Lorenzo Immell of Totten's battery went back for the gun. Aided by Private Nicholas Bouquet, who was part of the Iowa rear guard, the soldiers braved enemy fire to cut the dead horses from the traces, harness fresh animals, and draw the gun off the field. Immell received his medal in 1890; Bouquet in 1895. See Piston and Hatcher, *Wilson's Creek*, 283, 331–32.

40. Knox, *Camp-fire and Cotton-field*, 76.

41. Ibid., 105–7 (107).

42. Report of Maj. John M. Schofield, First Missouri Infantry and Acting Adjutant-General, Army of the West, August 20, 1861, *OR*, I, iii, 57–64.

43. Ben. McCulloch, Brigadier-General, Commanding, to General Hardee, August 24, 1861, *OR*, I, iii, 672.

44. Woodruff, *With the Light Guns*, 34; McCulloch to Hardee, August 24, 1861, *OR*, I, iii, 672.

45. Franz Sigel, "The Pea Ridge Campaign," in Robert Underwood Johnson and Clarence Clough Buel, eds., *Battles and Leaders of the Civil War* (New York: Century, 1887–1888), 1:318–19; Cutrer, *McCulloch*, 218, 245.

46. McCulloch to Hardee, August 24, 1861, McCulloch to Hon. J. P. Benjamin, Secretary of War, December 22, 1861, *OR*, I, iii, 672, 746.

47. McCulloch to Benjamin, December 22, 1861, ibid., 746.

48. McCulloch to Hardee, August 24, 1861, *ibid.*, 672; quotes from McCulloch to Benjamin, December 22, 1861, *ibid.*, 746.

49. O'Flaherty, *Shelby*, 88–89; McCulloch to Hardee, August 24, 1861, and to Hon. J. P. Benjamin, Secretary of War, December 22, 1861, *OR*, I, iii, 672, 746.

50. Shalhope, *Price*, 179–80.

51. Engle, *Yankee Dutchman*, 90–95.

52. M. Jeff. Thompson, of Saint Joseph, Mo. To His Excellency Jefferson Davis, President of the Confederate States, July 2, 1861, *OR*, I, iii, 601.

53. Peter Cozzens and Robert I. Girardi, *The Military Memoirs of General John Pope* (Chapel Hill: University of North Carolina Press, 1998), 17–18, 27.

54. [Grant], *Memoirs*, 1:245–51; Cozzens and Girardi, *John Pope*, 36.

55. [Grant], *Memoirs*, 1:253.

56. Duke, *Reminiscences*, 80; [Grant], *Memoirs*, 1:256–67; Hughes and Stonesifer, *Pillow*, 184–94.

57. Thomas L. Snead, Acting Adjutant, Missouri State Guard, to Brigadier-General Harris, Second Military District, August 26, September 13, 1861, *OR*, I, iii, 684, 701.

58. J. C. Fremont, Major-General, Commanding, to Col. Jefferson C. Davis, September 13, 1861, and Davis to Fremont, September 13, 1861, *OR*, I, iii, 173; Cozzens and Girardi, *John Pope*, 42.

59. Nathaniel Cheairs Hughes, Jr., and Gordon D.Whitney, *Jefferson Davis in Blue: The Life of Sherman's Relentless Warrior* (Baton Rouge: Louisiana State University Press, 2002), 46, 49, 53; *New York Times*, December 2, 1879.

Chapter 4

1. Sterling Price to Governor C. F. Jackson, September 4, 1861, *OR*, I, liii, 436.

2. Ibid. For the battle of Dry Wood Creek, see J. H. Lane to Captain Prince, Commanding, Fort Leavenworth, September 3, 1861, *OR*, I, iii, 162; Shalhope, *Price*, 180–81.

3. Price to Jackson, 21 September 1861, OR, I, iii, 185.

4. Thomas Wentworth Higginson, *Harvard Memorial Biography* (Cambridge: Sever and Francis, 1866)

5. See Geiger, *Financial Fraud*, 30, 81.

6. Col. R. T. Van Horn, "Recollections of the Battle," in *The Battle of Lexington* (Lexington: Lexington Historical Society, 1903), 5–10. Paroled after being captured at Lexington, Peabody took command of the Twenty-Fifth Missouri Regiment. He died at Shiloh in 1862. See Higginson, *Harvard Memorial Biography*, 1:150–66.

7. Price to Jackson, September 21, 1861, *OR*, I, iii, 185–86.

8. B. A. Rives, Colonel, Commanding, Fourth Division, Missouri State Guard, to Maj. Gen. S. Price, Commanding Missouri State Guard, September 13, 1861, *OR*, I, liii, 437. This account of the battle of Lexington also relies on Colonel R. T. Van Horn and Captain Joseph A. Wilson, "Recollections of the Battle," in *The Battle of Lexington*, 6, 10–16.

9. Price to Jackson, September 21, 1861, *OR*, I, iii, 186. See also Rives to Price, September 13, 1861, *OR*, I, liii, 437; M. M. Parsons, Brigadier-General, to Major-General Price, Commanding the Forces of Missouri, September 23, 1861, *OR*, I, liii, 448–50; Col. R. T. Van Horn, and Capt. Joseph A. Wilson, "Recollections of the Battle," in *The Battle of Lexington*, 6, 10–16.

10. *New York Times*, September 28, 1861; Castel, *Price*, 50.

11. Van Horn, "Recollections," in *The Battle of Lexington*, 5–10.

12. Wilson, "Recollections," ibid., 11; William E. Parrish, *David Rice Atchison of Missouri: Border Politician* (Columbia: University of Missouri Press, 1961), 1–5, 35, 46–49, 65–68, 215–19.

13. D. R. Atchison to General Price, September 21, 1861, and John Scott, Lieutenant-Colonel, Third Iowa Volunteers, to S. D. Sturgis, Brigadier-General, US Army, September 18, 1861, *OR*, I, iii, 193–94, 195; Parrish, *Atchison*, 218–19.

14. In August 1862, Scott was promoted to colonel of the newly formed Thirty-Second Iowa. This regiment was assigned to garrison duty at Cape Girardeau and New Madrid. Scott resigned from the army in May 1864 and returned to Iowa. He won election as lieutenant governor in 1867 and later befriended and employed the young William Ashley Sunday, the future evangelist Billy Sunday. Scott died in Nevada, Iowa, in 1903. See *Nevada Representative*, September 23, 1903; John Scott, *Story of the Thirty-Second Iowa Infantry Volunteers* (Nevada, Iowa: n.p., 1896), 399; A. A. Stuart, *Iowa Colonels and Regiments: Being a History of Iowa Regiments in the War of the Rebellion: And Containing a Description of the Battles in Which They Have Fought* (De Moines: Mills & Company, 1865), 475–86.

15. Scott to Sturgis, September 18, 1861, *OR*, I, iii, 193–94.

16. Atchison to Price, September 21, 1861, *OR*, I, iii, 195; A. E. Steen, Brigadier-General, Fifth Division, Missouri State Guard, to Col. H. Little, Adjutant-General, Missouri forces, September 22, 1861, *OR*, I, liii, 444.

17. Wilson, "Recollections," in *The Battle for Lexington*, 10–13 (11); Price to Jackson, September 21, 1861, OR, I, iii, 187. The report cited is J. T. Hughes, Colonel, First Regiment Infantry, to Col. B. A. Rives, Commanding Division, September 21, 1861, *OR*, I, liii, 44.

18. Price to Jackson, September 21, 1861, and Thomas A. Harris, Brigadier-General, Second Division Missouri State Guard, to Maj. Gen. Sterling Price, Commanding Missouri State Guard, September 23, 1861, *OR*, I, iii, 187 (quotes), 189–93. See also Van Horn, "Recollections," in *The Battle of Lexington*, 5–10.

19. B. A. Rives, Colonel Commanding First [sic] Division, Missouri State Guard, to Major-General Price, September 23, 1861, *OR*, I, liii, 439–41.

20. Rives to Price, September 23, 1861, and Hughes to Rives, September 21, 1861, *OR*, I, liii, 439–41, 441–44.

21. For the most part, the Third Division and Steen's new command were held in reserve. Clark was absent, having been "detailed on business for the army." Steen had been ill for more than a week and was able to be present only at the end of the battle. See Congreve Jackson, Colonel, Commanding Third Division, Missouri State Guard, to Col. Thomas L. Snead, Acting Adjutant-General, Army Corps., September 23, 1861, and J. C. Thornton, Major, Commanding, to Brig. Gen. A. E. Steen, September 23, 1861, *OR*, I, liii, 438–39, 444–46.

22. J. C. Fremont, Major-General, Commanding, to Col. E. D. Townsend, Asst. Adjt. Gen., Hdqrs. of the Army, September 15, 1861; Jno. Pope, Brigadier-General, to Fremont, September 15, 1861; Fremont to Brigadier-General Sturgis, September 18, 1861; *OR*, I, iii, 493, 495, 500.

23. Van Horn, "Recollections of the Battle," 5–10; J. T. Hughes to Rives, September 21, 1861, *OR*, I, liii, 441–44. Van Horn had moved to Kansas City in 1855. Although he expressed proslavery views before the war, he became active in the Republican Party after the war and served five terms in congress. He died near Kansas City in 1916. See *Biographical Directory of American Congresses* (online); *New York Times*, January 4, 1916; James A. Mulligan, "The Siege of Lexington, Mo," in *Battles and Leaders*, 1:307–13. This account was adapted from a newspaper report of a lecture delivered by Mulligan in Chicago.

24. John R. Boyd, Lieutenant-Colonel, Commanding, to Lieut. Col. D. W. Flowerree, Acting Assistant Adjutant-General, September 22, 1861, *OR*, I, liii, 446; Capt. Joseph A. Wilson, "Recollections of the Battle," in *The Battle of Lexington*, 10–13.

25. Report of Brig. Gen. Thomas A. Harris, Missouri State Guard, September 23, 1861, *OR*, I, iii, 191–92; J. H. McBride, Brigadier-General, Seventh Division, Missouri State Guards, [sic] to [Major-General Price], September 20, 1861, *OR*, I, liii, 451–52; Shalhope, *Price*, 182; Castel, *Price*, 52–54.

26. Capt. Joseph A. Wilson, "Recollections of the Battle," in *The Battle of Lexington*, 10–13; Castel, *Price*, 53; Mulligan, "The Siege of Lexington, MO.," in *Battles and Leaders*, 1:307–9. Regarding Mulligan's exchange, see Winter, *Civil War in St. Louis*, 140; Banasik, *Missouri in 1861*, 185n85. After his exchange, from January until June 1862, Mulligan served as commander of Camp Douglas, the Federal prisoner-of-war camp in Chicago. He and his regiment then returned to the field. He died in the Shenandoah Valley in July 1864. See George Levy, *To Die in Chicago: Confederate Prisoners at Camp Douglas, 1862–1865* (Evanston: Evanston, 1994), 53–76.

27. Castel, *Price*, 56; Geiger, *Financial Fraud*, 81.

28. J. H. Lane to Major General Fremont, September 24, 1861; Lane to Captain Prince, Commanding, Fort Leavenworth, September 4, 1861; W. E. Prince, Captain, First Infantry, Commanding, to John C. Kelton, Asst. Adjt. Gen., Western Dept., September 5, 1861; *OR*, I, iii, 162, 163–64, 196.

29. Shalhope, *Price*, 183, 184.

30. Matthews, *Basil Duke*, 34–35, 39.

31. Dr. William M. Polk, Captain C.S.A. (the son of Leonidas Polk), "General Polk and the Battle of Belmont," in *Battles and Leaders*, 1:348–57.

32. *New York, Times*, October 6, 1903; Piston and Hatcher, *Wilson's Creek*, 181–82; James Grant Wilson, *Biographical Sketches of Illinois Officers in the War Against the Rebellion of 1861* (Chicago: James Barnet, 1863), 26–28; Robert I. Girardi and Nathaniel Cheairs Hughes, Jr., eds., *Memoirs of Brigadier General William Passmore Carlin, U.S.A.* (Lincoln: University of Nebraska Press, 1999), 29–48.

33. [Grant], *Memoirs*, 1:264–68.

34. M. Jeff. Thompson, Brigadier-General, Commanding, to Col. M. N. Moore, Brigade Quartermaster, Memphis, Tenn., October 11, 1861, *OR*, I, iii, 224. On the uncertainties of the Confederate command structure in the West, see Richard M. McMurry, *Two Great Rebel Armies: An Essay in Confederate Military History* (Chapel Hill: University of North Carolina Press, 1989), 118–22.

35. Thompson to General A. S. Johnston, C.S.A., Columbus, Ky., October 18, 1861, *OR*, I, iii, 225.

36. Thompson to Johnston, October 15, 18, 1861, and Aden Lowe, Lieutenant-Colonel, Commanding, to Thompson, October 17, 1861, *OR*, I, iii, 224–26, 236.

37. Thompson to Johnston, October 18, 1861, and Thompson to Col. W. G. Phellan, commandant at Bloomfield, Mo., October 20, 1861, *OR*, I, iii, 225–26, 229.

38. W. P. Carlin, Colonel, Commanding, to Capt. C. McKeever, Asst. Adjt. Gen., St. Louis, Mo., October 15, 1861, and U.S. Grant, Brigadier-General, Commanding, to Col. J. B. Plummer, Commanding Forces at Cape Girardeau, Mo., October 16, 18, 1861, *OR*, I, iii, 202, 204–5.

39. Plummer to Grant, October 26, 1861, and Carlin to Capt. John C. Kelton, A.A.G., Hdqrs. Dept. of Missouri, Saint Louis, Mo., December 15, 1861, *OR*, I, iii, 206, 218–20.

40. Carlin to Capt. C. McKeever, A.A.G. Western Department, St. Louis, MO., October 22, 1861; Carlin to Kelton, December 15, 1861; J. M. Schofield, Major, First Missouri Light Artillery, to Capt. George Edgar, Act. Adjt. Gen, October 26, 1861; *OR*, I, iii, 217–20, 222–23.

41. Thompson to Maj. Gen. Leonidas Polk, C.S.A, October 22, 1861, *OR*, I, iii, 227–28.

42. L. F. Ross, Colonel, to Plummer, October 28, 1861, and C. C. Marsh, Colonel, Twentieth Regiment Illinois Volunteers, to Capt. George P. Edgar, Acting Assistant Adjutant-General, October 26, 1861, *OR*, I, iii, 210–13.

43. Warren Stewart, Captain, Commanding Squadron of Cavalry, to Plummer, October 22, 1861, *OR*, I, iii, 215; Plummer to Assistant Adjutant General, Hdqrs., District of S.E. Missouri, Cairo, Ill., October 31, 1861, *OR*, I, iii, 206–9.

44. Plummer to Assistant Adjutant General, October 31, 1861, and Carlin to McKeever, A.A.G., October 25, 1861, *OR*, I, iii, 206–9, 217–18.

45. Castel, *Price*, 59, 67–68; Shalhope, *Price*, 186. Sterling Price, Major-General, Commanding, Mo. S.G., to General A. S. Johnston, October 16, 1861, and Ben. McCulloch, Brigadier-General, Commanding, to Price, October 22, 1861, *OR*, I, iii, 720–21.

46. Joseph W. Morton, Jr., *Sparks from the Camp Fire. Or, Tales of the Old Veterans* (Philadelphia: Keystone Publishing Co., 1890), 114–24.

47. Knox, *Camp-fire and Cotton-field*, 82; Gerteis, *Civil War St. Louis*, 246; Castel, *Price*, 57.

48. Chas. Zagonyi, Commanding Body Guard, to Col. J. H. Eaton, Acting Asst. Adjt. Gen., October 28, 1861, *OR*, I, iii, 251–52. In his report, Zagonyi minimized the role played by the Prairie Scouts. Captain Naughton (who was wounded in the fighting) later protested Zagonyi's account. See P. Naughton, Captain, Irish Dragoons, to Maj. Gen. H. W. Halleck, Commanding Dept. of the West, December 18, 1861, OR, I, iii, 252–53.

49. Cozzens and Girardi, *John Pope*, 35.

50. [Grant], *Memoirs*, 1:271–72.

51. Ibid., 271.

52. Hughes and Stonesifer, *Pillow*, 198.

53. [Grant], *Memoirs*, 1:274.

54. Ibid., 274–80; Hughes and Stonesifer, *Pillow*, 197–205; Polk, "Battle of Belmont," in *Battles and Leaders*, 1:348–57.

55. Sterling Price, Major-General, Commanding Mo. S.G., to General A. S. Johnston, November 7, 1861, *OR*, I, iii, 732.

56. Leslie Anders, "The Blackwater Incident," *Missouri Historical Review* 88, no. 4 (July 1994): 420; Nathaniel Cheairs Hughes, Jr., and Gordon D. Whitney, *Jefferson Davis in Blue: The Life of Sherman's Relentless Warrier* (Baton Rouge: Louisiana State University Press, 2002), 66; Cozzens and Girardi, *John Pope*, 36–37.

57. Anders, "Blackwater," 417, 420; Cozzens and Girardi, *John Pope*, 36–37; Hughes and Whitney, *Jefferson Davis in Blue*, 66.

58. Cozzens and Girardi, *John Pope*, 38.

59. Piston and Hatcher, *Wilson's Creek*, 157; Anders, "Blackwater," 417, 428. Robinson was later exchanged and served as adjutant general of Marmaduke's division during Price's 1864 Missouri raid. He died in 1896.

60. Beriah Magoffin resigned as governor of Kentucky in August 1862 at the insistence of the state's unionist legislature. See Roy P. Basler, ed., *The Collected Works of Abraham Lincoln* (New Brunswick: Rutgers University Press, 1953–1955), V, 170; Anders, "Blackwater," 422.

61. Cozzens and Girardi, *John Pope*, 39.

62. Castel, *Price*, 60, 64; O'Flaherty, *Shelby*, 97.

63. Prentiss was captured at Shiloh and rose to the rank of major general after he was exchanged. He spent the last twenty years of his life in Bethany, Harrison County, Missouri, where he practiced law and was a leader of the Republican Party. He died there in 1901 at the age of eighty-two. See George W. Wanamaker, *History of Harrison County* (Topeka: Historical Publishing, 1921), 852–55.

64. In the 1870s, Glover won election to Congress from Missouri as a Democrat. See *Biographical Directory of United States Congresses* (online).

65. Birge's sharpshooters were later transferred to Illinois as the Sixty-Sixth Illinois Infantry. Frederick H. Dyer, *Compendium of the Rebellion: Regimental Histories* (online); Newton Bateman and Paul Selby, eds., *Historical Encyclopedia of Illinois* (Chicago: Munse's Publishing, 1905), 2:559; Victor A. Paul, *A Composite Roster of the 66th Illinois Infantry: "The Squirrel Brigade"* (Washington, MO: Obscure Place, 1995), i.

66. *New York Times*, December 30, 1861; William F. Switzler, *History of Boone County, Missouri* (St. Louis: Western Historical Company, 1882), 412–17.

67. *New York Times*, February 3, 1862; *The History of Appanoose County Iowa* (Chicago: Western Historical Company, 1878), 244; W. M. G. Torrence, Major, First Battalion, First Iowa Cavalry, to Brigadier-General Pope, January 10, 1862, *OR*, I, viii, 50–51.

68. Lewis Merrill, Colonel, Commanding Merrill's Horse, to Capt. J. C. Kelton, Assistant Adjutant-General, January 10, 1862, *OR*, I, viii, 51–52; Arlington National Cemetery (online).

69. Torrence to Pope, January 10, 1862, and John M. Palmer, Brigadier-General, to Major-General Halleck, January 10, 1862, *OR*, I, viii, 49–51.

70. Palmer to Halleck, January 10, 1862, and Thos. J. Turner, Colonel, Commanding Cantonment, to Capt. J. C. Kelton, Assistant Adjutant-General, January 14, 1862, *OR*, I, viii, 49.

71. Cozzens and Girardi, *John Pope*, 39; Hughes and Whitney, *Jefferson Davis in Blue*, 69–70, 73–74.

72. Engle, *Yankee Dutchman*, 87–89.

73. Ibid., 97.

74. Ibid., 90–95; H. W. Halleck to Maj. Gen. George B. McClellan, February 2, 1862, *OR*, I, viii, 828–29. See also Earl J. Hess, "Sigel's Resignation: A Study in German-Americans and the Civil War," *Civil War History* 26 (1980): 5–17.

75. Engle, *Yankee Dutchman*, 105.

76. Ibid., 121, 146–47, 152, 159, 163.

77. Ibid., 169, 194, 208, 215, 221; Gerteis, *Civil War St. Louis*, 337.

Chapter 5

1. Unless otherwise noted, the following discussion of Eads's gunboats follows Gerteis, *Civil War St. Louis*, 236–52.

2. Quoted in Florence L. Dorsey, *Road to the Sea: The Story of James B. Eads and the Mississippi* (New York: Rinehart, 1947), 67.

3. H. W. Halleck, Major-General, to Brig. Gen. D. C. Buell, February 7, 1862, and G. T. Beauregard, General, C.S. Army, Confidential Circular, February 21, 1862, *OR*, I, vii, 593, 899. Larry J. Daniel and Lyann N. Bock, *Island No. 10: Struggle for the Mississippi Valley* (Tuscaloosa: University of Alabama Press, 1996), 21. On Confederate efforts to establish a defensible northern border in the West, see McMurry, *Two Great Rebel Armies*, 119–24.

4. Daniel and Bock, *Island No. 10*, 27; Eicher and Eicher, *High Commands*, 184, 375–76.

5. Peter Cozzens, *General John Pope: A Life for the Nation* (Urbana: University of Illinois Press, 2000), 53–54; Cozzens and Girardi, *John Pope*, 47.

6. Cozzens, *Life of Pope*, 55. See also Cozzens and Girardi, *John Pope*, 47.

7. Later in the war, after the Atlanta campaign, Stanley won the Medal of Honor for his heroism at the Battle of Franklin, Tennessee. He retired from the army in the late nineteenth century and died in 1902. Poor health caused Hamilton to resign from the army in February 1863. He died in 1903. See Ezra J. Warner, *Generals in Blue: Lives of the Union Commanders* (Baton Rouge: Louisiana State University Press, 1964), 358–59, 374–75, 470–71; Daniel and Bock, *Island No. 10*, 36, 39, 152–54; John F. Marszalek, *Commander of All Lincoln's Armies: A Life of General Henry W. Halleck* (Cambridge: Harvard University Press, 2004), 19; Cuyler Reynolds, *Genealogical and Family History of Southern New York and the Hudson River Valley* (New York: Lewis Historical, 1914), 3:1388.

8. Palmer resigned from the army in 1868 and later won election as Republican governor of Illinois. Paine resigned from the army in April 1865 after being reprimanded for acts of cruelty against civilians. Plummer died of wounds in 1862. See Daniel and Bock, *Island No. 10*, 39, 58, 152–54; John Y. Simon, ed., *The Papers of Ulysses S. Grant* (Carbondale: Southern Illinois University Press, 1977), 6:427; *New York Times*, September 26, 1900.

9. Daniel and Bock, *Island No. 10*, 10.

10. Cozzens, *Life of Pope*, 56. See also Daniel and Bock, *Island No. 10*, 60–65.

11. Daniel and Bock, *Island No. 10*, 72–74.

12. Ibid., 78–87 (82, 87).

13. Ibid., 87–91 (91).

14. Ibid., 105.

15. Gerteis, *Civil War St. Louis*, 245. On Walke's career, see *New York Times*, March 9, 1896.

16. Gerteis, *Civil War St. Louis*, 248, 249. Foote received a promotion after the victory at Island Number Ten, but he continued to suffer from a wound received in the fighting at Donelson. He took sick leave in May, and Captain Charles H. Davis took command of the gunboats until David D. Porter arrived five months later to command the Mississippi Squadron. When Davis boarded the *Benton* on May 9, he found Foote confined to his bed. His wounded foot cause him a great deal of pain, but he also suffered from intestinal problems that Davis thought were caused by the atmosphere of the lower Mississippi Valley. Foote returned to his home in New York City hoping to recuperate. He died there in June 1863.

17. Marszalek, *A Life of Halleck*, 117, 123–24; Report of Brig. Gen. John M. Schofield, U.S. Army, of Operations in Missouri and Northwest Arkansas, April 10–November 20, 1862, *OR*, I, xiii, 8.

18. *OR*, I, xiii, 15.

19. E. M. Violette, "The Battle of Kirksville," *Missouri Historical Review* 5 (October 1910–July 1911): 95–98.

20. Joseph A. Mudd, *With Porter in North Missouri* (1909; Iowa City: Press of the Camp Pope Bookshop, 1992), 204; Michael E. Banasik, ed., *Confederate "Tales of the War" in the Trans-Mississippi, Part One: 1861* (Iowa City: Press of the Camp Pope Bookshop, 2010), 7:162n94.

21. Violette, "The Battle of Kirksville," 99–100.

22. Ibid., 101–9.

23. Ibid., 102.

24. *OR*, I, xiii, 13–14.

25. Porter made his way back to Arkansas and joined Marmaduke's first raid into Missouri in January 1863. He died of wounds he received at the Battle of Hartville. McNeil was promoted to brigadier general after the Battle of Kirksville. See William Jewett Tenney, *The Military and Naval History of the Rebellion in the United States* (New York: D. Appleton & Company, 1866), 315.

26. W. L. Webb, *The Centennial History of Independence, Mo.* (Independence: W. Webb, 1927), 190–96; Allardice, *More Generals in Gray*, 132–33.

27. Albert Castel, *William Clarke Quantrill: His Life and Times* (New York: F. Tell, 1962), 88–90.

28. Francis H. Kennedy, ed., *The Civil War Battlefield Guide*, 2nd ed. (New York: Houghton Mifflin, 1998), 155; Edwards, *Shelby and His Men*, 78–79.

29. Castel, *Quantrill*, 88–93; William Elsey Connelley, *Quantrill and the Border Wars* (Cedar Rapids, Iowa: Torch Press, 1910), 259–67.

30. Badly wounded in 1864, Cockrell resigned his commission. After the war, he settled in Texas and won election to Congress, where he served for two terms. He died in Abilene in 1915. See *Biographical Directory of American Congress* (online); on Coffee, see Kennedy, *Battlefield Guide*, 155.

31. Edwards, *Shelby and His Men*, 74.

32. Edwards, *Shelby and His Men*, 74. Foster's account is from Peter E. Palmquist and Thomas R. Kailbourn, *Pioneer Photographers from the Mississippi to the Continental Divide: A Biographical Dictionary, 1839–1865* (Stanford: Stanford University Press, 2005), 262. See also George S. Grover, "Major Emory S. Foster," *Missouri Historical Review* 14 (April–July 1920): 425–32. Foster survived the war and later edited the *St. Louis Journal*, an activity that brought him into contact

and conflict with John Newman Edwards. Foster never fully recovered from his wounds. The *New York Times* reported that his war wounds caused his death in Oakland, California, in 1902. *New York Times*, December 25, 1902.

33. "General Blunt's Account of His Civil War Experiences," *Kansas Historical Quarterly* 1, no. 3 (May 1932): 211–65; O'Flaherty, *Shelby*, 117, 119.

34. Connelly, *John M. Schofield*, 37–40.

35. O'Flaherty, *Shelby*, 124–26; *New York Times*, December 10, 1862. On Cooper, see Warner, *Generals in Blue*, 184; Oklahoma Historical Society, *Encyclopedia of Oklahoma History and Culture* (online); Richard Lowe, ed., *A Texas Cavalry Officer's Civil War: The Diary and Letters of James C. Bates* (Baton Rouge: Louisiana State University Press, 1999), 19–31.

36. Bruce S. Allardice, *Confederate Colonels: A Biographical Register* (Columbia: University of Missouri Press, 2008), 82, 173–74.

37. J. M. Schofield, Brigadier-General, to Maj. Gen. Samuel R. Curtis, November 9, 1862, and Report of H. E. Barstow, Capt., Company C, 10th Ill. Cav., November 10, 1862, *OR*, I, xiii, 354, 355–56.

38. Marmaduke submitted an initial report of his raid on January 18 and a full report on February 1. See J. S. Marmaduke, Brigadier-General, Commanding, to Col. R. C. Newton, January 18, February 1, 1863, *OR*, I, xxii, pt. 1, 194–98.

39. Ibid., February 1, 1863, *OR*, I, xxii, pt. 1, 198.

40. Ibid., 196.

41. E. B. Brown to [Samuel R. Curtis], January 8, [1863], *OR*, I, xxii, pt. 1, 179–80. Brown survived the war and died in West Plains, Missouri, in 1901.

42. Brown to Curtis, January 8, 1863, *OR*, I, xxii, pt. 1, 180.

43. Curtis to Halleck, January 8, 1863, *OR*, I, xxii, pt. 1, 178–79.

44. Curtis to Brown, January 8, 1863, *OR*, I, xxii, pt. 1, 179.

45. Marmaduke to Newton, *OR*, I, xxii, pt. 1, 194–95; Frederick W. Goman, *Up from Arkansas: Marmaduke's First Missouri Raid including the Battles of Springfield and Hartville* (n.p., 1999), 65–79. On the burial of MacDonald and Wimer, see Winter, *Civil War in St. Louis*, 123.

46. Curtis to Brown, January 12, 1863, and to Governor Gamble, January 12, 1863, *OR*, I, xxii, pt. 1, 179.

47. Marmaduke to Newton, February 1, 1863, *OR*, I, xxii, pt. 1, 198.

48. Marmaduke to Maj. W. B. Blair, Assistant Adjutant-General, May 20, 1863, *OR*, I, xxii, pt.1, 285–88; O'Flaherty, *Shelby*, 171–75.

49. Marmaduke to Blair, May 20, 1863, 286.

50. Curtis to Halleck, April 26, 1863, and Marmaduke to Blair, May 20, 1863, *OR*, I, xxii, pt. 1, 252, 285–88.

51. Marmaduke to Blair, May 20, 1863; Curtis to Halleck, April 26, 28, 1863; Wm. Vandever, Brigadier-General, to Brigadier-General Davidson, April 27, 1863; *OR*, I, xxii, pt. 1, 288, 252–53, 274. Vandever fought the rest of the war with Sherman's army. After the war he returned to his law practice in Dubuque. In 1884 he moved to California and from 1887 to 1891 he again served in Congress. He died in Ventura, California, in 1893. See the *Biographical Directory of American Congress* (online).

52. Marmaduke to Blair, May 20, 1863, *OR*, I, xxii, pt. 1, 288; G. W. Thompson, Colonel Commanding Brigade, to Capt. [W. J.] McArthur, Assistant Adjutant General, May 15, 1863, *OR*, I, xxii, pt. 1, 293; Anne J. Bailey, "Texans Invade Missouri: The Cape Girardeau Raid, 1863," *Missouri Historical Review* 84 (January 1990): 166–87.

53. Connelly, *Schofield*, 53–65; Gerteis, *Civil War St. Louis*, 181.

54. C. B. McAfee, Captain, Third Battalion, Sixth Mo. State Mil. Cav., to Col. J. Edwards, Comdg. Southwestern District of Missouri, October 10, 1863, ibid., 656.

55. O'Flaherty, *Shelby*, 193–95 (195); Emory S. Foster, Major Seventh Missouri State Militia Cavalry, to General E. B. Brown, October 9, 1863, *OR*, I, xxii, pt. 1, 647.

56. Jo. O. Shelby, Colonel, Commanding Expedition, to Maj. L. A. Maclean, Assistant Adjutant-General, Price's Division, November 4, 1863, *OR*, I, xxii, pt. 1, 672. See also McAfee to Edwards, October 10, 1863, ibid., 656–57.

57. Shelby to Maclean, November 4, 1863, *OR*, I, xxii, pt. 1, 673.

58. G. W. Kelly, major, Fourth Missouri State Militia, to Col. George H. Hall, October xxii, 1863; E. B. Brown, Brigadier-General Volunteers, Commanding, to Maj. Oliver D. Greene, Assistant Adjutant-General, October 28, 1863; Wm. Gentry, Major, commanding Battalion, to Brig. Gen. E. B. Brown, October 31, 1863; *OR*, I, xxii, pt. 1, 635–36, 626–29, 636–38.

59. Shelby to Maclean, November 4, 1863, *OR*, I, xxii, pt. 1, 675. See also T. T. Crittenden, Lieutenant-Colonel, Seventh Missouri State Militia Cavalry, to Maj. Lucien J. Barnes, Assistant Adjutant-General, October 12, 1863, *OR*, I, xxii, pt. 1, 670–78, 642 (see 679 for a map showing the Boonville–Marshall road).

60. Shelby to Maclean, November 4, 1863, and John McNeil, Brigadier-General of Volunteers, to Major General Schofield, November 1, 1863, *OR*, I, xxii, pt. 1, 670–78 (678), 650–52.

Chapter 6

1. John B. Sanborn, Brigadier-General, Commanding, to Maj. O. D. Greene, Assistant Adjutant-General, May 21, 1864, *OR*, I, xxxiv, pt. 1, 941–42. The compilers of the *OR* documented nearly seventy skirmishes and scouting expeditions in Missouri during the first six months of 1864. Most were south of the Missouri River, but they stretched across the state from the Mississippi River to the Kansas border. For a sympathetic treatment of Rosecrans's command in Missouri and during Price's 1864 raid, see William M. Lamers, *The Edge of Glory: A Biography of General William S. Rosecrans, U.S.A.* (New York: Harcourt, Brace and World, 1961; Chapel Hill: University of North Carolina Press, 1999), 415–39.

2. S. R. Curtis, Major-General, to [Major-General Halleck], Chief of Staff, January [n.d.], 1865, *OR*, I, xli, pt. 1, 464–523 (464).

3. E. Kirby Smith, Lieutenant-General, to Maj. Gen. Sterling Price, March 15, 1864, *OR*, I, xxxiv, pt. 2, 1043–44.

4. W. R. Boggs, Brigadier-General and Chief of Staff, to Maj. Gen. S. Price, by command of General E. Kirby Smith, August 14, 1864, *OR*, I, xli, pt. 2, 1040–41.

5. Ezra J. Warner, *Generals in Gray*, 85–86; Allardice, *More Generals in Gray*, 133–34; Castel, *Price*, 204–5; *Biographical Encyclopedia of Texas* (online); *Confederate Veteran* 22 (March 1914): 123. Cabell was captured during the raid and spent the rest of the war as a prisoner. After the war he returned to Arkansas and practiced law before moving to Texas where he served as a US marshal. He died in Dallas in 1911. Jackman briefly went to Mexico after the war and then settled in Texas where he died in 1886. Like Cabell, he served as a US marshal. Shanks was killed at Osage Crossing during the raid.

6. Castel, *Price*, 208–9; Eicher and Eicher, *High Commands*, 492–93; U. S. Grant, Lieutenant-General, to Hon. E. M. Stanton, Secretary of War, July 22, 1865, *OR*, I, xxxiv, pt. 1, 34.

7. Frank Eno, Assistant Adjutant-General, General Orders, No. 220, December 8, 1864, *OR*, I, xli, pt. 1, 318; Castel, *Price*, 209; Shalhope, *Price*, 263.

8. Thomas Ewing, Jr., Brigadier-General, to Col. J. B. DuBois, Chief of Staff, Headquarters Dept. of the Missouri, October 20, 1864, *OR*, I, xli, pt. 1, 445–52 (446); Ronald D. Smith, *Thomas Ewing, Jr., Frontier Lawyer and Civil War General* (Columbia: University of Missouri Press, 2008), 236.

9. *Biographical Directory of the United States Congress* (online); Smith, *Ewing*, 14–17, 44–48, 164–67.

10. Castel, *Price*, 210; Shalhope, *Price*, 264, 285.

11. Ewing to DuBois, October 20, 1864, *OR*, I, xli, pt. 1, 445–52 (447); Castel, *Price*, 210.

12. Ewing to DuBois, October 20, 1864, *OR*, I, xli, pt. 1, 445–52 (447).

13. Ibid. (447–48).

14. Castel, *Price*, 213–14.

15. Ewing to DuBois, October 20, 1864, *OR*, I, xli, pt. 1, 448.

16. Castel, *Price*, 214–15.

17. Ewing to DuBois, October 20, 1864, *OR*, I, xli, pt. 1, 449.

18. Ibid.; Castel, *Price*, 217.

19. W. S. Rosecrans, Major-General, to Lieutenant-Colonel Christensen, A.A.G., December 7, 1864, *OR*, I, xli, pt. 1, 307–17 (309).

20. Ewing to DuBois, October 20, 1864, *OR*, I, xli, pt. 1, 449.

21. Ibid., 450; General Orders, No. 189, Hdqrs. Dept. of the Missouri, October 6, 1864, *OR*, I, xli, pt. 1, 452; Smith, *Ewing*, 236–45.

22. Rosecrans to Christensen, December 7, 1864, and Price to Brig. Gen. W. R. Boggs, Chief of Staff, Shreveport, La., December 28, 1864, *OR*, I, xli, pt. 1, 307–17 (310–11), 625–40.

23. Albert Castel and Thomas Goodrich, *Bloody Bill Anderson: The Short, Savage Life of a Civil War Guerrilla* (Mechanicsburg, PA: Stockpole Books, 1998; Lawrence: University Press of Kansas [2006]), 59–61.

24. Castel and Goodrich, *Anderson*, 88–114; Shalhope, *Price*, 267–68.

25. Price to Boggs, December 28, 1864, *OR*, I, xli, pt. 1, 625–40; Castel and Goodrich, *Anderson*, 120.

26. Chester Harding, Jr., Colonel Forty-Third Missouri Volunteers, to Lieut. W. T. Clarke, Assistant Adjutant-General, District of North Missouri, November 12, 1864, *OR*, I, xli, pt. 1, 434–39; Bay, *Bench and Bar*, 553–56. After the war, Harding returned to his law practice in St. Louis. In 1875 he died in St. Louis, not yet fifty years old.

27. Harding to Clarke, November 12, 1864, *OR*, I, xli, pt. 1, 434–39.

28. Ibid.

29. G. A. Holloway, Captain and Assistant Adjutant-General, to Brigadier-General Fisk, Commanding District of Northern Missouri, October 18, 1864, and Jno. B. Clark, Jr., Brigadier-General, Commanding Division, to Lieut. Col. L. A. Maclean, Assistant Adjutant-General, Price's Army, December 19, 1864, *OR*, I, xli, pt. 1, 430–31, 678–85 (681–82). See also Castel, *Price*, 225–27.

30. Holloway to Fisk, October 18, 1864; Clark to Maclean, December 19, 1864; W. S. Rosecrans, Major-General, to Lieutenant-Colonel Christensen, A.A.G, Mil. Div. of West Mississippi, December 7, 1864; *OR*, I, xli, pt. 1, 430–31, 678–85 (681–82), 307–17.

31. Clark to Maclean, December 19, 1864, and Holloway to Fisk, October 18, 1864, *OR*, I, xli, pt. 1, 678–85 (681–82), 430–31.

32. Castel and Goodrich, *Anderson*, 117–22; *New York Times*, November 20, 1864.

33. Castel, *Price*, 228.

34. Curtis to [Halleck], January [n.d.], 1865, *OR*, I, xli, pt. 1, 464–523; Castel, *Price*, 228–29.

35. Jas. G. Blunt, Major-General, to Maj. C. S. Charlot, Ast. Adjutant-General, Department of Kansas, December 21, 1864, *OR*, I, xli, pt. 1, 571–79.

36. Ibid.; Shalhope, *Price*, 269.

37. Blunt to Charlot, December 21, 1864, and T. Moonlight, Colonel, Eleventh Kansas Cavalry, Commanding, to Capt. George S. Hampton, Assistant Adjutant-General, December 15, 1864, *OR*, I, xli, pt. 1, 571–79, 591–95; Eicher and Eicher, *High Commands*, 394; Castel, *Price*, 229; Shalhope, *Price*, 270. Despite its name, the Little Blue River is not a tributary of the Big Blue. Both rivers flow north and empty into the Missouri River on either side of Independence. After the war, Moonlight became active in politics. He served as governor of the Wyoming Territory and US minister to Bolivia. He died in Leavenworth, Kansas, in 1899.

38. Stephen Z. Starr, *Jennison's Jayhawkers: A Civil War Cavalry Regiment and Its Commander* (Baton Rouge: Louisiana State University Press, 1973), 134–38, 333–35, 366–68, 385–86; Shalhope, *Price*, 271. After the Federal victory at Westport, a court-martial dishonorably discharged Jennison for plundering in Missouri during the pursuit of Price. After the war Jennison won election to the Kansas state legislature and died in Leavenworth in 1884.

39. Curtis to [Halleck], January [n.d.], 1865, *OR*, I, xli, pt. 1, 464–523 (480, 481). On the fighting at Byram's Ford, see also Monnett, *Action before Westport*, 79–86.

40. Curtis to [Halleck], January [n.d.], 1865, *OR*, I, xli, pt. 1, 484.

41. Ibid., 486 (Deitzler, 489). See also Starr, *Jennison's Jayhawkers*, 335–37. The Ohio-born Coloradan Colonel James H. Ford would be promoted to brigadier general and serve for the rest of the war in Arkansas. See Eicher and Eicher, *High Commands*, 239.

42. Curtis to [Halleck], January, [n.d.], 1865, *OR*, I, xli, pt. 1, 485–86, 491; Starr, *Jennison's Jayhawkers*, 337–39.

43. Curtis to [Halleck], January, [n.d.], 1865, *OR*, I, xli, pt. 1, 491–93.

44. Ibid., 497.

45. Chas. W. Blair, Colonel, Fourteenth Kansas, to Maj. Gen. S. R. Curtis, January 1, 1865, and F. W. Benteen, Lieut. Col., Tenth Cavalry Missouri Vols., To Maj. Gen. A. Pleasonton, November 3, 1864, *OR*, I, xli, pt. 1, 601–6, 333. The honor of capturing General Cabell belonged to Sergeant Cavalry M. Young also of the Third Iowa Cavalry. Both men later received the congressional Medal of Honor. See Iowa Medal of Honor Heroes, State Historical Society of Iowa (online).

46. Curtis to [Halleck], January, [n.d.], 1865, *OR*, I, xli, pt. 1, 501–10.

47. Ibid., 510–23.

48. Lamers, *Edge of Glory*, 437–39; E. B. Brown, Brigadier-General, Commanding, to Maj. J. W. Banes, Assistant Adjutant-General, June 16, 1865, and Thos. Gannon, 1st Lieut. Company G. 9th Cav. Missouri State Militia to Capt. Thomas B. Reed, Commanding Sub-District, January 12, 1865, *OR*, I, xlviii, pt. 1, 30, 32–33; Gerteis, *Civil War St. Louis*, 313; Sutherland, *A Savage Conflict*, 204; Stiles, *Jesse James*, 164.

Conclusion

1. Parrish, *Frank Blair*, 202–29.

2. Gerteis, *Civil War St. Louis*, 307–38; Parrish, *Frank Blair*, 223.

3. Louis Gerteis, "The Legacy of the Dred Scott Case: The Uncertain Course of Emancipation in Missouri," in David Thomas Konig, Paul Finkelman, and Christopher Alan Bracey, eds., *The Dred Scott Case: Historical and Contemporary Perspectives on Race and Law* (Athens: Ohio University Press, 2010), 68–82.

4. Gerteis, *Civil War St. Louis*, 327, 334.

5. *The Encyclopedia of Arkansas History and Culture* (online).

6. *Biographical Directory of American Congresses* (online).

7. [Grant], *Memoirs*, 1:249, 259, 2:542.

8. For an examination of slavery's demise in Missouri, see Louis S. Gerteis, *Civil War St. Louis* (Lawrence: University Press of Kansas, 2001), particularly Chapter 9, "Slavery Dies Hard," 260-93.

Index